RONALD FIRBANK
MEMOIRS AND CRITIQUES

edited with an introduction by

MERVYN HORDER

DUCKWORTH

First published in 1977 by
Gerald Duckworth & Co. Ltd.
The Old Piano Factory, 43 Gloucester Crescent
London NW1

ISBN 0 7156 0763 4

Made and printed in Great Britain by
The Garden City Press Limited
Letchworth, Hertfordshire SG6 1JS

RONALD FIRBANK
MEMOIRS AND CRITIQUES

Contents

Introduction

We are assured by a competent technical observer of the subject* that people tend to meet the moment of their death in the same manner as they lived—the self-effacing quietly in their sleep, the egocentric giving the maximum trouble to all concerned, the theatrical speechifying away *con brio*, the athletic with one foot out of bed, and so on. Is it too much to seek the same sort of link between the life styles of authors and artists and the fate of their works and reputations after their death—the respectable Tennysons, Maughams and Kiplings of this world with scholarship funds, uniform editions, an official Life and Works, their houses reconstituted as tourist museums and rediscovery of their merits every twenty years; less fluent or more *avant-garde* practitioners, who have found the going more troublesome, with lost manuscripts, bankrupt ex-publishers, intricate copyright wrangles, textual cruxes and other manifestations of widespread neglect?

With Ronald Firbank in particular there is something wildly appropriate in his negligently managing to get himself buried in the wrong cemetery; and in the fact that his last novel, *The New Rythum*, did not even turn up till thirty-five years after his death—this due to the singular incuriosity of his sister and next-of-kin, Heather, who for the whole of the rest of her life apparently left his possessions unexamined in the tin boxes in which they reached her. Firbank was himself hard-headed enough to leave a sum of £1,000 with the express aim of getting published after his death the uniform edition of his works which had eluded him all his life; but this took over two years to organise—the British Consul in Rome needed many months to deal with the effects of the mysterious stranger who had died in his bailiwick, and Messrs Duckworth's first contract for these books was with the Public

---

* Pamela Bright: *The Day's End*, a neglected book of 1956. The author speaks from long experience in the Middlesex Hospital cancer ward.

Trustee; nor, in 1929, was an edition of more than 200 copies thought necessary, for sale both here and in America.

Paradoxical too—and does the well-tuned ear detect a faint, undulating giggle arising from that cemetery in Rome on this matter?—is the fact that the first two full-length detailed books about him have both been by a class of person with which he felt not the slightest personal sympathy, that is to say, by women:

Ronald Firbank: a Biography, by Miriam J. Benkovitz, London and New York, 1970.

Prancing Novelist: a Defence of Fiction in the Form of a Critical Biography in Praise of Ronald Firbank, by Brigid Brophy, London and New York, 1973.

Both these works are admirable for their enthusiastic sponsorship of their subject, the first strong on fact, the second on fancy; and both have to be digested and weighed by all who hold the modern view that a knowledge of the details of an author's life helps to a better appreciation of his work.

It is for these reasons that last year, half a century after Firbank's death in May 1926, it seemed time to dot i's and cross t's by assembling in one volume whatever can still be found in the way of eyewitness accounts by those who knew him personally in life; and to support these with a few useful critiques of his work not easily accessible elsewhere. Centre-piece of such a collection, and its real *raison d'être*, must be a reprint of the *Memoir* edited by Firbank's fellow Celt Ifan Kyrle Fletcher, published in 1930 and out of print ever since a bomb destroyed much of the stock of it in 1940—the editor's own contribution to this book being the most valuable part of it, the base on which all subsequent biographers have built. How disarmingly he reminds us in his early pages: 'It is to misunderstand Ronald Firbank completely to suggest that any scientific law can reveal his mystery.'

At first it was thought best to present all the material in chronological order, which would have had the happy result of giving the place of honour to Carl Van Vechten, the only wholehearted literary champion that Firbank ever found for his work during his lifetime. Van Vechten corresponded with Firbank but never met him, got Brentano in New York to publish *Prancing Nigger* (though they couldn't stomach *Cardinal Pirelli* which followed it), and himself thought up the title *Prancing Nigger* for the book which appeared at first in England as *Sorrow in Sunlight.* His pioneering support gave Firbank almost the only undiluted critical approval he ever knew in his lifetime, to say nothing of a substantial royalty cheque or two; and he must still be honoured for it.

For reference purposes, however, the more conventional 'Life and Works' division has its advantages, and this scheme has been preferred, with each contribution acknowledged and dated in a footnote. No attempt has been made to point out, much less to iron out, the several inconsistencies thrown up by these varied pieces. A mosaic is for apprehension as a whole, not stone by stone.

Those who read or re-read Harold Nicolson's *Lambert Orme* have to bear in mind that, like all the chapters of *Some People* from which it is taken, it is fiction, and fiction by a writer who had excellent reasons for disliking Firbank, a dislike which smouldered on in him to the end of his life. Though Lambert Orme is modelled on Ronald Firbank, the portrait is nothing like an exact one—unlike Lambert Orme, Firbank did not have red-gold hair, was neither poet nor composer, nor diplomatist, nor yachtsman, nor did he meet his death gallantly in war. The piece, however, comes into its own for its wonderfully exact physical description of the victim in his Madrid days.

Compiling the book has not been all gas and gaiters. Several obvious names, which might as well remain nameless, have professed themselves too busy, or proved too idle, to contribute; quite a number of others have left letters steadfastly unanswered. By contrast, it is a pleasure to acknowledge the help given by Alan Clodd, Sewell Stokes, Mrs C. A. Kyrle Fletcher, Anthony Hobson and Alan Harris—in particular the first three.

Let us hope, therefore, that these rescued perceptions from those who knew Firbank in life may help to give substance to a character not merely elusive in itself but fast receding from our view altogether. For now, fifty years on, Firbank needs all the friends he can get. 'That camp old thing—who reads him now?' snort the *literati*, ever ready to 'hear some new thing'; and indeed these austere, impatient days make it hard for us to dally in the Valmouth air with Mrs Yaj, or to agonise in sympathy with poor stagestruck Miss Sinquier. Somehow the novelty has worn off, the outrage is no longer so outrageous, the stylistic tricks have been so often copied. The standard *Collected Firbank* is no longer published in America at all; over here, though his worst enemies would allow him some merit as an innovator, he never made the august columns of *Scrutiny*, the practice of reading him aloud (recommended by E. J. Dent) has not caught on at all widely, nor has he ever found exactly the right illustrator to help spread his fame among those who can assimilate word fantasies quicker when they are made explicit in pictures.

However, Firbank-lovers—if that is the right word—can be sure that the doldrums will not last for ever. 'Sophisticated virgins and demi-puceaux,' as Van Vechten wrote, 'will adore these romances.' Their hero will be critics' fodder for decades to come, a permanent magnet for undergraduates of all ages, not a big figure, but a bright one, endearing and evergreen. Meanwhile, if earnest students coming new to him really must have some kind of label to help place him, there is always the French word that Anthony Powell uses (coins, in fact, since it appears in no reputable French dictionary) in his preface to the *Collected Firbank*: 'hopelessly *insortable*'. For the rest, in a collection of eyewitness accounts of a person so resolutely narcissistic as Ronald Firbank, pride of place must surely be given to his own accounts of himself, on the ground that no one else has devoted so much concentrated thought to the subject. So here are assembled the passages from his own published works and correspondence in which he refers, or seems to be referring, to himself. They are printed in any old order so as to give confirmed Firbankians the pleasure of identifying them:

'He has such a strange, peculiar style. His work calls to mind a frieze with figures of varying heights trotting all the same way. If one should by chance turn about it's usually merely to stare or to sneer or to make a grimace. Only occasionally his figures care to beckon. And they seldom really touch.'

'He's too cold. Too classic, I suppose.'

'Classic! In the *Encyclopaedia Britannica* his style is described as *odd spelling, brilliant and vicious*.'

'Considered a cult, but everybody reads him.'

'I used to have the reputation of always wearing the most harmonious ties, your ladyship.'

'I once met him,' Miss Hopkins said, dilating slightly the *retinae* of her eyes. 'He told me writing books was by no means easy.'

'I think nothing of fileing fifty pages down to make a brief, crisp paragraph, or even a row of dots.'

'I am a *spinster,* sir, and by God's grace intend to stay so.'

'I believe strawberries are the clue to my heart.'

'I always feel a sort of *malaise* in Florence. Why, I can't tell.'

'If I'm a little disappointed at present, I believe always in my own eventual star.'

A dingy lilac blossom of rarity untold.

'I adore the mauvishness of him.'

An elaborate young man who, in some bewildering way of his own, seemed to find charming the fashions of 1860.

'I am all design—once I get going.'

'I should have loved to have lived in the Bible period. . . . How beautiful to have followed the Saints.'

He was usually considered charming. He had gone about here and there, tinting his personality after the fashion of a Venetian glass. Certainly he had wandered. . . . He had been into Arcadia, even, a place where artificial temperaments so seldom get—their nearest approach being, perhaps, a matinée of *The Winter's Tale.* Many, indeed, thought him interesting. He had groped so. . . . In the end he began to suspect that what he had been seeking for all along was the theatre. He had discovered the truth in writing plays. In style—he was often called obscure, although, in reality, he was as charming as the top of an apple-tree above a wall. As a novelist he was almost successful. His books were watched for . . . but without impatience.

'Modern life is only remarkable for its want of profile, and lack of manners. To be smart is to be artificial. To be artificial is to be smart. There is not a man or woman in London society that dares to be him or herself. We are surrounded by invisible laws and conventions, we all sin, and cover our sins in chiffon and diamonds. The chiffon is quite transparent, everyone can see through it, still chiffon is a veil, and then the diamonds! We are all vulgar at heart, and if the diamonds glitter, what does it matter where they come from or how they are bought? To be artificial, and to be a little more improbable and impossible than one's neighbour, is to be a perfect success!'

'Drifting, if you can bear it and are resigned, is probably less painful than grappling with the cruelty of the world, but I do not think we are here to drift.'

'Ah the East... I propose to return there, some day, when I write about New York.'

Hardly had he been angling ten minutes today when lo! a distinguished mauvish fish with vivid scarlet spots. Pondering on the mysteries of the deep, and of the subtle variety there is in Nature, the veteran ex-minister lit a cigar. Among the more orthodox types that stocked the lake, such as carp, cod, tench, eels, sprats, shrimps, etc., this exceptional fish must have known its trials and persecutions, its hours of superior difficulty...

'My writing must bring discomfort to fools since it is aggressive, witty and unrelenting.'

So much for Ronald Firbank's views of himself. Now for the views of others.

M.H.

London
January 1977

Part One

RONALD FIRBANK: A MEMOIR

IFAN KYRLE FLETCHER

I

The Chinese have a saying that, in judging a man, it is essential to look back at least three generations in order to discover the state of education of the family. In the case of Ronald Firbank, the enquirer, even if he be as astute as Tu Fu, would be puzzled to find the roots of his talent in the life of his great-grandfather. A glance back to the third generation reveals a Firbank who could neither read nor write. He worked all his days as a coal-miner at Bishop Auckland, in the county of Durham, and his sons seemed destined to follow the same life. One of these, Joseph Firbank, commenced work underground at the age of seven. By means of evening classes he augmented his scanty schooling, with the heroic intention of leaving the mine when opportunity arose. His chance came at the end of fourteen years, and it took the form of a glorious offer to work as a labourer on the railway construction scheme between Bishop Auckland and Weardale. There was something in the new railway work which called up the genius in Joseph Firbank. The steps of his development were as rapid as they were remarkable. The next year he obtained a subcontract on the Woodhead Tunnel. In 1854 he went to Newport to undertake work for the Monmouthshire Railway and Canal Company. There he was quick to buy land which was shortly to be required by the Great Western Railway Company. In 1866, as one of the largest contractors in the country, he was triumphing over innumerable difficulties of construction at Carlisle.

In spite of his success, he remained pleasantly unaffected. Those who knew him throughout his career have vouched that their memory of him was the same, in essentials, in poverty and in affluence. They remembered a man about six foot tall, his

---

Ronald Firbank: A Memoir by Ifan Kyrle Fletcher, with personal reminiscences by V. B. Holland, Augustus John R.A., Osbert Sitwell and Lord Berners, was published by Duckworth in 1930, and a part of the stock was destroyed by enemy action in 1940. The book is reproduced in full here, with a few minor additions and corrections to the Kyrle Fletcher contribution supplied by Mrs C. A. Kyrle Fletcher.

head set low on a wide neck, his small eyes twinkling at the top of his spreading nose; a man who worked with a fury of energy and spoke with disconcerting directness. At the beginning of his career, he was offered, by a generous friend, a loan free of interest to start a contract. He replied, in his rich dialect: 'I values at nowt what I gets for nowt.'

Years later, when everyone with money to invest endeavoured to secure his advice free of charge, he adhered firmly to his principle. A solicitor, who was anxious to discover in what companies Firbank was investing his money, planned to travel to London by the same train and to worm out the information during the journey. As though by accident he got into the same compartment. After the usual greetings he opened a conversation which could be led to the subject of the companies. All seemed to be going well, when Firbank leaned across and said: 'And what takes you to London?'

The solicitor was quick with his reply. 'A little business, for a client.'

Firbank looked at him out of his small eyes and then said steadily: 'Mr Leslie, you're a damned liar!'

He sat back and said not another word.

By the time of his death in 1886 he had reached an eminence which enabled him to command respect from all the business men of the country. They were able to say over his grave that 'he was an excellent specimen of the Englishmen who rise up not so much by any transcendent talents, as by intelligence and energy, and above all by honesty and inspiring confidence in those for whom they have to work.'

Admirable memorial as this may be, it is more revealing of its age than of its subject. While it may have satisfied the Victorian commercial conscience, it did far less than justice to the robust individuality of Firbank. There must have been many who longed to bring sincerity to this stilted epitaph by recalling his lively methods of maintaining an enthusiasm for work in his gangs. Polite these methods might not have been, but at least they were tokens of imagination and verbal range. Or someone should have remembered his affection for the men working under him, and how he provided immense consignments of beef and beer for his labourers. The affection was amply returned. There was not a railway worker on the line who had not a kindly word to say of 'old fairther Firbank'. This nickname, with its sense of friendly intimacy, is a more lasting memorial than the business men's fine speeches.

The small details of his life, apparently unimportant but full of meaning when related to one another, all point to the conclusion that the business men were wrong in their estimate of him. Energy he had, but educated intelligence he lacked. There can be no other explanation of his refusal to accept tempting contracts out of the country. He explained that it was because foreigners did not pay in English gold. Even Ireland was a foreign country in his narrow view. He had no hobbies himself, and disapproved of them in others. In his later years he entrusted much of the management to his son, Thomas, who had other views about relaxation. But the old man paid periodical visits of inspection. On one of these he found a spruce hunter in the stables with the cart-horses. He looked at it sourly, and then said to his son: 'Eh, lad! That woarnt pull a load o' muck!'

Similarly, he disliked holidays. When persuaded to go away, he usually returned long before the date fixed. Like all men of limited interests, he hated idleness, from which arose his habit of retiring to bed at eight in the evening and rising again at five.

In these habits there are signs of his lack of education and his cramped environment. Yet his business deals prove that he possessed natural genius. His calculations for tenders were worked out by mental arithmetic. Himself he told the story of how he laid the foundations of his fortune by trebling an already profitable estimate. By such incidents did he prove his inherent aptitude for big business. It is not absurd to claim that there was something of the artist in Joseph Firbank. Although he made only 'the most beautiful railways' (as his grandson called them), he had such overwhelming zeal, such fixity of purpose, and such skilled technique, that his work passed beyond the usual confines of craftsmanship. His life was wholly absorbed by his work. Even religion failed to secure entrance. His neighbours in Newport whispered the shocking rumour that he was a free-thinker!* A free-thinker in 1870! His genius must have been paramount to preserve his business in the face of such a suspicion. It is terrifying to conjecture what would have happened if they had known of his playfulness with the corpses in St Pancras Churchyard. It was in 1864, when he was building the Midland line into London.

* His daughter Mary insisted that throughout his life he was in fact Church of England and never missed Sunday matins.

The work necessitated the removal of part of the burying-ground of St Pancras Church. Reverence was shown to the disturbed remains by removing them to consecrated ground elsewhere. In the midst of the work a message was received that the body of a French Roman Catholic dignitary was to be taken back to his native land. Unfortunately, the digging operations had disturbed the grave. When it was opened, it was found to contain three sets of bones! From this dilemma the ingenuity of Firbank found an escape. The man was a foreigner; therefore he must have been dark. They would choose the darkest skull and find rights and lefts to fit it. Solemnly the workmen carried out the instruction. Some days later an eminent French Roman Catholic dignitary was buried with great pomp in his home place. If Ronald ever heard this story he would have appreciated it.

Joseph Firbank died at St Julian's House, Newport, on 29 June 1886. His immense fortune was divided between his seven children, not, however, without the usual litigation. His business was inherited by his eldest son, Joseph Thomas, later to become Sir Thomas Firbank. This title and his honours as Member of Parliament and Deputy Lieutenant gave an air of great dignity to the new head of the Firbank family. His resemblance to old Joseph in feature and build increased the respect which was shown to him as his father's son. It seemed likely that he would become very popular, especially as he contrasted favourably with Joseph in the matter of hobbies and social recreations. But the contrast, to bring him real fame, would need to have extended to many things other than hobbies. When the contrast was made it was found in every case that the rare personality of the father was unassailable. The step from autocracy to pomposity is small.

Joseph Firbank used to boast that 'the Firbanks have a knack of marrying the right women'. This was true of himself and of his three marriages. His first wife, by her intelligence and grace, did much to smooth his social rough corners, but died childless. It was no less true of Sir Thomas. When he married Miss Jane Garret, his life became coloured by the sensitiveness to beauty which guided her temperament. By birth she was Irish, being the daughter of the Reverend James Perkins Garret, of Kilgarron, County Carlow. She was a beautiful woman, sensitive and attached to lovely things. Due to her influence, Sir Thomas gathered around him collections of *objets d'art.* His French furniture and prints, and English furniture and porcelain, were famous among connoisseurs, who visited him at Petworth and Tunbridge Wells in order to admire his treasures.

Arthur Annesley Ronald Firbank, Sir Thomas and Lady Firbank's second son, was born in London in 1886, the year of his grandfather's death. That he never saw his grandfather does not prevent the playful law of heredity from drawing them much nearer together than obvious family ties drew father and son. Towards his mother he maintained a steadfast and affectionate regard. From her he first learned to be fleet in the pursuit of beauty. But, if any of the secret of his strange personality is to be found in his ancestry, the immovable force of his isolated independence must be sought in his grandfather as much as his unwavering devotion to beauty was derived from his mother. But it is to misunderstand Ronald Firbank to suggest that any scientific law can reveal his mystery. The blunt forthrightness of Joseph underwent a profound change to become the nervous retirement of his grandson, just as Lady Firbank's love of beautiful things was twisted into a strange shape when it became her son's deceptively casual aestheticism.

II

The boyhood of Ronald Firbank was lived under the contrasting influences which play upon a family passing upwards through the social strata. Railway contracts, politics, Moreau prints, and ormolu furniture typify the influences. Big business and *The Yellow Book* strove for his affection. Very early in his life two factors decided the issue. He suffered from ill-health and, perhaps as a result, he was a spoilt boy. Frequently he was taken to warm climates to repel the advances of the throat affection which, even then, was troubling him. In 1901, at the age of fourteen, he was sent to school for the first time. The arrival at Uppingham of this tall weed of a youth, entirely incapable of holding his own in the rough-and-tumble of school life, must have been the signal for outbursts of ragging. From his point of view, the atmosphere of an English Public School, antipathetic to his trend of thought and definitely opposed to his taste for the poets and painters of the nineties, must have seemed Philistine and reactionary. He had no place in a system of education based upon classwork, games, and communal life. Details of his life at Uppingham are not available, but a small tragedy is concealed behind the bare entry in the school register:

> 'Arthur Annesley Ronald Firbank: Entered September, 1900. Left April, 1901.'

He continued his education under a private tutor at Buxton. While there he met R. St C. Talboys, who directed him in his reading and encouraged him to write. Such gentle guidance found a response in his nature. The experience of normal education at Uppingham had the effect of deepening his inherent reserve, without in any way lessening his self-consciousness. Two terms at Uppingham made him react from all forms of mediocrity; two years might have had a very different effect. For so nervous a boy it would not have been easy to withstand the inroads of a powerful system, although his behaviour in later years must convince us that his resilient nature was capable of astonishing resistance.

About this time he was reading the works of Lord Herbert of Cherbury, and he determined to visit Newport, where, at St Julian's House, Lord Herbert had written *De Veritate*. It was this Tudor mansion, then decayed into a farmhouse, which had inspired Joseph Firbank to call his new house and estate by the same name. Ronald arrived at Newport and hired a hansom cab. 'Drive me to St Julian's House.' The cab rattled through the drab sreets of Maindee (built from the remains of a London suburb demolished during a railway contract) and pulled up in front of a Victorian neoclassical mansion.

'What is this?'

'St Julian's, Sir. Fairther Firbank's old 'ouse.'

'But I want the old St Julian's. Lord Herbert's house.'

In vain Ronald protested. This was St Julian's. And, still protesting, he was driven back into the town. Then began an excited questioning of policemen. No one could help, until he was directed to a student of local history. Eventually, after a morning which had completely exhausted his small store of nervous energy, leaving him in a state of hysterical giggling, he achieved his desire to see the real St Julian's.

The next step in his education had the effect of widening his horizon, while leaving his liberty unfettered. In the summer of 1904 he was sent to a château at Tours to learn French. At this time the suggestion was first made that he should enter the Diplomatic Service, and a period of study in France was considered a suitable preliminary. Whether it was, we shall never know; the Diplomatic Service was never embarrassed by the strangeness of his talents. In other directions his stay at Tours was valuable training. He learned French, and, more important, he studied French literature. He read Maeterlinck, Baudelaire, Mallarmé, Flaubert, Gautier, and Henri de Régnier. His education was not only literary but liberal. He acquired the graceful habit of wearing ties from Doucet's and from Charvet's. He felt for the first time the attraction of the Roman Catholic religion. And he found in the scenery of the Touraine the focus of his growing literary powers. The aura of grey and gold and soft rose, in which the château had its being, he hung around his story *Odette d'Antrevernes.*

> In the long summer evenings, when the shadows crept slowly over the lawn, and the distant towers of the cathedral turned purple in the setting sun, little Odette d'Antrevernes would steal out from the old grey château to listen to the birds murmuring 'good night' to one another amongst the trees.
>
> Far away, at the end of the long avenue of fragrant limes, wound the Loire, all amongst the flowery meadows and emerald vineyards, like a wonderful looking-glass reflecting all the sky; and across the river, like an ogre's castle in a fairy-tale, frowned the château of Luynes, with its round grey turrets and its long, thin windows, so narrow, that scarcely could a princess in distress put forth her little white hand to wave to the true knight that should rescue her from her terrible fate.

In 1905 he published a slim volume containing this story and another sketch called *A Study in Temperament.* Some of the copies were bound in pink wrappers and some in blue. The pallor of these colours offended his eye, now quick in aesthetic sensibility. He expressed his detestation in a letter to his publishers which foreshadowed his later ironical work. From the point of view of the public, he need not have been concerned. His book was ignored. One cannot blame the critics that they did not recognise in it the first work of a potential genius. One cannot blame his present admirers if they find it tiresomely precious, lacking the humour which farced his novels. It was written at a time when literature was more important to him than life. He was powerfully under the influence of Maeterlinck, and mystic simplicities drew him to writing which today sounds hollow and pretentious. But what Firbank the writer then ignored, Firbank the wit stored up in his mind. In after years, he often talked about the château and its inhabitants. His conversation never attempted to recapture the solemn mystery, but always dwelt on some hilariously funny episode of his stay. Alas! in a way which was habitual to him, before he had said many words he shook with uncontrollable laughter—and his listeners were forced to accept the joke on trust.

A signed copy of *Odette* which he sent to Henry Ainley was coupled with a request—which Ainley found himself too busy to grant—to be given elocution lessons.

Other works showing the influence of his visit to France are a dream play, entitled *The Mauve Tower*, and an episode called *True Love*, possibly written after his first visit to Paris and attempting to recapture some of the glamour of the city. The play shows, too clearly, his indebtedness to Maeterlinck and his love of touching in his scenes, as though with heavy dabs of pigment.

It was now decided that he should proceed to Cambridge, and, as the next step in his preparatory studies, he was sent to Madrid in March 1905. His stay lasted two months, during which time he studied Spanish, made a few friendships amongst literary people, and appeared much in fashionable society. He lived in rooms in the Calle Mayor, where he entertained his friends with exquisite grace. The room was heavy with the aroma of incense and the fumes of candles burning in tall sconces. The tea-things gleamed sharply against the dull patina of old wood. Ronald sat near the fire in a chair hung with red silk. As he talked witty French in a high voice the flames flickered rosily on his cheek-bones and forehead. Antonio de Hoyos y Vinent, remembering such an occasion, wrote that his host was '*alto, rubio, delgado y un poco presumtuoso, aunque con chic, un tanto afectadillo*'.

Returning to England, he entered Scoones' in October of the same year. During his stay with Mr Scoones he lived at 49 Nevern Square, the house of Mr de V. Payen-Payne, one of the tutors. His fellow-boarders were the Hon. John Mitford and Mr

Lascelles, son of Colonel Lascelles, of Petworth. Mr Payen-Payne has described the advent of Firbank:

'Mr Scoones suggested to Firbank that he should live in my house. He was entirely spoiled by his mother, who was the cause of the weakness of his character. When he came to live with us she sent a footman and a housemaid to prepare his room with a new bed, complete with eiderdown, and a special armchair. Mitford and Lascelles dominated this weakling, and used to borrow his eiderdown and anything else they desired. Firbank, although weak, had a sweet nature and perfect manners.'

Whatever preparations he may have made for the Diplomatic Service, he remembered his stay with Mr Payen-Payne for another reason. In a letter written years afterwards he said: 'Of course I have not forgotten, and very well I remember that it was at your house that I first heard of Dowson and read first Verlaine.'

Throughout these years prior to Cambridge his personality was rapidly forming. His tastes for *fin de siècle* literature both French and English, Impressionist painting, and Russian music were already acquired. Modifications and extensions of his outlook were to take place, but at the end of 1905 his was a developed personality. The changes which were to come were only those which accompany increased knowledge and experience. Already he despised people whose feeling for beauty was not as keen as his own. He hated 'the mob', as he called the vulgarians of all classes. He was nervously self-conscious, and had already learned to conceal it behind a barrier of reserve, when his gestures grew long and sinuous and his voice slithered without control over his sentences. His friends sometimes thought that he was playing to the gallery, but, as A. C. Landsberg wrote: 'He was really too fastidious ever to be cheap—unless it is cheap to be for ever striving *not* to be so!'

In that sentence lies a hint of Firbank's self-torturing complexity. Landsberg continued: 'No one could be more full of contradictions than he was, being one of those people who are naturally artificial and sincerely paradoxical.'

It is this twisting of qualities which today makes him appear so remote, like a figure from a Restoration comedy. And it was this twisting of qualities which, in his life-time, made him so vitally baroque. His life seemed all grotesque ornamentation. His love of beauty was skilfully disguised. But it was always apparent in his hatred of pretentiousness. He suspected his own expressions of admiration as strongly as he questioned the sincerity of all rodomontade. Growing out of this was his refusal to talk seriously about art and life, even to kindred spirits. He feared that serious talk would become sober tosh. Therein lay the cause of the mocking isolation of his later life. Like the Sleeping Beauty, he lived in a shadowy haven of retreat, secure from the world behind an impenetrable barrier of briars.

III

It was in October 1906, that Ronald Firbank went up to Trinity Hall, Cambridge. The choice of college was curious. In the words of a Cambridge correspondent, 'Trinity Hall in those days was chiefly a college of rowing, hunting, and racing men, who seldom passed examinations successfully.'

Although not a sporting man, Firbank did something to maintain the reputation of the college. He sat for no examination —not even Little-go—and he completed only five of the nine terms. His time was devoted to more personal studies than academic training embraced. He attended rehearsals of the Footlights' Club, being in some position of unofficial authority; he made long and delighted visits to the Fitzwilliam Museum; frequently he disappeared from Cambridge, to return full of impressions of concerts and exhibitions in London. Although he was out of his element at Trinity Hall, he probably made more real friendships than at any other time in his life. As long as the sporting men did not rag him, which they did only once, when he appeared in ridiculous running togs, he was happy in the congenial company of Vyvyan Holland, A. C. Landsberg and Rupert Brooke. Amongst the older generation he won the esteem of the late Charles Sayle, who loved to entertain undergraduates interested in literature and the arts, and S. C. Cockerell, the director of the Fitzwilliam Museum, who remembers him as 'a sensitive and rather shy young man with fine discernments in art and literature and rather exotic tastes'.

When A. C. Landsberg went up to Cambridge in 1907, he found Firbank already at Trinity Hall. Recalling their friendship, he wrote:

'Neither Firbank nor myself fitted into the college particularly well. The great advantage to both of us was that one was not bothered too much about passing exams. As he was a little older than myself, he seemed to me without age—for he gave one the impression both of being old and of being under-developed in some ways. He and I were the only members of the college who took the least trouble about making our rooms beautiful, or who took any interest in art generally. Through him I was introduced to *The Yellow Book*, Savoy and Wilde tastes, and to modern French poets and novelists. As I was at the time fresh from Harrow and English coaches, and full of the usual schoolboy prejudices and mistrust of originality, I was both thrilled and a little suspicious (this is not quite the right word, but it will have to do). In any case, in some ways I confess that I sympathised no less with the general college atmosphere than with him, especially at first. I both admired him and found him a little ridiculous—and even sometimes pathetic! You see, ours was such a very sporting college that I was myself conscious of not being in my right element, and he was even less so, and looked—I thought at that time—terribly feminine, sophisticated, cosmopolitan, and "elegant".'

His rooms were on the chapel side of the entrance-court of the college. Those who knew him best, remember him most vividly in the strange beauty which he created out of the drabness of college rooms. His room was arranged with old red silks, masses of flowers, and a number of dainty tables, covered with books and statuettes, and, in a place of honour, a photograph of his mother in Court dress. The statuettes were a fascination to him; mostly they were reproductions of Gothic religious figures, but sometimes they were Pompeian and Tanagra work, paganly attractive. Once he brought back from London an Egyptian bronze statuette. His whim was to have an opal set in it. When his friends remonstrated, and urged that this would mar the dull green surface, he replied: 'It must be done, as a propitiatory offering!'

In his room he would sit in curtained and shaded twilight, behind his head the yellow glimmer of candles set in carved and gilded candelabra. As he talked in his high-pitched voice, the silhouette of his face, large and fleshy, with low brow, aquiline nose, and full lips, would pass across the light. His hands, clasping his ankles or circling his head in frequent gestures, glinted with the sombre colours of his rings. Usually he wore a green jade Chinese ring, but occasionally he preferred the colour of some blue Egyptian rings, made of earthenware. In appearance, he always reminded A. C. Landsberg of the portraits of society women by Boldini, 'as he was always writhing about and admiring his hands'. His clothes—although made by the best tailors—always looked a little foreign. The same Continental atmosphere surrounded the parties which he gave, parties at which E. P. Goldschmidt and Mario Colonna were frequent visitors. The dinner in honour of Robert Ross is described in detail elsewhere by Mr Vyvyan Holland, but this was only the most famous of many elegant parties. Firbank entertained very exquisitely, choosing the menu, the decorations, the company, and the conversation with delicate care. Professor E. J. Dent remembers a dinner-party at which he and Rupert Brooke were the guests, when the room was decorated with masses of white flowers. Often on these occasions, Firbank talked little, but, if he had recently been to London, he would be full of news of pictures by Shannon and Ricketts, concerts of the music of Granados and Debussy, new French books and plays. He seldom directed the conversation, but added to its piquancy by a well-timed anecdote. Frequently his stories were unfinished. Either his mind would fly off at a tangent, leaving his listeners to bridge the gap, or he would lose his climax in torrents of hoarse, helpless laughter.

Much of his time was spent with Monsignor A. S. Barnes, the Roman Catholic chaplain to the University. The leaning towards mysticism, which had first become apparent in France and which revealed itself later in his reverential awe for Egyptian deities, now became prominent. It is difficult to understand how a nature such as his, delighting always in the tangibility of visual beauty, finding refuge from the reality of existence in the ordered elegance of his own life, was attracted by the tradition, dignity, and colour of the Roman Catholic service. Harder to understand is his intellectual reaction to the Church. While proclaiming that he hated the mob, he was being drawn to a religion which demanded subjection of his personality. His spiritual privacy, the result of a deliberate withdrawal from the world to hold a satirical watching brief, was in danger of invasion by doctrines of self-sacrifice and communal worship. The explanation afforded by the aesthetic satisfaction of the Church ritual is not upheld by the testimony of a friend who met him in Paris in 1910 and found that the service made no appeal to him, but that he was still profoundly moved by the mystic element of religion. The thought arises that, under an exterior of nervous elegance, Firbank concealed spaces of his mind where reason had no sway, where the vast ideas of infinity and eternity and immortality moved helplessly except for the guidance of faith. The explanation of one friend that it pleased him to coquette intellectually with priests gives place to the subtler belief that his aloofness, like his nervousness, was deeply rooted in his nature. He turned from people not intellectually but instinctively. Unlike others, who attempt to conceal their real motives by logical explanations, Firbank never gave reasons. But it is as certain as anything can be that, at times, he was conscious of the loss inflicted upon him by his unnatural nature. Not that he seriously missed social amenities, but that he was deprived, in himself, of the poise and self-possession which were, in his eyes, the most precious of virtues.

In spite of the fact that his Cambridge friends believed his mind to be too comprehensive to be held within one creed, he was converted to the Roman Catholic faith in 1908.

'I remember,' wrote Professor Dent, 'being at Sayle's house one evening and talking about Firbank. Sayle pulled out his watch (it was about 9 or 9.30 p.m.) and remarked: "Yes, that young man is at this moment being received into the Catholic Church." '

Firbank was always reticent about his beliefs and his religious activities. At the time that he left Cambridge he spoke to a few friends about his connection with the Church. In later years it was a subject which he avoided, and, except for the occasion on which he said to Lord Berners, 'The Church of Rome wouldn't have me and so I mock at her,' he confided in no one.

When Professor Dent took Rupert Brooke to see Firbank he had no inkling of the curious friendship which was to spring up. At first glance it seems that Brooke's avid delight in the world contrasted so markedly with Firbank's nervous retirement that no intimacy could have existed. But the attachment occurred during Brooke's ninetyish phase, of which Firbank approved. The so-called unpleasant poems in Brooke's 1911 volume awakened a response in a mind which was then considering the necessity of belief in wickedness. About the time that Firbank was accepted into the Roman Church he was immersed in a theory that positive evil has a place in man's spiritual life. 'If for no other purpose, to add colour to life,' he said. Rupert Brooke, it will be remembered, felt that 'the rosy mists of poets' experiences' had been rather overdone. His biographer claims that 'ugliness had a quite unaffected attraction for him; he thought it just as interesting as anything else; he didn't like it—he loathed it—but he liked thinking about it'. Two men with such ideas must have found much in common, and the bond was strengthened by their senses of humour. Again, in this respect, they were alike, yet different. J. T. Sheppard has written of Brooke's ironic habit of laughing at his friends and treating their most cherished enthusiasms as amusing, if harmless, foibles. This gift of irony was possessed to a higher degree by Firbank. In the cold light of his wit all enthusiasms appeared valueless. Even the pursuit of beauty without pretension, almost by stealth, was not proof against his wit. Brooke's society was, as Sheppard wrote, 'in the good sense, comfortable'. Of Firbank it might be written that his society was, in the pure sense, comminatory.

From contemporary evidence, their friendship seems to have been real, and Firbank's regard for Brooke's poetry sincere and unaffected. The years following Cambridge brought a change of mind. One evening in 1914, 'Eddie' Marsh, Brooke's biographer, was at Drury Lane for a performance of the Russian Ballet:

'I went out between the acts,' he wrote, 'and noticed a strange figure pirouetting about in the corridor and making little faces to itself. I got the impression of a waxwork that had escaped from Madame Tussaud's and met with a good but injudicious Samaritan who had taken it to a public house. Everyone stared, and I was idly watching the scene without any notion that I'd be involved in it, when the figure suddenly darted up to me, took my right hand out of my trouser pocket and shook it warmly, saying in a rather mincing voice:

' "I'm going to Kamschatka. Do you think I'm wise?"

'While I was wondering what to say, he went on still more urgently:

' "Do say I'm wise."

'I made the only answer which occurred to me:

' "I don't see what else you could do."

'He then changed the subject and said:

' "You knew Rupert Brooke, didn't you?"

' "Yes," I said.

' "Did you admire him very much?"

' "Yes."

' "You're wrong—I'm better than he."

'This was more than I could bear, and I executed the manoeuvre known as turning on one's heel. Later in the evening someone told me the man was Ronald Firbank. And so if in my old age I am asked, "And did you once see Firbank plain?" that is what I shall have to tell.'

Early in 1909, when his period at Cambridge was coming to an end, Firbank thought of applying for a post at the Vatican. He no longer mentioned the possibility of a position in the Diplomatic Service. In preparation for this Papal preferment, he talked of going into retreat, adding, as the spirit of absurdity asserted itself, 'As much for my looks as for the welfare of my soul.'

This was the time when he became jealously proud of his good looks. Charles Shannon had just drawn a pastel of him which revealed the sensitiveness of his features and the charming slimness of his profile. His dismay at discovering that he was becoming plump was genuine—and faintly amusing. He used to diet himself, take long walks in all weathers, and even tried running. It was only the preservation of his looks which persuaded him to appear in running shorts and so make himself the butt of the sporting men. He had a horror of growing old. To the methods of preserving his youth may be attributed a characteristic of his later life—his inability to eat—just as his fear of age may account for the narcissistic habit of having his portrait painted. Observers of his habits have noticed that he ate little while he drank much and have presumed from his weakly health that his ailment prevented mastication. There is no evidence to support this theory, and it is more likely that his habits of dieting engendered a dislike of food by suggestion. In the same way, his vanity has been blamed for the number of portraits which he commissioned. Shannon, Augustus John, Wyndham Lewis and Guevara drew him at various times. But his vanity was always at the mercy of his malice, and pride in his own features would not have lived long against his devastating sense of absurdity. The swift passage of the years made personal his theory that only art was enduring. If he was to bar the way of time, it must be done through art. His features, which he hated should become old and sunken and wrinkled, were to be made into lovely patterns by great artists.

All his fine discernments were used to choose the artists who should preserve him against mortality.

The years at Cambridge, so full of experiments in which music, painting, acting and literature all took their place, left their most definite mark upon his writing. The literary tradition of the University helped him to outgrow his desire to exemplify in himself a unity of the arts. The equality of the art forms in abstraction might be taught, but in practice every influence in Cambridge served to orientate him towards verbal expression. A. C. Landsberg remembers that 'his sensitiveness was such that it was obvious when one saw him what book he had last been reading—especially, of course, if it was something very strong like *Hamlet* or *Volpone*, when he would behave like Hamlet or Volpone, and speak to one almost as if he were Hamlet or Volpone!'

In his private reading at this time, Maeterlinck and Huysmans were his favourite authors. Their influence was heavy upon him, like a luxurious scent. He admired their deliberate withdrawal from forms of realism, their reaction from the Trade Union tendencies of late Victorian literature, their celebration of the solemn mystery of beauty. This was his Impressionist period, and it was many years before he passed out of its rich, overheated atmosphere into the disciplined rigours of Post-Impressionism. But already his experiments were leading him in that direction. He was working at a sort of mosaic, in which the pattern was picked out in pretty touches and amusing details lifted from life. He watched people and events with detached and malicious observance. Always he was listening for scraps of conversation which would give the right emphasis or colour to his design. Returning from a trip to London, he would be as excited about a *faux pas* he had seen at Rumpelmayer's or an *incongruité* he had overheard in the train as if he were bearing a new book by 'Max' or an Egyptian amulet of rare potency.

In spite of the deference which was shown him as the author of a published work, he aroused the hostility of those who were affrighted by the fantastic. A Cambridge contemporary said that, 'being so strongly marked a personality, there were people who couldn't bear the sight of him'. But justification, if ever it were needed, was to be found in his whimsicality, his love of beauty, and what Roger Quilter called 'his impish sense of the ridiculous'.

IV

Firbank went down from Cambridge in June 1909. His life there had done little to break the barrier of his reserve or to widen his sympathies. The congeniality of his few friends served but to emphasise the antagonism of 'the mob'. His deliberate isolation, a token of his nervousness and refinement, was a proof of his claim that he lived like a hermit. Poverty he hated, but he hated vulgarity still more. To live in the world was constantly to be touched by vulgarity. Only in a world governed by his sense of perfect manners and swayed by his obscure rules of conduct could he remain undisturbed by errors of taste. In spite of this, he adored luxury and the world, although he was continually wounded by it through his over-self-consciousness and sensitiveness. The sense of freedom which came to him on leaving Cambridge did not compensate for the irritation and annoyance bred by the discovery that in the world the percentage of gigmanity was even higher than in a university microcosm. Although some had hated him at Cambridge, his eccentricities had largely been accepted as the deviations from the normal to be expected of an aesthete. They were smilingly condoned. The same eccentricities transplanted to the bleak air of London appeared absurd and unforgivable. They were frowningly condemned. From his pampered upbringing he had learned to expect acquiescence in every whim. In its place he now encountered the sharp mockery of people who did not trouble to understand him. Even his friends found him pathetic and rather absurd, while acquaintances jeered openly at his silly behaviour and his ridiculous belief in his own literary powers. Reacting against these oppositions, he allowed his desire to live in solitude to develop into a craving for isolation.

The death of his father in 1910 revealed consequences of far-reaching importance to the conduct of his future life. It is idle to suppose that Ronald can have felt deeply the death of one who had little sympathy with the ideas and desires which actuated his life. He welcomed the increased sense of freedom and the hope of a larger income. It was an unpleasant shock when the reading of the will revealed the fact that Sir Thomas had been losing heavily on his contracts. The Firbank fortune, enviously large in the days of old Joseph, had dwindled to no more than a comfortable income. Sir Thomas had concealed this unpleasant news from his family. Only after his death did they find it coldly revealed in his will. The unpleasantness of this sudden deprivation was increased by the secrecy with which it had been concealed. Lady Firbank, formerly the most charming of women, became terrified of finance, and suspected every business arrangement of being another means of taking advantage of her financial ignorance. The effect upon Firbank was to increase the barrier between himself and the world. Poverty was hateful, even his very comparative poverty. But more hateful was the vulgarity of acknowledging the importance of money. He knew that many only tolerated him because he entertained lavishly. If the vulgarity of mundane conversations with his friends appalled him, how much more odious was the thought that the dilettanti who drank at his expense should know of his mortification. So, everyone who met him was impressed with the luxurious distinction of his surroundings. He wore exquisite clothes, massed rare flowers in his rooms, ate little but delicately, drank quantities of champagne, and mocked at those who had the low taste to drink ale and stout. Behind such masks did he save himself the necessity of explanation. And everyone talked with awe of his immense wealth.

The expected sense of freedom was somewhat curtailed by this monetary consideration. In any case, for some years he had possessed all the freedom he required. It was only the sense of it which was lacking and which he welcomed eagerly. For a little time he lived with his mother in Curzon Street. Then, in the winter of 1911, he paid the first of many visits to Egypt. The attraction of this ancient and mysterious civilisation was to grow in power throughout his life. But this did not prevent him from writing: 'I dare say, dear, you can't judge of Egypt by *Aïda*.'

The fascination exercised on him by Egyptian antiquities had been checked by the influence of Catholicism. That influence was waning; in 1911 he had ceased to show any interest in Christian mysticism. As his mind swung, momentarily unguided by a powerful faith, he felt again the attraction of Egypt. During his visit he found that its antiquities had for him an esoteric significance, the secret of which, he believed, would one day be revealed to him through a supernatural agency. His mind was entangled by the mystery of the Sphinx. But there may have been some truth in the belief that his mind was too subtle to take one creed as being the only possible form of absolute Truth. On his return to England, he met a disciple of Aleister Crowley, who was then carrying out magical work in Paris and London, and was writing *The Equinox* and *The Scented Garden of Abdullah*. Probably Firbank read these works; certainly he passed through a short phase of profound interest in magical ritual.

Visits to Constantinople and Vienna were events in the wanderings of this period. His travels were so extensive and were made so unobtrusively that it would be impossible, even if it were necessary, to keep a record of his journeys. Their value is to emphasise his unromantic outlook. To Englishmen, leaving the shores of their small island, comes some of the glamour of adventure and discovery—a natural emotion to a nation of explorers. Firbank knew nothing of this imaginative excitement. He did not penetrate into the fastnesses of Tibet; he did not climb in the Himalayas. His trips were made, calmly and almost casually, to well-known tourist resorts. 'Ducking always the touch of must and shall', he contrived to make his leisurely excursions fit the imperative needs of his health. But never did he show himself conscious of those needs, nor of the attractions of his journeys. He would be found living at Rome, Florence, Madrid or Bordighera in a state which was neither naturalised nor alien, but a strange, intermediate grade of his own devising. Fringing the English colony, with whose members he maintained no more than a bowing acquaintance, he yet, by his unconscious eccentricities, seemed to flaunt his foreign origin before the natives. When one of the importunate English visitors said to him, as Lady Rocktower said in *The Princess Zoubaroff*, 'Although you live within a stone's throw, one sees simply *nothing* of you,' perhaps he replied in the same words as the Princess: 'Yes, *how is it*, I wonder?'

Only the small group of his chosen friends—A. C. Landsberg, Evan Morgan and Albert Rutherston—were allowed to see more than the surface of his life. He met them frequently in London and Paris. He talked to them much about the book he was going to write. Since *Odette* he had published nothing, although throughout his Cambridge days he had been gathering material and fashioning it into his clear patterns. He seemed unable to bring himself to the final effort of production. Not even his intimates took seriously his intention to write, not because they doubted his ability, but because he was gay and heedless, always willing to drop the occupation of the moment to loiter on the boulevards. There he would sit far into the night, forming, in the high tones of his voice and the sinuous gestures of his arms, an impression of the novel in the manner of Gautier that he would one day write. Gautier had become his literary model, although Wilde and Beardsley still maintained an influence. What Ezra Pound has called 'the muzziness' of the nineties was ceasing to attract; the riot of half-decayed fruit was giving place to the glitter of gems. He talked so much of writing, but he never seemed to write. He was so taken up with attractive theories—the affinity between prose narrative and Impressionist painting and the ineluctable brightness of *le mot juste*—that his friends, in the midst of discussion, agreement and disagreement, would smile dubiously when he mentioned his own work. Their doubts would increase when, giggling with nervous excitement, he would suggest a round of visits to some of the 'restful' places he knew in Montmartre. The early morning would find him still drinking champagne and talking, his voice switchbacking over tabooed subjects. For one so weak, he was amazingly unafraid. Dangers seemed never to exist to him. So, lacking the discretion which is the better part of valour, he often proved a sore trial to his companions. Once, when the forbidding character of the haunt occasioned suspicions of the youths with whom he was drinking, he had to be removed by force, protesting hysterically against the maliciousness of the friend who was robbing him of his amusement. After such events he would punish his misguided friends by withdrawing from them the grace of his company. When next they met, the subject would not be mentioned, as though Firbank, in his forgiveness, had consented to forget their indiscretion.

In London he was often to be found at Le Tour Eiffel, the headquarters of the Vorticist group. This restaurant lingers on the outskirts of Tottenham Court Road as though to give a masochistic stimulation of ugliness to its aesthetic clientèle. Firbank, with his powerful sense of contrasts and his detestation of squalor, must have felt some such emotion as he sauntered past the cheap furnishers or paused to look at the French magazines fluttering outside the enigmatic general shops. By a conscious mental attitude he was able to position vice within his field. At Cambridge he was arguing that wickedness added colour to life. But vulgarity always repelled him. Like most men of sensitive nature and unusual instincts, with strong attractions and repulsions, he came to derive a perverse pleasure from being hurt. The thrill, at once exciting and nauseating, which came over him in Percy Street was akin to the nervous delight which he took from the spectacle of a gang of greasy bookmakers mocking him in the Café Royal. Outside Le Tour Eiffel he could contrast the mean street, lined with frowsy windows, with the discreet gloom of the restaurant, each table a rosy reinforcement of pleasure and elegance. At the Café Royal, when on a race night he sat, pink cheek by heavy jowl, with the exulting bookmakers and heard their coarse witticisms as he twisted his glass with carmined fingers, his pleasure was intense. No smile of his full lips or glint of his cold eyes revealed that it was his joke and not theirs. In his own time he finished his drink, set down his glass with a gesture which emphasised his limp elegance, casually drew out a wad of banknotes and paid his bill. With malicious enjoyment he noticed how the small eyes of his neighbours narrowed with avarice and how ingratiating smiles crept upon their faces. When one of them passed the time of day with him his triumph was complete. Appeased was his hatred of vulgarity, revenged was his outraged shyness!

At Le Tour Eiffel he shared a table with Augustus John, Evan Morgan and Thomas Earp. In this casual fraternity he was the most irregular. There was no means of ensuring his presence. Generally he would come alone, but sometimes he would bring a chance acquaintance, one of a group of people who formed a shadowy background to the events of this period. From this distance it seems that Firbank's progress through the life of Paris and London is chequered by consecutive lights and shadows. At one moment he is quite clear, sitting in a restaurant, drinking champagne and eating a persimmon, extolling the beauty of a Conder fan to Albert Rutherston; at the next he has passed into an obscurity. Although he passed through a phase, in which to use his own words, he 'experimented with life', the shadowed portions of his progress were to no large extent hectic superimpositions. They were a definite part of the pattern of his life. To know Firbank is to see elements of grace, wisdom, wit, reserve, nervousness, masochism, and perversion mixed in strange but attractive proportions. Never did he pose; never was he deliberately eccentric. To accept his characteristics as data is to be in a position to judge the normality of his actions and reactions. Those to whom conduct should be maintained on the basis of a seventeenth-century homily, those to whom the word 'unnatural' brings elemental fear and the anger of indignation, those to whom eccentricity spells charlatanism, will never appreciate Ronald Firbank. While others thought of vice and virtue, he was concerned about vulgarity and elegance. There are so few people in the world who will not read a book because its cover is ugly, and who build up friendship on the nicest subtleties of unspoken intimacies. And in the end, morality and immorality are both just a little tedious.

In his friendships he was greatly influenced by personal appearance. More than most people he believed in the indicative qualities of form and manner. With an ugly or commonplace person he refused to speak. Many were the occasions on which he embarrassed his friends by his refusal to be introduced to a new arrival. Lord Berners noticed that 'it was difficult to get him to accept any invitation—especially if there was a probability of there being other people present'. Once, when he was taken to meet an American staying in London, he paused in the doorway, looked once, muttered, 'He is much too ugly', and walked away. The object of this curt treatment could console himself with the thought that Firbank was drunk. Undoubtedly he was, but when sober he would have *thought* the same, though lacking the courage to say it. Albert Rutherston he admired because of the trim youthfulness which lingered in his face and figure. In Evan Morgan's features he found an amazing resemblance to those of the mummy of Rameses in the British Museum. In this case his delight in good looks was reinforced by the mysterious influence pervading everything Egyptian. This mummy exercised an influence strange and superstitious. When Firbank first met Evan Morgan he hurried him off to the British Museum to see 'his original'. Whenever they met, Firbank would feverishly suggest a visit to the Museum. His interest became almost an obsession. He came to believe that Evan Morgan was a reincarnation of Rameses, and must, therefore, be possessed of cosmic secrets. If he waited long and patiently he too might be initiated.

At this period he found pleasure in collecting the literature of the nineties. He made a small but choice collection of association and presentation copies of Oscar Wilde, Beardsley, Dowson, Crackanthorpe, Mrs Ros, Beerbohm and their friends. Most of these copies he enshrined in costly bindings. Although he pursued this hobby carelessly, it afforded him real pleasure. An addition to his Beardsley collection was an event of importance and the new treasure would be carried triumphantly to Le Tour Eiffel, that its merits might be discussed. Many of these books came from the shop of C. W. Beaumont, the bookseller in Charing Cross Road, who remembers his customer very clearly and has written a charming description of him:

'Ronald Firbank was a customer of mine before the war. He was tall and slender in figure; his physique was almost feminine in its delicacy; he had the wasp waist affected by Victorian exquisites. His hair was dark and sleek and brushed flat to the head; his eyes were blue or bluish-grey; his features were oval in shape, the eyebrows thin and arched, the nose long, the chin weak; his complexion was fresh, with a delicate rosy blush on the cheek-bones. He was clean-shaven.

'Firbank was always dressed in a dark, well-fitting lounge suit, and he wore a black bowler almost invariably tilted far back on his head. He carried gloves and a cane. His hands were white and very well kept, the nails long and polished, and what was unusual in a man is that they were stained a deep carmine. I might mention that before my wife and I learned his name we always spoke of him as "the man with the red nails".

'He walked with a kind of leisurely saunter, as though time had no claims upon him. All his joints seemed to be loosely attached, like those of a marionette, and his movements in fact closely resembled those of a marionette, the controlling threads of which had been slackened. In short, he was a decidedly limp specimen of mankind.

'His tastes in literature were rather "ninetyish", although he was interested in eighteenth-century French literature of the more frivolous type. His stock question on entering was: "Have you anything in my line today; you know, something vague, something dreamy, something restful?" He was very fond of the word "restful"; all the books he liked he termed "restful". Even a study in the baroque such as Beardsley's *Venus and Tannhäuser* he would term "restful", although the normal male would doubtless consider such a work, on the contrary, disturbing.'

V

It is pathetically easy to realise how the War smashed Firbank's life. Even people whose needs were primitive found themselves forced to readjust themselves to an atmosphere charged with exulting enmity—an atmosphere which crept into every cranny of the mind, turning out comfortable preferences and thoughtless dislikes, and setting in their place one ruthless prejudice. In the business of the day this was reflected in a thousand inhibitions, mandates, newspaper exhortations—'It is forbidden . . .' 'England expects . . .' changing for the multitude of men into 'Défense de . . .' 'Vive la France . . .'

Firbank never suffered this sea-change, but his needs were more than primitive. Where others could, with effort, readjust themselves, he was entirely lost. Europe at war held no haven for him. On 4 August 1914, the gay, easy life vanished with the slickness of a conjuror's set piece and left no fragments of frivolity to console those who had loved its rococo splendour. The symbols of Firbank's happiness ceased to be vital and became memorials of departed pleasure. Lilies in Constantinople, scarabs in Cairo, music in Vienna, the ballet in Paris, books and pictures and theatres in London, with witty conversation wherever he went—these were the bright elements of his life, which, like a kaleidoscope, he had arranged in symmetry and which now were so rudely tumbled. The people who easily readjusted their outlook were to him 'the mob'; the same sort of thoughtless, unsympathetic, credulous people who had laughed at him in Cambridge and sneered at him in London. The war was their triumph. In the life he had made for himself he had been able to avoid obligations and to shun human encroachments. No one had the right of interference. The war gave everyone the excuse to demand to know what he was doing with his life and to force upon him the duties of the true-born Englishman. They peeped into his privacy, they tried to order his life, they tried to order everyone's lives. It was all done with the best of motives. But he hated it. And more still he hated the patriotic heartiness with which they believed that he would love it. This jingoism was responsible for his final desolation, when everything foreign began to disappear from the world of art. Foreign composers, artists, poets, dramatists and performers disappeared, and Art, emasculated perhaps but British through and through, was allowed to do its bit by holding concerts and exhibitions in aid of war charities. Such a mixture of pious humbug and salacious humour was revolting to those who still cherished their memories of Massine and Granville Barker and the first Post-Impressionist Exhibition. To a mind such as Firbank's, whose realities were those of culture, whose ridicule was reserved for the pretentious, the sombre and the moral, the war could be nothing but an irreparable disaster.

At the outbreak of the war he was living at Old Square, Lincoln's Inn, having just returned from a long stay at Bath with his mother. A. C. Landsberg remembers visiting him in August 1914, when he found him worried but inclined to allow himself to be soothed by the peacefulness and dignity of his surroundings. The panelled rooms, glinting with the patina of old wood, seemed a reassurance of stability. He spoke with enthusiasm of a new black carpet he had bought. On the wall was hanging another recent purchase, a drawing by Gordon Craig, which gave him great pleasure. Such solace was fleeting. During the first months of the war there was a general feeling of financial insecurity, which in the case of the Firbanks, with their small fortune, produced something of a panic. Pressure was brought to bear upon Ronald to urge him to augment the family revenue by his personal efforts. He was genuinely alarmed. For a time he seems to have had a vision of himself as a clerk at fifty shillings a week, becoming dismally suburban and riding to work by tube. The pressure must have been powerful and continuous, because he actually reached the stage of deciding that if he had to do work he would prefer it to be in a publishing house to anywhere else. He asked Wilfrid Meynell to help him in the matter. Mr Meynell remembers a visit when Firbank burst out in nervous exasperation against the war. From the time of that visit no more was heard of his intention to secure work. As the months passed people began to realise that, although there was a war, they had not gone bankrupt.

He spent the first year of the war in London, trying to hold together some of the scattered elements of his pre-war life. But the disintegrating force was too strong. In the summer of 1915 he stayed some months at Pangbourne, in Berkshire. There, probably, the idea first came to him to give up his attempt to live as though nothing had happened. It is amusing as a gesture to fiddle while Rome is burning, but as an occupation it is impossible. He would withdraw from the world. The place he chose for his retreat was Oxford. It was not his university and as a writer and aesthete he would be entirely unknown to the older generation of academic thinkers, to whom the city of learning had been abandoned. The chances were that he could live undisturbed and yet within easy reach of London. He took rooms at 71 High Street; later he moved to No. 66 in the same street. With the exception of a few visits to London and Torquay, he remained in Oxford four years.

Coincident with this retirement from London was his change of name. Hitherto he had been known as Arthur Firbank, his family having chosen to call him by his first name. As though to symbolise his change of life, he announced that in future he was to be called Ronald Firbank. This announcement was of the same nature as the advertisements of his arrivals from abroad which he caused to appear in *The Times* and the *Morning Post.* In their purpose they were half serious, half a parody of the pretentious people who regularly announce their movements. That this change of name was a deliberate gesture is shown by a letter of reproval which he sent to an old friend, who, knowing nothing of his literary ambitions, persisted in addressing letters to 'Arthur Firbank, Esq.' He wrote that he thought Arthur a horrid name. It had always pained him that his family insisted upon using it. The author of his books was to be Ronald Firbank.

To assert his detestation of the war he was frequently very rude to men in uniform. It gave him a meagre pleasure to make even so ineffective a gesture of defiance. One day in 1915, when he was lunching at the Café Royal with Grant Richards, his publisher, they were joined by C. R. W. Nevinson, in khaki. Firbank and Nevinson had not met before. At Grant Richards's invitation, Nevinson drew up a chair to join them. For a few moments the conversation flowed easily between the publisher and the artist, until they realised that Firbank had withdrawn into a silence which chilled the atmosphere with its malicious purpose. From this no pleasantry could arouse him. It was months later that he discovered that Nevinson's opinions about the war coincided with his own. A little later he met the Hon. John Mitford, a fellow-student at Scoones's, while travelling from Oxford to London. Conversation turned to the war, and its tenor can be gauged from John Mitford's tactful remark that 'I remember the meeting in the train during the war, but my only recollection of that is that, as far as I can remember, he did not then seem to be contemplating joining the Army'.

In another section of this book Osbert Sitwell refers to Firbank as 'in the best, and least boring, sense a war writer'. Revolted by the war, he forced himself away from it, and, in this reactionary movement, he was forced away from himself. Intense subjectivity had grown until it was torturous self-centredness. In such an atmosphere of introversion, with all energy poured inwards in an attempt to establish personal balance, he had little chance of writing his book. At that time he had been confined in a small world which was pro- or anti-Firbank. Unable to find his place in the scheme of things, he had thought the action to be centring around himself—and he thought it mostly hostile. His hysteria, apart from its sexual diagnosis, probably had one of its causes in his inability to see himself in the contemporary setting. At the time of going into retreat at Oxford, he achieved, as far as he ever achieved it, the business of development and detachment. The achievement was effected by the simple, magical process of introducing himself as Ronald Firbank. Now he saw himself as before he had seen the world—sharp and unblurred by the softest bloom of sentiment. He became able to laugh at himself; not publicly and raucously, as do those who seek an empty cheerfulness, but privately and bitterly. Later he learned to laugh in the discreet publicity of his work. It was his work which was the greatest result of the final stage of development and detachment. His work, flowering so easily after so long and painful a period of gestation, came from the same primal force which broadened his interests; which gave him a curious but effective comprehension of men and events; which made his mind, at least in part, aware of the claims of objectivity.

His first novel, *Vainglory*, was published in 1915. In its black cover, and decorated with a favourite pastel by Félicien Rops, it made a shy and beautiful entry into a world quite unprepared to receive it. Even was it difficult to find a publisher to open some quite small and discreet door. Martin Secker claims:

'My only distinction, and it is a negative one, is that I declined to publish both his first and second novels. He paid me several visits, I remember. I was amused by his first book, when I read it in typescript, but I saw no reason at all why it should sell, and, not being gifted with second sight, I had no idea that one day he would become a cult and that monographs would be devoted to him and his work. I recommended him to take his book to Mr Grant Richards, so that I feel I am in a very small degree responsible for his career.'

Having made its entrance, the book remained in a state of virgin neglect. It was read by friends who received free copies from the author, and it was supposed to be read by critics who received free copies from the publisher. The friends felt it incumbent upon them to be polite, but the reviewers felt no such constraint. Until a few years before his death, when he received evidences of appreciation from readers in America, he never encountered sufficient intelligent criticism to shake from him the feeling that he was deliberately or foolishly misunderstood. The urge of creation must have been strong in him to force so nervous and sensitive a man to subject himself repeatedly to neglect or disdain. It is difficult to know which hurt him most—the calculated coldness of the academic critics who gave him two lines at the end of their weekly budget of the latest fiction, or the well-meaning idiocy of the provincial reviewers, one of whom said that *Inclinations* was 'pleasant, vivacious, and stimulating'. One appreciates the bleak wit of Firbank's retort: 'Stimulating to what?'

His isolation and neglect were not relieved by the circumstance that he deliberately discouraged his friends from talking to him about his work. At Oxford he was almost without companions of any sort, and necessity forced him to dispense with the friendly exchange of opinions so valuable to most authors. This bred a habit of reserve with regard to his work, which was in direct contrast to his eagerness to talk of theories and methods in pre-war days. He confided in no one, and even his nearest friends did not know what experiments he was carrying out. At a time when he was accused of being obscure and well-nigh incomprehensible, he made no attempt to defend himself or to explain his method of writing.

From this distance it is amazing that anyone should have been perturbed by *Vainglory*. It is so charming, so full of early ardour, with the simple sophistication of dainty, gay figurines of porcelain. Almost it seems cruel to rifle its charms in search of hints about its author. But to study *Vainglory* is illuminating. A first reading reveals wit and satire and crystal dialogue. It is a close acquaintance which reveals the rhythm, by means of which all the elements are surely linked into a slight pattern. This rhythm ordained that Mrs Henedge's party, with battalions of guests deployed in each room, should be followed by the slim austerity of the scene in Mrs Shamefoot's flower-shop, and that the party should be gravely remembered in Lady Anne's dinner conference 'for women alone'. It was the rhythm which determined the precise juxtaposition of Mrs Henedge and Lady Castleyard, the Bishop and Monsignor Parr, Professor Inglepin and Claud Harvester. Unless it is possible to believe that an author is able to create in words what he cannot create in any other medium; unless the dictum that '*Le style c'est l'homme même*' may be rejected entirely, *Vainglory* must be recognised as a significant cenotaph. It commemorates the death of Arthur Firbank, a charming dilettante, and it proclaims the birth of Ronald Firbank, an artist in the rhythm of thoughts and verbal forms; an artist, moreover, who, if he found it more difficult to force a pattern from the overwhelming material of life, at least set an example of grace and elegance. After the publication of *Vainglory* he worked assiduously to issue *Inclinations*, *Caprice*, and *Valmouth* before 1918—one black-covered volume each year. For each group of characters he created a vivid and suitable setting. Each had its individuality while remaining a member of one family. Of them all, perhaps *Caprice* has made the most direct appeal to his admirers. It is not that the coruscations of wit are brighter and more numerous, or that the passage of the plot is more intricate and more richly decorative, but that the reactions of Miss Sinquier to the sophistication of London—so foreign to her simple nature—provides a theme which can suavely carry all its author's gentle malice. Especially amusing are the pages on which the Dean's daughter desiring the comfort of 'some nice tea-shop, some cool creamery', wanders, all unaware, into the Café Royal:

> She advanced slowly through a veil of opal mist, feeling her way from side to side with her parasol. It was like penetrating deeper and deeper into a bath.

And who can resist the solemn absurdity of her end? She dies while executing a few athletic figures to shake off sleep, on the stage of the Source Theatre. It is presumed that she was killed in a mouse-trap, but she died alone, and all that was heard was a cry:

> a cry that was heard outside the theatre walls, blending half-harmoniously with the London streets.

Writing did not absorb all Firbank's time and energy. Deprived by the war of many personal contacts, he found a substitute in his books. At Cambridge he had been a perfunctory reader, except for his devotion to a few authors. In Paris and London people were more fascinating than their shadowy images in words. But at Oxford he found his books a permanent delight and consolation. He flitted from author to author, from language to language, always within the narrow limits of his taste. The poetry and prose of the nineties always attracted, but he made delighted excursions into the comedies of the Restoration and the gay novels of eighteenth-century France. He read as a jackdaw steals—not for immediate gain, but to form a hoard of *bons mots*, from which one day he would select the brightest and most attractive to create his pastiche. He never allowed books to obscure his view of life. Even when his only intellectual contacts were made through books, they were substitutes. No one who saw him in the British Museum could fail to realise this. A friend wrote:

'I have seen him in the Reading Room with rows of tomes around him, keeping up an elaborate and entirely effective mockery of study. He read one book because it was the most trivial ever written on its subject, while he pushed away the standard work with a gesture of contempt. He handled an Italian volume so that he might derive the pleasure of touch from its leather binding. Another lay open in front of him an hour or more, that he might appreciate fully the pleasant proportions of its page. This book was discarded for the solemn reason that it looked dull, while that, a Greek Testament, with a jewel set in the cover, was amusing because it reminded him of the Cyclops. Such easy contempt of sober knowledge! And in that atmosphere! The effect was shattering.'

His delight in beauty of form was always revealed in his passion for beautiful books. In his rooms at Oxford he often derived pleasure from the typography and bindings of his books. Because he was so conscious of their external beauty, he found them difficult to fit into his schemes of decoration. Although they were lovely, they intruded. He kept them in closed cupboards, so that the colour of their bindings and the gold of their titles should not ruin the harmonies of his room. He quarrelled with his first publisher about the colour of the wrapper in which his story was bound. Again, during correspondence about a later book, he wrote:

'The "crocodile paper" would be very effective with a dull silver label edged with blue—turquoise—and palm or emerald green top. The silver should be quite dead, almost oxydised and subservient to the gold—and in any case the blue border would relieve a too sharp contrast.'

In spite of the care with which he designed the formats of his books, he was bored by the job of correcting proofs. His disconcerting habits of spelling, in which he allowed himself to be guided by the sight and sound of a word rather than by the *Oxford Dictionary*, brought him into conflict with compositors. From their wrath he escaped by soliciting the help of friends and even casual acquaintances. But until his work was in the hands of the publisher it was jealously guarded. Not even his friends should know what he was writing. In an expansive moment he offered to read a portion of his last book to Lord Berners. At the appointed time he arrived with the script. Nervously he curled himself into a chair and ruffled his hair with a long hand. At length he took up the first page and his mouth opened to read the words. But he jumped to his feet, muttering, 'No! no! I can't read it. It isn't finished', and hurried out.

Perhaps the loneliness of his life at Oxford has been overemphasised. It has been said that for two years he spoke to no one but servants and railway officials. But this picture is more pathetic than true. A few friends visited him from London and from amongst the residents he was able to make one or two pleasant acquaintanceships. Occasionally he left his retreat to attend a concert or an exhibition in London. For the rest, his isolation was profound. Intelligent people, who would not be affrighted by the fantastic and who would have relished his company, had no inkling that he was living in Oxford. Today, at his two addresses in 'the High', he is not even a legend. He has been forgotten entirely. But, possibly, some Oxford housewife or shopkeeper used to notice a strange willowy figure mounting a bicycle and used to wonder who he was. Perhaps, as an indolent pedaller in 'the Broad', he remains a memory in some obscure Oxford mind.

VI

The explosion of elation which burst over England at the signing of the Armistice, flinging up showers of hopes, desires, joys and resolutions, sent up one tiny private hope for Ronald Firbank. Hovering above the chaos of four years, it shone portentously during the few months that he lingered on at Oxford. Europe would be the same again! Refreshed by his long hibernation, he would enjoy the spring-like gaiety of Europe after the war. The warm cities of the south, whose healing air he had missed in the cold, damp winters of Oxford, would welcome him again. Once again he anticipated the solemn delights of Egypt. The cities that he loved—London . . . Paris . . . Rome . . . Vienna . . . Constantinople—their names sounded infinitely caressing now that he was to be restored to them.

In the February after the war he was visited by Osbert and Sacheverell Sitwell, who had long known and admired his work. He was then engaged in writing *Valmouth*, a chapter of which, under the title of 'Fantasia in A Sharp Minor', Osbert Sitwell published in *Art and Letters*. A few months later he decided to leave Oxford. As a gesture to signify that he was leaving a forced seclusion to take up his rôle of indolently critical spectator, he sold his library of books. It is certain also, although it is not recorded, that he sold his bicycle. The paraphernalia of life at Oxford were entirely discarded. He took rooms in Jermyn Street. The theatres soon saw him again. A friend wrote: 'I remember how much he enjoyed a play at the Haymarket that we saw together—*Frocks and Frills*.'

As though to celebrate his delight in the release of the theatre from war conditions, he wrote *The Princess Zoubaroff*, a comedy which elegantly held within an archaic form the agelessness of wit and the timeliness of satire. Always he had loved the theatre, and it seemed apt that he should desire to hear the bland tones of his dialogue. His earlier effort, *The Mauve Tower*, may be put aside as the exercise of a talented youth, who felt vividly the visual beauty of the stage. The process of detachment which made it possible for him to write *Vainglory*, now enabled him to lose the formlessness of his theatrical experiment. He realised how vitally the theatre depends upon the portrayal of character. But it did not need more than one glance at the contemporary stage to warn him that characterisation unrestrained by a sense of style makes an imitation of life and is a reproach to the reality of the theatre. His master was Congreve. To read *The Way of the World* and *The Princess Zoubaroff* is to become aware of relationships stronger than those of blood and more enduring than those of contemporaneity. Across two hundred years Congreve and Firbank look from the same angle at a facet of life, from which they draw the same desire to make, in exquisite creations of people and events, a microcosmos bounded by the footlights and the flies and subject only to the laws of fine wit and swift perception.

No managers rushed to secure the rights of *The Princess*

Zoubaroff. This neglect was no greater than that he had suffered with his novels. But perhaps it seemed greater in view of the hopes engendered by the peace. It was in his mind that the play might appeal to one of the private producing societies. At a time when the Phoenix Society was reviving the Restoration comedies to enthusiastic audiences, it seemed pathetic that no one saw a potential audience for *The Princess Zoubaroff*. By the time the play was published, in 1920, Firbank must have known that his expectation was not to be realised. The world was not the same as it had been in July 1914, and by the most optimistic outlook the signs of a return to pre-war conditions could not be found. There were furious recriminations between Governments, paralleled at home by bitter class hatreds. There were mad outbursts of spending, followed by a devastating period of poverty. The world was strident and strenuous. Only too clear was it that the comfort of the old order would return no more.

Even if it had been otherwise, the fact would have remained that Firbank himself had changed. His friends, most of them seeing him for the first time for five years, found a great and subtle difference. The manner was the same. He still sat curled in a chair; he still turned up the collar of his coat when he was indoors and turned it down when he went out; he still talked in a low gurgling voice, his hands circling around his head, making a rhythmic commentary on his conversation; he still undulated down Piccadilly so that people stopped to stare as he passed; he still ate almost nothing and drank and drugged a great deal. But those who remembered him as an amusing, slightly ridiculous disciple of the cult of aestheticism, must have noticed that his wayward tastes were now under some control and that his rather childish enthusiasms were seldom apparent. While retaining the finest flower of his sense of absurdity, the quintessence of elegant impishness, he had contrived to widen his interests and deepen his sensibilities. To say this is, perhaps, to give the impression that he had become serious or sober or profound. He had not. He had grown up, but he had not lost his view of the comedy of life. At no time was Firbank anything but the gayest of jesters, to whom life was far too portentous to take seriously, and whose echo of the ridiculous would have deceived Ridicule herself.

To a certain extent Firbank was able to recapture the flavour of his pre-war life. The restaurants where he had spent his nights soon saw him again. The theatres were a constant pleasure. The advent of flying made trips to the Continent even more frequent than they had been in the years after he left Cambridge. His behaviour was still as singularly individual. About this time he celebrated Armistice Night by taking one of his Bohemian friends to a very sedate political club. There they drank hilariously and insisted upon remaining until the early hours of the morning. The next day, the one clear impression which remained to them was the atmosphere of outraged decorum in which they finally made their exit. During the season he met Aldous Huxley, who has written:

'I used to see him from time to time at the theatre when I was doing dramatic criticism. He often attended First Nights, in spite of an overwhelming shyness which made the presence of other people an agony to him. Sometimes the agony was so great that he would do extraordinary things that made him very conspicuous and so increased his self-consciousness (e.g. he would get up in the middle of an act, or start rummaging under his seat). He must have derived some curious painful pleasure from his embarrassments. The last time I saw him was at Robert Nichols's wedding. We sat with various other people in the Café Royal. As I took my seat at the table opposite him, Firbank gave his usual agonised wriggle of embarrassment and said:

' "Aldous—always my *torture*."

'Which must, I think, have been his spontaneous reaction to most people, at any rate at first.'

Holt Marvell, who knew and loved the old 'Café', has written:

'Ronald Firbank is dead. He was truly a *habitué* of that faded, jaded room. Some days he sat from noon till midnight in his accustomed seat—to the right as you swing through the door. A thin man with a black felt hat. A narrow man and restless—writhing like a basket of serpents. Clutching at the lapel of his coat, dipping his head like an embarrassed governess. Always paying for drinks. . . . "My dear, I saw a crossing sweeper in Sloane Street today with the eyes of a startled faun!". . . "My dear, when you talk like that you give me a distinct feeling of plush!" It was he who gave me the life story of the lavatory attendant at the Café whose children were never told about their father's profession until they were sixteen and old enough therefore to know the facts of life. To an undergraduate, hoping to find the Café Royal the embodiment of all that was most fine and free and desperate, Firbank seemed, in his appearance and his talk, to keep alive a little of the spirit of the nineties. He was friendly and generous and tolerant of the conversation of undergraduates. Because of his charm, his queer uncoiling movement and his mannered, coloured talk, one undergraduate at least bought *Valmouth* meaning to read it in the train.'

These memories of Firbank in the Café Royal bring to mind Miss Sinquier's visit, in *Caprice*, when she sat drinking China tea and eating a bun with currants in it, listening to the conversations of 'stage folk, artists, singers'. She felt drawn to speak:

> 'Can you tell me how I should go to Croydon?' she asked. The words came slowly, sadly almost.
>
> 'To Croydon?'
>
> 'You can't go to Croydon.'
>
> 'Why not?'
>
> The young man of the whiskers looked amused.
>
> 'When we all go to Spain to visit Velazquez——'
>
> 'Goya——!'
>
> 'Velazquez!'
>
> 'Goya! Goya! Goya!'
>
> "... We'll set you on your way.'
>
> 'Goose!'
>
> 'One goes to Croydon best by Underground,' the pale-looking girl remarked.
>
> Miss Sinquier winced.

His friends heard again his hysterical laughter. He knew it was a shy man's most valuable weapon. When C. R. W. Nevinson was leaving for America, a dinner was given in his honour. Firbank, as a friend of Nevinson, was invited. With typical contrariness he broke his rule of refusing to attend soirées and banquets and took his place at the principal table. During dinner his behaviour was exemplary. The valedictory address was delivered by an eminent journalist, who took advantage of the occasion to embark upon a sea of rhetoric. Period crashed upon period, working to a brave cadenza of farewell. Subdued and indefinite noises were heard. The speaker continued, undisturbed. But the noises grew louder and took shape as a rush of shaking, irresistible laughter. All eyes were turned on Firbank. In his nervousness, perhaps, he aggravated the noise by stuffing a handkerchief into his mouth, until the sound became a muffled booming. The eminent journalist was still wishing the famous artist 'God speed', but obviously he was labouring under difficulties. Firbank shook with uncontrollable mirth. At last he left the room.

Although he sat in his accustomed place at the Café Royal and jested as easily as ever, he had left the old casual life far behind. His work occupied the central place in his thoughts. *The Flower Beneath the Foot*, which he was now writing, was using all his most delicate perceptions. At this time he seemed to give some thought to his relation to the reading public. His neglect by critics and readers gave him no encouragement to write. Perhaps in the hope of convincing the critics of their error, he allowed a friend to arrange a dinner at which he was to meet some of the despised reviewers. The idea was that if they found him a gracious host and charming companion, they might think more kindly of his next book. The dinner was arranged to take place at the Savoy. Firbank was in a frenzy of nervousness. As soon as the critics had arrived, he drank several glasses of champagne and subsided beneath the table. The critics ate the dinner and remained blissfully unaware of the publicity campaign arranged for their benefit. This amused concern with what people thought of his work is found exemplified in a letter which he wrote at this time to Mr Payen-Payne, a former tutor:

'I hope Mrs Payen-Payne has not forgotten me and that my novels don't shock her more than perhaps just a little.'

In June 1921 he went to Versailles for the summer. In the house in Rue des Reservoirs he wrote most of *The Flower Beneath the Foot.* A friend who visited him there had the impression that he was more happy than at any time after the war. The spacious splendour of the town, set in the gay artifice of park and garden, seemed to soothe Firbank's restlessness. For a short time he was undisturbed by the pathological hysteria which so miserably wrecked the tranquillity of life in Paris and London. Perhaps it was that he was enjoying a transmigration to Pisuerga, where he studied in detail the lives and habits of Madame Wetme, Count Cabinet, Mrs Montgomery, Laura de Nazianzi, and, in moments of special condescension, those even of her Dreaminess the Queen and King Willie. Certainly he carried this rare country and its orchidaceous people with him in the autumn to Montreux, where, under the trees by the green lake, they developed a warmth of blood and gaiety of mood unknown in western Europe. As the keen winds crept even over Lac Leman, he removed his creatures to Florence, where, the winter through, they flourished in his company. With none of his creations did he linger so long as with these of Pisuerga. Even when the warm breezes reminded him that at home people were beginning to think of Brighton or Bognor and that therefore it was time for him to smell the tarry heat of Piccadilly, he still clung to his characters. They remained with him throughout his visit to Havana, and not until his return did he bring himself to part with the unique distinction of being their only friend. When at last the binder's covers, stamped with their passport, *The Flower Beneath the Foot*, had closed upon them, they became at once more and less his own. More his own, because the world, if it wished, was now able to hail him as the creator of the King, 'who had the air of a tired pastry-cook'; of Mademoiselle de Nazianzi, who taught herself to read so quickly 'on the screens at cinemas', and of the Honourable Eddie Monteith and Mrs Harold Chilleywater, who reflect reality in a dazzingly distorted mirror. They became less his own because he knew with prescience that the world would bovinely disdain his offering.

While he was in Rome during the winter of 1922 a few friends offered him proof of their affection and esteem. They procured a life-size reproduction of the particular statue of Psyche which, through an accident, has lost the crown of its head and has, instead, a marble plateau. On this convenient memorial plaque they inscribed their names—Gerald Tyrwhitt, Evan Morgan, Aldous Huxley, and some others. With solemnity the statue was sent to Firbank at the Hotel Quirinale. He received it calmly, perhaps in the spirit of a master accepting homage from admirers of his art, perhaps as a slightly puzzled practical joker, suspecting that he was being pleasantly victimised. It was amusing that a symbol of the spirit was sent to one whose concern was paramountly with *la mondanité*.

VII

In August 1922 Firbank left London for Haiti. His departure, although sudden, was not unexpected. Some months before, he had been telling Aldous Huxley of his intention to go to the West Indies to live among the Negroes so as to collect material for a novel about Mayfair. His friends had noticed a growing interest in the black races. The number of his visits to coloured entertainments, such as *The Blackbirds*, was a source of amusement to his friends and of discreet suspicion to his acquaintances. Many who met him after the war remember him best lying at an uncomfortable angle in the stalls at the Pavilion, his neighbours eyeing him nervously, while he waited, quite unconscious of the agitation around him, for the appearance of Florence Mills. He was happy in watching Negroes. He loved their powerful vitality; their languorous sense of rhythm, waking to fierce movement with the flick of wrists and ankles; the dull gleam of oiled bodies; their range of muted colours—ebony, brown-black like iodine, blue-black like tar, bronze, wrinkled brown like an old morocco binding, the dull mouse shades where yellow is softened with grey. He watched the creole boys, fair, with a hint of green around the eyes and pink at the elbows and knees. Under the shadowless glare of footlights and battens, these figures moved in uncreasing rhythm, an endless excitement and a perpetual provocation. With the draughts from the stage, smelling of grease-paint, powder, and dust, came the heavy odour of human flesh, to rise in the theatre like incense to a pagan god. In swirling circles the dancers followed every jerk of syncopation, delighting in a primitive, animal merriment, to which the audience was forced to respond. The people who had come to the theatre as so many individuals, cool and compact as ice-bricks, found the sharp edges of their personalities yielding and rounding under the pressure of this insistent rhythm. Gradually they ceased to feel their isolation and became an entity having one mind and one purpose—to sway in unison, a thousand dark heads dipping in the drowsy gloom. There is no guessing if Firbank yielded his individuality and swayed with the crowd. While the sensual stimulus streamed through the theatre, beating eagerly upon everyone, its reception was private. No one could tell how much or how little his neighbour responded. Least of all could Firbank's neighbour have guessed.

He was away three months and visited Haiti, Havana, and Barbados. Moving indolently through unfamiliar scenes, he accepted all impressions. The colour and form of the scenery, the manners and customs of the people, their talk, he allowed everything to remain on the retina of his mind. When he came to record his impressions in *Sorrow in Sunlight* he remembered the dark savannah as vividly as he did 'the brainy district' of the city of

Cuna-Cuna, and he pictured 'Mamma Luna' in the tiny tropical village as truly as 'Madame Ruiz' in the modish *faubourg* of Farananka. In his prose he caught the fascination of Negro rhythms:

> The Latest Jazz, bewildering, glittering, exuberant as the soil, a jazz, throbbing, pulsating, with a zim, zim, zim, a jazz all abandon and verve that had drifted over the glowing savannah and the waving cane-fields from Cuna-Cuna by the Violet Sea, invited, irresistibly, to motion every boy and girl.

Among the natural phenomena which caught his attention were the miraculously shaken cocktails of Havana ('the surpassing excellence of thy Barmen, who shall sing?') and the prevalence of sexual diseases amongst the natives.

At the end of his stay with the Negroes he went straight to Bordighera, where he spent the winter preparing his material for *Sorrow in Sunlight*. During this preliminary work he made a definite break with his earlier method of writing. Till then he had built up a framework of amusing incidents and witty snatches of conversations, around which the story was plastered on. It was like putting up a ferro-concrete building. This device, at best a vivid reflection of life, at worst a flat imitation, produced the rather uncomfortable air of mock reality, which took some of the fresh gaiety from *Vainglory*. The method of his later books was little concerned with imitations of people and their conversation. The importance was transferred to created character and vividly imagined dialogue. The Mouth family in *Sorrow in Sunlight* are bewilderingly, deliciously fantastic, jolting their way through colossal, exotic vegetation to the city of Cuna, 'full of charming roses, full of violet shadows, full of music, full of Love, Cuna . . .!' It is impossible to believe in the actual existence of these laughing Negroes, whose low, rolling speech seems made to conceal a thousand innuendoes. But, the more on that account, it is possible to believe in them as creatures of Firbank's imagination. Unlike the characters of his earlier books, they are fully drawn, they have depth, they are observed in the round.

Sorrow in Sunlight, although one of the first works of the modern Negro vogue, still impresses by reason of its witty sanity. It belongs neither to the Ku-Klux-Klan nor to Harriet Beecher Stowe. And most emphatically does it not belong to those modern novelists, dramatists, composers, and scenarists who have found a regenerating force for the world's art in a black dancer, a spiritual, a carved head from Benin City, or a simple little Negro love-story. The material of the book is selected, the architecture designed, with tact and prudence and a sense of humour. There is no Negro problem to be solved; only the adventures of the Mouth family to be used to create a work which, in the words of Carl Van Vechten, 'hovers delightfully between a Freudian dream and a drawing by Alastair, set to music by George Gershwin'.

From Bordighera he went to Rome, where he remained at the Hotel Quirinale until late in the spring of 1925. *The Flower Beneath the Foot*, which had been so long in manuscript, now made its appearance, and it was soon followed by a short story in the Oriental style, called *Santal*. When he returned to London he suffered a reaction towards mysticism. The undercurrent was always present, but occasionally it burst through, like a stream surging from the darkness of the earth. This time it took the form of a superstitious belief in an Egyptian fortune-teller. This necromancer was established as firmly as the Delphic oracle. He gave opinions on every subject connected with his client. In a short time Firbank was unwilling to make any decision if he had not first consulted this man. He turned to him for guidance when he wished to sell a portion of the family estate which included a quarry. The fortune-teller's opinion was that the quarry contained valuable stone and that he would make a great mistake if he sold the land without having expert advice. He obtained a local opinion that the quarry was valueless, but he determined to visit the estate in person, accompanied by the greatest London authorities. On the day chosen for the visit he was suffering from a heavy attack of nasal catarrh. During the tedious train journey he found relief in rubbing his forehead and nose with a block of solidified eau-de-Cologne. Wherever he went during the day he left this block, and the party of experts was forced to wait on street corners while messengers were sent to look for it. In acute discomfort, but supported by the prophecy of the fortune-teller, Firbank followed the experts to the quarry. He waited in eager silence while they examined the stone. As they drove back into the town he received their verdict that the quarry was quite valueless.

During the summer months which he spent in London, he was finding himself increasingly lonely. Some of his friends had married, and they found it difficult to reconcile Firbank and the placid atmosphere of matrimony. In any case he would have deliberately avoided their houses, as he was awkward and embarrassed in the company of women. His conversation, never fluent for more than a few moments, disappeared entirely in most female company. Others of his friends he met only to quarrel with them. C. R. W. Nevinson wrote:

'I loved his sense of fantasy, he appreciated my life, we both knew each other to be absolute 'men of the world', and in spite of a thousand acquaintances we were both the "loneliest". A loathing of the mob, a capacity for drink, and a worship of beauty, all helped to make us friends, in moments of enthusiasm "his only friend", which he always hastily denied again!'

When his friends attempted to break off the relationship, for their wives' sake or some other reason, he conveyed sharply, by his manner, that he did not care whether he ever saw them again. In this mood he was once guilty of a melodramatic reply to a friend who asked if he felt lonely. With a gesture, he said: 'I can buy companionship.'

That he was not always able to save his absurdity with his wit is revealed in an anecdote from a friend of this period:

'Once or twice we had supper together at the Eiffel Tower, and he would get wildly excited and murmur faster and faster while his voice dropped lower and lower. Champagne went straight to his head, and, when he became slightly drunk, he would lose all sense of direction and put caviare on the end of his nose instead of in his mouth.

'One night I had just put him in a taxi, and, as I shut the door, I said: "Good night, Firbank."

'The taxi moved off, but before I had had time to move, there was a violent rattling and banging and the taxi stopped. Firbank leaned out of the window and called to me.

' "I wish," he said, "you wouldn't call me Firbank; it gives me a sense of goloshes."

'Then he drove away down Rathbone Place.'

VIII

On 25 March 1924, Firbank's mother died. His affection for her had remained constant from early boyhood. It was the one emotional contact not only which he preserved, but which gave him real joy. Lord Berners has wisely said: 'I don't think he wished for intimacy. I think he was terrified by the idea of being subjected to any kind of tie or obligation.'

Yet at Cambridge he showed so much affection for his mother that A. C. Landsberg wrote: 'I remember that he seemed to be very fond of his mother and to admire her tremendously. I gathered that she was in every way a great and beautiful lady.'

And, in July 1920, when a friend invited Firbank to dinner, he replied: 'Unhappily, Saturday 31st is my last night in London before leaving for Italy and I will be with my people.'

He returned from Rome during his mother's illness and was in London when she died. Grief was not an emotion which had an easy place in his nature. When it came, it made him eager for sympathy. He went to Lincoln's Inn in search of Albert Rutherston. They had not met for years, but in Paris, before the war, they had been close friends. When he arrived he saw Mrs Rutherston, who told him that her husband was very ill and could not be seen. He stood as though paralysed by this new blow. At last he said: 'My mother died this morning. I knew Albert would understand. And now *he* is ill.'

In a sort of despair he turned and left without another word.

After the funeral he went back to Rome. He busied himself with arrangements for the publication of *Sorrow in Sunlight*. To an English publisher he wrote, 'I bring you the book. It is . . . rather like a Gauguin.' Its Negro interest suggested that it might have an American market, and he offered the manuscript to Brentano's of New York. A difference of opinion occurred over the title. Firbank's own choice was *Sorrow in Sunlight*, 'although', he wrote, 'the book is extremely gay'. The publishers wished to call it *Prancing Nigger*. Early in 1924 he wrote:

'I am still sufficiently vague as to the American publication of *Sorrow in Sunlight*. The title in New York will be *Prancing Nigger* (after a character in the story), which they suggest will sell "at least a thousand more copies" than if the book were called *Sorrow in Sunlight*.'

Although he allowed himself to be persuaded to make the change, his sense of the rightness of his own choice was so strong that he insisted on *Sorrow in Sunlight* being used for the English edition.

Due to the flamboyant title or not, the American edition sold well. For the first time Firbank tasted the pleasant fruits of success. He was simply, almost childishly, pleased by the appreciations of his talent which appeared in the American Press and letters which were sent to him from enthusiastic readers. Particularly he was excited by the praise of men like Carl Van Vechten, Philip Moeller and Stuart Rose. Soon after the publication of the book, Philip Moeller visited Firbank in Rome. The story of that meeting, charmingly told in a letter Moeller wrote to Van Vechten, is here in full.

ROME,
June 6th, 1924

CARLO CARO—

Your letter took me instantly to Palazzo Orsini. It was all quite bewildering. Nothing more so than the delicious wiggly bewilderment of Firbank himself. The doorman insisted that he was in and led me to two stories over a beautiful court to knock for myself. I stayed and knocked. It seemed a pity to bruise the beautiful door, deep gold and shining like old wood shines that the years have polished. I did want to see him, as probably I'll be leaving Rome tomorrow for Subiaco, where a friend of mine is teaching in a monastery.

And then the door opened and I knew instantly that it was he. No one but he could have so delightfully seemed to get behind himself. Then he began to read the letter, drifting as he did so into three different places. Apparently I had awakened him. I was abject and in my abjection I did my best. He seemed to be responsive. I thought that any moment his leg would lift in an unexpected wriggle and wind about his neck. I have never seen anyone seem to droop so in fifteen different ways and still stay standing. He said you had been so charming. I told him you were a sort of high priest of the cult and he squirmed like a very sly lizard, in a sort of oncoming and, at the same time, reticent delight. He graciously asked me to dine with him tonight. Of course, I was delighted, but begged him to work out whether or no the mood was really auspicious. I apologised for breaking in in so hideously abrupt a manner and explained that I knew perfectly how stupid things like that could be— Yes, that I understood that maybe the moment wasn't a very blessed one. But I think we were getting on. I am not sure he wasn't standing on his left ear when he gurgled in a syncopation of tiny gasps that it was 'all perfectly wonderful'. By that time we were in his apartment and he told me to sit down, and when I sat down he got up and then I got up and he didn't. And then, as he didn't, he did. Then I said: 'But you haven't read all of Carl's letter.'

And then he began reading your note to me and then he said: 'Oh—you wrote *Madame Sand*. How divine!'

And then, with a glance of despair about him, he suddenly ejaculated:

'But there aren't any flowers! None! None! Perhaps it doesn't matter. I am moving out. I have been hunting places. It's all too dreadful! Nothing matters. Do sit down. Yes, it will be charming tonight. Where shall we go? How hot Rome is—but how cold your winters are! Tonight, then.'

Then I said again:

'I shall be delighted.'

And we were out in the little hall and he made a terrific pounce and closed a door—a trunk, actually a trunk, in the next room had been visible. He seems to be delightful, but my only impression so far is that if he suddenly stood still, I don't think he would be there. I look forward to the dinner quiveringly, don't you?

Unfortunately, Philip Moeller did not write another letter to describe the details of the dinner and so he remembers the first meeting more vividly. 'The name of the restaurant I have forgotten,' he wrote recently, 'but I know it was opposite the most fashionable of the Roman churches—the chic shrine of Catholicism, if I may so word it. We sat in the back room of the restaurant; as I remember, it was beyond two or three other rooms and the walls were frescoed with fruits and flowers and, I think, vistas of the Italian scene. I did my best to be practical with an omelet, if I remember rightly; but all that Firbank ate were peaches and champagne. Yes, I am sure of that—innumerable peaches and a bottle or two of champagne.'

The success of *Prancing Nigger* led to a tragi-comedy which is here related in Lord Berners's words:

'Ronald Firbank was coming to luncheon with me one day in Rome.

'It was shortly after the publication of *Prancing Nigger*.

'Thinking I heard Ronald approaching the house, a sudden

impulse seized me to put on a Negro Mask and surprise him by appearing at one of the windows.

'However, it was not Ronald after all. And a small boy who happened to be passing on a bicycle looked up and was so frightened that he fell off and was run into by a motor.

'He was luckily unhurt—but a crowd collected.

'At this juncture Ronald himself arrived, and when I explained to him what had happened he said, "That will teach him to concentrate in future." '

In the late autumn of 1925 he arranged to go to Egypt. He seemed perceptibly weaker in health. His cough was monotonously insistent and his breath often came in short gasps. Some of his friends, alarmed by his symptoms, urged him to visit a doctor. For a time he vacillated—he had a horror of doctors—but one day he agreed to go. An appointment was made and everyone wondered if he would keep it. His friends awaited the diagnosis with anxiety. The night of the interview Mr and Mrs Nevinson arrived rather late at the Café Royal and found Firbank, drunk and hysterical, the centre of undesirably prominent attention. He was weeping. As the Nevinsons hurried to him he cried out: 'I don't want to die!'

They consoled him as best they could and determined to remove him from the publicity of the Café Royal. With some difficulty they got him to a car and drove to the Tour Eiffel. Away from the crowds he was calmer. They persuaded him to eat a little. When he had done so he recovered considerably. He seemed grateful to them for the care they had taken of him. Knowing that he was safe in the kindly charge of M. Stulik, they left him for the night. Early the next morning he was knocking on the door of their studio. He was alert and excited. He said he had come to ask for his scarf, which he thought he had left in the car the night before. The car was searched, but no trace of the scarf could be found. Probably he had left it behind at the Café Royal. Firbank became very agitated. He was certain he had had the scarf in the car, and he hinted pointedly that his rescuers knew more about it than they admitted. They laughed at such a suggestion, but Firbank was convinced. With high dignity he walked away, and until the time of his departure for Egypt he refused to speak to them.

His suggestion to spend the winter in Egypt seemed wise. His friends thought that the warmth would effectively combat his ailment. It was at the Tour Eiffel that he spent his last night in England. He arrived early in the morning and sat alone in a corner drinking cocktails. He refused to eat, as he did not wish to spoil his appetite for dinner. When dinner-time came he took a caviare sandwich and a bottle of champagne. He said his final farewells to his friends. He was nervous and they were faintly amused. As on many previous occasions, his fortune-teller had warned him that he was making his last journey. Those who were acquainted with this ridiculous and morbid ritual had no premonition that at last superstition had chanced upon the truth.

The avidity with which the Americans read *Prancing Nigger* suggested that they would like his earlier books. Brentano's published a corrected edition of *Vainglory* in the autumn of 1925. Firbank was delighted when two American authors, Stuart Rose and Thurston Macauley, considered the project of dramatising *Prancing Nigger*. He gave them permission to use his book as they desired, and he was keenly interested in the play which they made. It took the form of a colourful extravaganza, to be played against a shifting background of jazz rhythms. Narrative was abandoned in favour of a vivid series of kaleidoscopic views. The important accessories of music and scenic designs were prepared for a possible production, which, however, has yet to be given. Although Firbank had never visited America, he began to think seriously of writing a book on the manners and customs of New York. In November 1925, he wrote to Brentano's from Cairo: 'This winter, in Egypt, I propose to begin my book on New York, and as I never was there you may be sure it'll be the New Jerusalem before I've done with it. However, I hope to come out next year to develop it all.'

Seven weeks later he wrote: 'I have just begun the second chapter of my American novel and it ought to be amusing. Is there such a thing as a dictionary of American slang and colloquialisms? I expect to be soon in sore need of a few really racy words—expressions of the *soil.*'

A copy of Mencken's *The American Language* was sent to him. In the same letter he ventured to give an opinion upon the comparative merits of his books:

'Would you be inclined to do *Valmouth* or *Caprice* in the spring? Possibly I could improve *Valmouth* here and there by modifying certain passages. I have also written an entirely new, and as yet unpublished, dinner-party chapter scene for *Inclinations,* if this would suit you better; but of the three novels, I believe *Caprice* would find most favour with the public, although *Valmouth* is more finished and complete.'

A sentence in a letter to C. R. W. Nevinson from Egypt proves how seriously he considered taking a trip to America. He said: 'I am anxious to get to New York before this cough gets me.'

This Faustian picture of a game of hide-and-seek with Death, like a sequence from a German film of the best period, was ludicrous even to the participator. Death seldom intruded into his work. But when St. Laura de Nazianzi saw the great crowds gathered for her lover's wedding, the street paved with heads, she reflected, 'Just so shall we stand on the Day of Judgment.'

And Charlie Mouth's heart stopped still when he thought of heaven hereafter.

In Egypt, Firbank finished writing the book which he had commenced during his visit to Spain in the summer of 1924. Often the appearance of places and people gave him the initial impetus, the first glimpse which enabled him to see how amusingly related were some casual names and happenings. In this case, although he could write: 'Spain! The most glorious country in God's universe. His admitted masterpiece, His gem', it is certain that the absurdities and incongruities were not first in his mind. When he said of himself: 'His work calls to mind a frieze with figures of varying heights all trotting the same way', he had not written *The Eccentricities of Cardinal Pirelli.* It was something more vital than snatches of conversation, more definite than impressions of events, which formed the mainspring of his last book. It was a character and a plot. The figures do not all trot one way; they circle around the Cardinal as though for the celebration of a Rabelaisian rite. Indeed, their antics at the Cathedral of Clemenza during a fashionable ceremony—a christening, and not a child's—are worthy of the supreme Master Francis himself. Some, however, have noticed that, in spite of their graceful movement and their witty speech, there is around them a darkening atmosphere, an incensation connected with strange and phallic ritual. In the midst of this 'Sarabandish and semi-mythic dance' stands Don Alvaro, the Cardinal, the pivot of all its macabre gaiety. If there is 'a Firbank character' it is the Cardinal. He is compounded of wit and grace, corruption and prurience, in such nice proportions that, on reflection, the whole book is tinted by his prismatic colours of decay.

Those who will may see in *Cardinal Pirelli* the signs of change affecting Firbank's work. They may notice that plot was ceasing to be a framework to carry an amusing fancy dress; it was changing into the bones and muscles of a corporate body. Even more may they notice how Time cooled the first exuberance, so that the prodigal fecundity of the early books, each teeming with characters, has given place to a rich reservation, whereby Pirelli and his friends could move freely, unjostled by the crowd. But most of all, the observant will have noticed that the distance from the chaste château of little Odette to the end of the Cardinal, lying 'nude and elementary now as Adam', while above him stirred the wind-blown banners in the nave, makes a long and subtle journey, accomplished by the aid of innuendo and covert suggestion. It is idle to guess at the next stage, but the certainty that his admirers would have revelled in its free and delicate humour is only enhanced by the thought that it would have earned the distinction of causing a conference between the Home Secretary and the Director of Public Prosecutions.

Firbank returned from Egypt to Rome in the spring of 1926. He stayed at the Hotel Quirinale. The story of his last days and death is fully told by Lord Berners elsewhere in this book. Firbank died on 21 May and was buried in the Testaccio Cemetery.

Within a few weeks rumours were current, both in England and America, that he was not dead. It was suggested that he was perverse enough to test the reaction of his death upon the literary world. So, said the legend, he was wandering in distant lands, like Ambrose Bierce, enjoying with cynical amusement his obituary notices. The rumours were given encouragement by an article in *The New York Evening Post* in October, hinting that there was no actual proof of his death. The excitement which prevailed in New York convinced the papers that they had found a first-class literary sensation. They played the solemn farce out to the end. The Rome correspondent of *The Evening Post* was instructed to pay a formal visit to examine the city archives. He found duly recorded the death and burial of Ronald Firbank.

It seems opposed to the very spirit of Firbank to end his biography on an impressive minor chord. To write his epitaph would be the final irony to one of whom Philip Moeller has said that 'he, of all people, cared least whether he was alive or dead'.

Let his farewell be his own words, strangely and beautifully appropriate:

'Now that the ache of life, with its fevers, passions, doubts, its routine, vulgarity, and boredom, was over, his serene, unclouded face was a marvelment to behold. Very great distinction and sweetness was visible there together with much nobility, and love, all magnified and commingled.'

POSTLUDE

The biographer is frequently accused of vulgarly attracting attention to his subject's private life and obscuring real appreciation of his public work. A life of Firbank is particularly open to this charge. As an author he experimented but announced no doctrines, published no manifestos and converted no disciples, while in his life he was the prey of the fashionable paragraphist and was believed to court the most glaring notoriety. The biographer of Firbank would have performed two good services if he could preserve the authentic eccentricity but disperse the cloud of foolish legend, and if, through the interest of the life, he could send everyone to the writings. For—let there be no misunderstanding—there are ten reasons why Firbank should be remembered. They are his ten books.

The spur to biographical endeavour is the certainty that, just as Firbank's books are full of himself, his life was charged with potential fiction. On the one hand, in *Vainglory* he appears as 'Claud Harvester', the writer whose style 'was as charming as the top of an apple-tree above a wall'; in *The Flower Beneath the Foot* he is himself, moving as a discreet influence through Mrs Bedley's circulating library; while in *Sorrow in Sunlight* discretion has become almost impersonal and he exists as the exotic name of an orchid, 'a dingy lilac blossom of rarity untold'. On the other hand, many of the episodes of his life read like dashing improvisations of a new novel. They are curious and remote, with tender sophistication and outrageous simplicity. But alas! who but himself could have used them, placed each in position to add another sparkle to his glittering mosaic. To write of him one needs must be as detached as himself. From a pinnacle between heaven and earth, within easy reach of Parnassus and Piccadilly, one may find the gay solitude wherein to appreciate his aloofness. There his plots should be examined, judging them as exquisite designs of coloured stone. The connoisseur would notice the freshness and grace of *Caprice*, like an early Greek design; the heavy outline and bold colouring of baroque *Vainglory*; the dainty sadness of *The Flower Beneath the Foot*, like a Persian miniature; the grim riot of *Cardinal Pirelli*, full of mediaeval lust and laughter.

To mention his titles is to bring crowding back to the memory the fantastic creatures who people his books. They have every grace and scarcely a virtue, the gayest of manners to gloss their contempt of sobriety. There is the Mouth family, who are able to be the most Negroid of amusers as well as the most amusing of Negroes; Mrs Shamefoot, wrapt in her desire to be commemorated by a stained glass window; Miss Compostella, an actress, 'although so private looking'; the portentous figure of Mrs Yajñavalkya, most dubious of masseuses; Princess Zoubaroff, who harboured a desire 'to shake Switzerland, because there are no mountains as high as I could wish'. These are the stars around whom gather hundreds of brilliant supers, who live in the mind not for what they say but for what they are called—George Kissington, Miss Thumbler the dancer, Mrs Asp, Lady Blueharnis, Mrs Wookie, Lady Pantry, Madame Wetme, and the others whose every name is a prelude to delighted laughter.

It is the tragedy of wits that their polite motley is always supposed to conceal a Salvationist's uniform. The public turn his jokes inside out looking for the moral—and when he deals in *doubles-entendres* it is not difficult to mistake his meaning. Firbank, fortunately, was hardly suspect for a moment. The most earnest could find little that was uplifting in his humour, and if they could understand his *doubles-entendres* they were quite convinced that he was undesirable. From this has spread the belief that he has been misjudged and misunderstood. It must be emphasised that he hoped he would be misunderstood by certain people. It would have been his bitterest condemnation if they had understood him. In an age when earnestness and sincerity were marketable virtues, Firbank was an exception who provoked vain questions. Was he ingenuous or ingenious? What was his purpose? The questioners would not be satisfied with groping answers, with attempts to fit words to the startling uniqueness of his reactions. They expected, and still expect neat replies, whereby the work of Firbank may be parcelled and docketed, ready to be delivered to future purchasers. The true admirer, expecting no ready-made labels, will ask himself if Firbank's purpose was to be amusing and satirical and fashionable. Certainly Carl Van Vechten described him as '*plus chic que le futurisme*'. But the same admirer also called him 'the Pierrot of the Minute', a title which suggests a simple belief in a clear-sighted aesthetic. In that title there is a gay, sun-flooded vision of crisp humour, pricking innuendo, and elegant control of limb and mind, which reveals a quality very near the essence of Firbank. What is that essence? If it may not be found by direct statement, may it not be tracked in other sources? It must have been in Aristophanes's actors; to a degree it is in the Greek anthology; the Commedia dell' Arte surely knew it; Congreve was crossed with a strain of it; Wilde and Whistler had heard of it, but only above the sombre preaching of Tennyson and Browning; today it is more easily found in French music and painting than in any literature, though it would be churlish to deny that Max Beerbohm, Guillaume Apollinaire, Norman Douglas and Aldous Huxley have found some of its engaging charm. It is the authentic light touch—light of hand, light of heart, light of wit, light of mind. Firbank is the impudently illegitimate descendant of all the witty jesters who have seen wisdom in folly.

Even the fashionable paragraphists noticed the light touch. If English, they called him 'smart and stylish', while the Americans established his 'up-to-dateness' by the adjectives 'cunning' and 'cute'. Through the influence of such descriptions the legend grew in England of his elegant exclusiveness, while across the Atlantic our cousins fostered an image of a charmingly precocious child. Both reveal what errors of judgement can be made by the arbiters of taste. Indeed, the reception of Firbank's work is a pathetic example of the obtuseness of the professional critics. It is in the nature of things that every summer they must miss at least one swallow, but the cold discouragement with which they neglected this rare and delicious creature is hard to condone. Perhaps they felt perturbed that so mocking a cry was concealed by vivid plumage. Certainly he was farcically misjudged by those who did not understand him and vaguely feared by those who did. His humour, informed with a free and ample spirit, the heritage of the world's comic masters, was gravely questioned. His critics were wise enough to know that a passage of wit, taken from its context and placed in the midst of sentences of condemnation, had an air as forlorn as Mirabell's 'eye of a dead whiting', and was as certain to kill appetite. How full of relish are the same passages when encountered in their places, as orderly as the courses of a well-planned dinner!

> 'Whenever I go out,' the King complained, 'I get an impression of raised hats.'
>
> It was seldom King William of Pisuerga spoke in the singular tense, and Doctor Babcock looked perturbed.
>
> 'Raised hats, sir?' he murmured in impressive tones.
>
> 'Nude heads, doctor.'

No passage was more viciously abused than chapter twenty of *Inclinations*. With a brevity which is as witty as it is graphic, it carries the reader from the contemplation of Mabel Collins' plot to elope to its actual accomplishment. But all that it says is:

> 'Mabel! Mabel! Mabel! Mabel!
> 'Mabel! Mabel! Mabel! Mabel!'

If his humour was scorned, his plots were pilloried. The critics confessed that his books were meaningless to them, and then proceeded to drag unwilling stories from the texture of his writing. Is it possible that the critics of another age thus hailed the first appearance of *Incognita*; that, in spite of Congreve's warning that 'when I digress, I am at that time writing to please myself; when I continue the thread of the story, I write to please the Reader', they wrenched from its context this thread of plot, with which to entice readers? Or because Congreve had warned them of his pleasure in the digressions, did they solemnly praise the parts they liked least? But Firbank never warned his critics of his preferences, never hinted to them that perhaps they would mistake his intention if they placed importance upon his plots. Once he said of his characters that 'if one should by chance turn about it is usually merely to stare or to sneer or to make a grimace. Only occasionally his figures care to beckon. And they seldom really touch.'

But that hint was hidden in one of the books which the critics did not understand! So they continued to point to the incoherence of *Inclinations*, and failed to see how easily the figures trotted through the book, preserving the unhesitating movement of a Greek frieze. They complained of the riot of characters in *Vain-*

glory, and lost entirely the sense of a hot and overcrowded drawing-room which pervades the book.

The irony which he used with deadly effect served him ill when it decreed that his peculiar excellence of style should be most stupidly misunderstood. Much as a composer adds emphasis and strength to his symphony by 'thickening' his part-writing, so Firbank created a method of treating dialogue, by which was traced a pattern of sound, not polyphonic in character, but built upon subtle contrasts and delicate resemblance; a pattern, indeed, derived from the French composers Debussy, Fauré and Ravel, whom he admired so much. Each book contains an inimitable example of this technique, but chapter four of part two of *Inclinations* is the most richly typical. The intimate dinner given by Mrs Collins overflows with conversation, but each stray interjection has its place in a scheme of audible arrangement. At least one of the readers of *Vainglory*, as long ago as 1915, discovered the secret of reading Firbank.

'You can imagine how puzzled I was by its style,' wrote Professor E. J. Dent, 'but I enjoyed it hugely, and discovered at once that it was a book to be read aloud.'

The definite disapproval which characterised the official attitude to Firbank's work was no isolated phenomenon. It had its place in the literary lay-out of England during the years of the 'Great' War. Simplicity and sincerity were the fashionable virtues. A nation at war could not be expected to have time for subtleties or sympathy with ill-timed jests. And yet the mystery of Lord Kitchener proved as enthralling as a detective story, and Daly's and the Lyric were packed every night. Poetry and drama were still recognised as means of escape for the masses of people who wanted to forget Flanders, but under war regulations all exits had to conform to standard pattern. Poetry was to be heroic—not blatantly patriotic, but, of course, on the side of right. It was to be tenderly reminiscent, recalling the pleasantness of England, and emphasising the eminent soundness of

Oh! to be in England
Now that April's there.

The war provided evidence that, in the face of death, many have followed the example of Falstaff and 'babbled of green fields'. The theatre, also, had its war-work to do. Where else was light, colour and gaiety to be found? It did not matter if the light was garish, the colour tawdry and the gaiety a little thin. Men from the trenches were not particular.

It is miraculous how Firbank survived in such an atmosphere. He preserved his artistic integrity only by means of vigorous stimulation from the stupidity of others. But it was not to be expected that he would be understood. An artist with rigid standards, an artist who would say nothing trite or trivially sincere, whose wit and gaiety were born of his fantastic approach to life, whose plots held in the form of arabesque the unique discernments of his mind, to whom zeal was the cardinal sin, such an artist was not welcome in England in wartime. Sixteen years after the outbreak of the war we may wonder if such an artist would ever be welcome in England. Yet he is essential. He is salutary. But for the irony of such artists as Firbank, sobriety and prudery and temperance would descend upon us like a black and stifling pall.

VYVYAN HOLLAND

It is difficult to say anything definite about anyone as vague as Ronald Firbank. There seems to be nothing to grasp hold of, merely a fleeting impression here and there, of his gestures, of his half-said phrases, of his laughter and his tangled hair. Yet these impressions remain and leave one with an idea of a very lovable person, a dreamer of rather material dreams from which he drew inspiration in writing his books. For his books are surely the product of dreams, written in that nebulous state of mind one is in just before fully regaining consciousness, while the dream still holds one with its spell, and its improbability and absurdity are not yet apparent.

A few days after returning to Cambridge at the beginning of the October Term 1906, I heard that an undergraduate had come up to my college—Trinity Hall—a Freshman indeed, but one who was already a full-blown author with a published book to his credit, and of whom it was rumoured that he was expecting to write a series of novels in the course of his university career.

In common with most other undergraduates I had, at that time, distinct literary aspirations, and I immediately decided to make the acquaintance of this enviable prodigy as early as was consonant with my recent dignity of a second year man. Calling etiquette at Cambridge was quite sufficiently strict to be a nuisance. The first call could only be made by the senior member of the university upon the junior, irrespective of any social distinctions that might exist. There was no necessity for the caller to make sure that the callee was in; indeed, it was usual to take steps to ascertain that he was out. The junior returning the call, however, was compelled to go on calling until he found his host in. It is significant, therefore, of the awe inspired by this book, of which we did not even know the title, that those of us who called made sure beforehand that Ronald Firbank would be in. I do not remember if he ever repaid our calls officially, but I very much doubt it.

The only impression that remains to me of my first interview with Firbank is of his rooms. I cannot remember what we talked about, but he produced his book, '*Odette d'Antrevernes*, by Arthur Firbank', and gave me a copy with my name, wrongly spelt, and his initials A.R.F. on the flyleaf. It was the first book I had ever possessed with a presentation inscription from the author: I have it still, and I have not, even yet, lost the sense of importance that its possession gave me when I first got it. His rooms were on the ground floor in the Main Court—the actual number was F.2—and they were filled with unaccustomed things disposed in unusual places. The necessary sofa was not in its traditional place before the fire, but was pushed against the wall between the windows, and it was on a corner of this that Firbank liked to sit, his back to the light, his face in shadow, his legs drawn up beneath him, one hand always fluttering around his head, the other usually grasping his ankles or a book. A refectory table stood in the centre of the room, giving it a feeling of depth which no doubt it did not possess. The room was always full of flowers all through the year: no one knew where they came from and apparently no one ever saw them coming into college: yet such an occurrence in a Philistine college like the Hall would be bound to excite comment, possibly of an active and even retributive nature, if it had been noticed.

Instead of the picture one expected to find in undergraduate rooms in those unenlightened days, consisting, for the most part, of bad reproductions of sporting prints and of even worse pictures of insufficiently clad women, Firbank had Conder lithographs and paintings on his walls, and several etchings by Helleu, whom he had known in Paris. Paris! How impressed we were when he spoke to us of Paris. He had lived in Paris for a whole year by himself before coming to Cambridge. At least, so he said. Most of us had read *La Vie de Bohème*, and those who had not done so hastened to do so, at my instigation. For this was clearly the Paris of Murger, and Firbank was Rodolphe himself. Really I suppose the Paris in which Firbank had lived actually was a form of rather pecunious Bohemia; it included Pierre Louÿs, Willy and Colette Willy, the actor de Max, the actress Polaire with her sixteen-inch waist, and many other celebrities, most of whom we heard of for the first time with carefully concealed ignorance. Firbank spoke of these people with a kind of diffident familiarity, almost deprecatingly, and we, whose experience of Paris, if any, revolved round such centres as the Bois de Boulogne, the Louvre and Notre Dame, absorbed every word. He always stopped his recitals with a wave of his hand and his far-away, rather hoarse laugh, just when they were beginning to reach what we imagined were about to be the most interesting parts, and left us to guess at mystery and romance. It was very tantalising, but very effective.

Firbank never played games, though he occasionally appeared in the costume of sport, apparently returning from some strenuous and probably purely imaginary form of exercise. Seeing him once clad in a sweater and football shorts, I asked him what on earth he had been doing: 'Oh, football,' he replied. 'Rugger or soccer?' 'Oh, I don't remember'—and a laugh. 'Well, was the ball round or egg-shaped?' 'Oh! I was never near enough to it to see that!'

His knowledge of any form of game was negligible. Were he ever compelled to be present at any conversation about games his mind would disappear completely, to wander in some fantastic land of its own creation. We were once both bidden to a dinner-party by Monsignor Barnes, then Catholic Chaplain at Cambridge. An invitation from Monsignor Barnes had something of the nature of a Royal Command in its irrefusability, and Firbank, who hated dining out, felt compelled to go. The party consisted of about a dozen undergraduates, and soon after dinner began the conversation turned upon a hockey match that had taken place that afternoon, possibly between Cambridge and some rival university. Firbank's mind was far away, when a pause in the discussion brought him suddenly back to consciousness of his surroundings, and he beamed upon the undergraduate seated opposite him, nervously hoping that his mental absence had not been noticed. The undergraduate, confused by this unexpected sign of friendliness, felt that something was required of him and asked Firbank: 'Were you there this afternoon?' Firbank coloured deeply, cleared his throat and, clasping his hands together, glanced wildly round for help. He obviously had not the least idea of where he was suspected of having been, but, seeing every eye upon him, except possibly mine, for I knew the incident could not end well, he leant forward and replied in a voice trembling with assumed interest: 'Oh, no! I'm so sorry. I wasn't. But *do* tell me. Was it wonderful?'

And that was the end of the hockey conversation.

Trinity Hall produced, and no doubt still produces, a magazine called *The Crescent*, coming out once a term. I edited this during Firbank's first year, and I asked him to contribute something to it. In due course I received from him a weird phantasy which was really the precursor of all his later books. The simplicity of *Odette d'Antrevernes* was left far behind. At this date I have not even the vaguest recollection of what the story was about, but I still retain the impression that it was manifestly unsuitable for an undergraduate magazine, and I rejected it as tactfully as I could. I think Firbank was more indignant than hurt, though he pretended to be neither; but I am sure I was right by undergraduate standards. I returned the manuscript. I wish now that I had kept it; how seldom one appreciates the gifts of the gods at the moment of their bestowal!

The only undergraduate society to which he belonged at Cambridge was the Footlights (or it may have been the A.D.C.; as a member of neither, I am not competent to remember). He used to attend rehearsals regularly, and his opinions, as a man of clearly established literary reputation, based upon his published book, were listened to with respect. But his incurable shyness always prevented him from taking any active part in the performances, though he was often offered parts and used to read them through, and act them to himself in the secrecy of his rooms, before returning them.

I can imagine no college more inappropriate for Firbank than

Trinity Hall at that period. We were a small college, about 130 strong, and we were Head of the River, a position which gave us, in our own eyes, a marked athletic superiority over every other Cambridge college. Any energy left over after our athletic duties were performed was devoted to a thoroughly inattentive study of the Law. One could not imagine Firbank as a lawyer; there was something singularly un-law-like, almost illegal, about him. He never took exercise, he never worked, he never sat for any examination, even the Little-go; yet he was never sent down or bullied by the authorities; I think the Senior Tutor, the late Mr G. B. Shirres, a most charming and popular man, had a soft spot in his heart for him. And, strange as it may seem, his rooms were never 'ragged'; heaven knows why not; it was the golden age of ragging; everyone's rooms were ragged on one pretence or another; excessive popularity was as good an excuse as excessive unpopularity, and excessive eccentricity was the best excuse of all; so from the undergraduate point of view Firbank's rooms were an urgent invitation to a rag. I think that the reason they escaped was that in some way Firbank was beyond ordinary standards, and was therefore treated with the respect and awe frequently accorded by the simple-minded to things they do not quite understand.

He did not have a very great number of books in those days. He read a good many French novels, but as soon as he finished them he gave or threw them away. Most of his English books were poetry, especially poetry of the nineties. He was always enthusiastic about that period. Dowson and Conder, Arthur Symons and Beardsley, were his chief joys. He used to read poetry very slowly, often out aloud to himself, with long pauses to let the words and ideas sink into his mind. He preferred reading slim volumes which he could easily hold in his hand and slip, if interrupted, into his pocket. He liked, too, the look of slim books on his shelves. This preference for slim books seems to have persisted with him: once in 1918 he came to see me as I lay in bed in London with influenza. He kept a safe distance between himself and me, and I realised how great an effort he must have made to come to see me at all, as he had a morbid and perfectly natural horror of infection; but he brought with him half a dozen slim volumes of poems for me to read. Two of these I never returned: Walter de la Mare's *Songs of Childhood* and Ralph Hodgson's *Poems*. 'I just picked them out of my bookshelves,' said Firbank. 'I remembered; all the thin ones; you used to like the thin ones best.'

In May 1909, just before we both went down for good, Robert Ross came up to Cambridge to see me and Firbank, and I gave a dinner in his honour; endless was the consultation that took place about it. We discussed food at great length, though I have no doubt, from the menu, which I have before me, that, as was usual, the Trinity Hall chef did the actual choosing. We did, however, choose the guests ourselves, and there was a great deal of discussion about that too. We arranged to share the burden of the dinner-party so that I should be responsible for the food and Firbank should be responsible for the drink. The chief advantage of this arrangement was that Firbank possessed some 1884 Moët, originating, I think, from his father's cellar. There was quite a quantity of this, and it was just as well, as two bottles out of every three had departed this life apparently some years before, but when a bottle was good it was indeed good. The dinner took place in Firbank's rooms and developed into quite a famous affair in later years. Several more or less literary men who were not present have since told me how they enjoyed the party, in undisturbed ignorance of the fact that I had anything at all to do with it, and some of them have described it to me in minute detail, to my intense interest. There were actually nine people present: Ronald Firbank, Robert Ross, Rupert Brooke, Mario Colonna, Ernst Goldschmidt, A. C. Landsberg, myself, and two gentlemen whose signatures I cannot decipher upon the menu before me, but who were clearly of no vast importance or I should have remembered their presence, or at any rate their names.

We were very proud of this party, for it was there that Robert Ross met Ronald Firbank, Rupert Brooke and Mario Colonna for the first time. During dinner a violent altercation took place between Robert Ross and Mario Colonna over the way in which Colonna's father, then Syndic of Rome, did his job. Firbank, usually most pacific, joined in the argument and egged them on, taking alternate sides to prevent their ardour cooling.

Shortly after this we both left Cambridge, and I lost sight of Firbank for some months, until one day he came to see me and asked me if I could arrange for him to meet Ada Leverson, the Gilded Sphinx of Golden Memory. He was still absorbed in the nineties, and he was eager to meet 'the Sphinx', upon whom all the stars of that period had glittered, however wanly. Anyone who had sat on the floor in the half-light of a studio party with Aubrey Beardsley would surely be able to give particulars of him which would not be within the knowledge of his ordinary literary friends. So I called upon the Sphinx and told of this young man and of his interest in her. The Sphinx, who was always, and indeed still is, perfectly charming, made an appointment to receive us on the following Sunday afternoon at 4 o'clock, and on Sunday I lunched with Firbank at his house, in preparation and anticipation. For the occasion he had procured a silk hat of Parisian proportions and the most remarkable pair of trousers then in existence; they were, as I see them now, mauve in *motif*, with black lines of varying thickness running down them. He was really 'arrayed', in the noblest sense of the word, rather than dressed, and as we drove from Curzon Street to Radnor Street in a hansom cab his excitement infected me, and I was as nervous as he at the thought of the ordeal before us. We rang for some time at the door of No. 12 before we got an answer, and when we did get one it was in the form of the shattering words: 'Not at home.'

Firbank turned without a word and left me, and it was not until several days later that I saw him again and heard the rest of the tale. He was apparently under the impression that the Sphinx must have been looking out for us from an upper window and that the sight of his trousers had been too much for her and had decided her against the obvious risk of making his acquaintance: for aught I know this may have been the true explanation. Firbank seized the first hansom that passed and drove back to Curzon Street, where he removed the trousers and cut them up into small pieces, which he fed to his bedroom fire all through the rest of that sad Sunday afternoon.

Shortly after this I left London and for some years I lost sight of him. Indeed, except at rare intervals I saw very little of him for the rest of his life, to my very great regret. We used to correspond in a desultory way and make plans to meet, but they seldom came to anything. The last time I saw him was in London not long before his death. He telephoned to me one afternoon and suggested that he should come to see me. He arrived bringing with him a little Egyptian sandstone head which he had come across in Egypt before the war. He entered the room with it held out before him, and said: 'I have brought you a present!' impulsively, with his painful infectious shyness. He sat on the sofa in the old attitude of Cambridge days, his legs drawn up beneath him and his hand waving around his head or half-hiding his face from view. He spoke of his work and about the letters he received about it from all parts of the world; it always gave him great pleasure to get letters about his books from strangers, as it made him feel that his work was appreciated outside his own immediate circle of admirers. 'I have written twelve books now,' he said. 'I always meant to write twelve books and now I have done it. I am thinking of having a very limited edition done of my complete works. It would be wonderful to have one's complete works published whilst one is still alive. I don't think I shall write any more.'

As he left the house I watched him walk diagonally across the street to the corner of the square, and I thought how little he had changed since I first knew him. His hat on one side, his head tilted slightly into the air, the slow, swaying walk so peculiarly his own. And I shut the door with a deep regret and the unsatisfied feeling one has when parting with someone whom one has once known well but with whom one has lost touch with the passing years.

I always think of Ronald Firbank as an unhappy man who, luckily for him, had the power of expressing himself through his books. His brain was too tumultuous to allow him to express himself clearly in speech; his thoughts seemed to overlap one another, and whilst he was saying one thing the expression of his eyes gave one the impression that his thoughts had already shifted to some quite different plane. And then: 'Oh! I don't know. Don't you see? It's so difficult. No, no, I can't explain!' and his nervous laugh, deep in his throat; and his hands moving rhythmically around his head.

His loss was a very real one even to friends like myself who saw so little of him during the last years of his life. The little Egyptian head which he gave me is a symbol to me of what he would have liked to be, in the calm beauty of its self-possession, the lack of which was Firbank's great sorrow in life. Whenever I look at it, I think of this queer, gentle, lovable creature, full of kindness and a desire for happiness, who, had he been bold and confident, would have been a type of Regency beau, but would have lost most of the mysterious charm he had for those who, like myself, are of coarser and more invulnerable clay.

AUGUSTUS JOHN

If I terrified Ronald Firbank, as he used to say I did, he often quite unnerved *me* with his way of emitting a long, hollow laugh about nothing in particular, a laugh like a clock suddenly 'running down', accompanied by a fluttering of the hands (not the clock's), hands which he would then proceed to wash with the furtive precipitation of a murderer evading pursuit. Only rarely did his eye meet one's own, but when it did one was charmed by its brown and shy amiability; instantly deflected, however, behind the flushed bulge of his cheek-bone, the suitable look of humorous curiosity one had hastily assumed to meet it would glance ineffectually off the shining planes of his teeth, which he wore *à l'anglaise*, or else waste itself in the curly hair which crowned the apex of his back profile. His mother complained I had made him look almost an idiot with a head of such a shape, and received with only partial credulity my explanation that the illusion was merely due to the way he wore his hair. Lady Firbank, though, was quite sure Ronald was *clever*, but she did wish he would have somebody to look after him. He was always alone—even in company—except perhaps for the presence of some invisible familiar with whom he seemed to commune on terms of complete intimacy and understanding. He was, in fact, not as other men. One day while posing for me (if you could call it posing), in his nervousness he let fall a little Egyptian divinity in lapis with which he had been occupying his hands. Instead of saying 'Oh, bother' or something, as anyone else would have done, he glanced at the smithereens on the floor, remarking, '*There!*' just as if he had expected the disaster, and retired chuckling for another wash and brush-up. In his life as in his books he left out the dull bits and concentrated on the irrelevant. He made even *me* feel grossly realistic and matter-of-fact, and contact with him brought with it an element of discomfort only to be endured in a spirit of dog-like devotion. Indeed, the fragmentary sallies he would so often address to the apparently empty air were only to be met on my part by a kind of appreciative tail-wagging and a look of almost human unintelligence. Not that he didn't want sometimes to be 'serious', but the effort involved was so great and the result so possibly compromising or even tedious . . . There was Death, of course—much too unpleasant to think about—or wasn't it? Firbank believed in himself. He knew he could write beautifully. He wasn't really in the least affected, but he did so want to look his best. He suffered—very bravely I think—under more than one serious disability; his health, of course, was not of the best; the dreadful fact that his father had been an M.P., and then his profile—was it *quite* perfect? The last time I saw him was in Bond Street after a long interval. I hailed, but not too heartily I hope, the elegant slanting figure with the exquisitely poised bowler. He turned in alarm, screening his face with that beautiful hand, and, protesting that he wasn't 'fit to be seen', writhed confusedly into the nearest shop. Sometimes I wonder if I should have boldly followed him and, at the risk of appearing too robust, dragged him off somewhere for lunch. A series of cocktails, a shoot of asparagus, a bottle of wine or two, might have pulled him together, and we should have got on as well as usual, 'or perhaps', as dear Ronald himself would have said, 'not'.

OSBERT SITWELL

It was in 1912 that, most unexpectedly, I found myself in the Army—or, at any rate, on my way to that goal by means of being attached to a cavalry regiment. There was no sign, no chance of a way out, except mutiny, which would end this existence for me by ending me; and this seemed too drastic a remedy. Even a few hours' leave to London, away from the monosyllabic discussions on horses and dogs—discussions which regimental tradition prevented me from taking part in—was regarded with suspicion.

The regiment had an ancient history, yet assuredly was only now at its beginning, would continue indefinitely into the future. Never did I dream that which has now come to pass. For it was only a few weeks ago that I opened a paper and read that it had been struck—as a good fairy at the end of a fairy story taps the wicked with her diamond wand and turns them all into toads and beetles—into a tank corps; and of all that mute swagger and stupid insolence now lost in dull, mechanic routine, only their spurs are left to them.

It can, perhaps, be comprehended how, with but a few hours in which to look round, and even that with the black cloud of Aldershot hanging always over one like the spectre of the judgement Day for the evildoer, I strove to make the most of each minute, drinking in every detail of the performance and the audience, in order to elaborate them afterwards in my mind, luxuriating in the then new magic of *Boris* or *L'Oiseau de Feu*, of the Futurist Exhibition at the Sackville Galleries or of the Second Post-Impressionist show in Grafton Street. Nothing of these escaped my eager mind. And always I noticed in gallery, opera-house or theatre—so that afterwards when back at Aldershot, pondering over those few though vivid, now intolerably distant hours of happiness, his image would come back to me and set me wondering—the lonely, stooping, rather absurd figure of a man some ten years older than myself. With a thin frame, long head and a large, aquiline but somewhat chinless face, the cheek-bones prominent and rather highly coloured, showing that he was ill, he had something of the air, if one can imagine such a combination, of a witty and decadent Red Indian. And is it possible that there was, added to this, a touch of priest, or even curate? He haunted the background of my favourite scenes for me, just as those of Greco's pictures are haunted by a gaunt and spectral saint. The eyes of my phantom, I noticed, were full of wit, though he spoke never a word, being always alone. In the intervals he would stand at the bar, occasionally gulping down a drink, as though with difficulty, nervous and ill at ease, his long hands clutching the lapels of his coat, examining the correctness of his tie, smoothing his hair, or fluttering round him apprehensively. Rather ill and unhealthy, one judged him to be; but certainly, I decided, his silence differed from that of my brother officers. Often I would wonder who he might be, and why so much alone; for it was before I myself began to understand all the terrible mysteries of the nervous system.

Times changed, and with them my regiment; now I was stationed in London. And always, whenever I went, let us say, to the first performance of Scriabin's *Prometheus*, to a concert of Fauré's music conducted by the old composer himself, or to the first night of the *Rosenkavalier*, invariably would I see at it this curious figure. But never could I discover his identity.

Then the war came, with for me two winters in the trenches,

and the diminutive spiritual paradise of books, music and conversation into which I had recently found my way (in spite of constant drill and dull bouts of Pirbright and such places) was utterly smashed and broken. Thus one did not see him for several years: for there were no longer many, or even any, concerts in London at which—even if one could be present at them—to see this silent spectre. Indeed, music was under suspicion as a German agent.

It is impossible to remember quite when it was, but certainly towards the end of the 'Great' War, that I opened a weekly review and read a short criticism of a novel called *Vainglory*. The critic owned manfully that he could make nothing of it, but fortunately quoted a short passage in which a mother describes a quarrel with her child's nurse. To this day the quotation remains in my memory almost word for word, so much did it amuse me. Enchanted, we bought the book and all else that issued from the same pointed, absurd, yet indeed magic pen.

Here was to be found a new if minute world, which existed in its own pulse of time and exhibited its own standards of behaviour that thus could never for a moment be questioned. Strange, fresh tides of rhythm played and lapped round its breathless shores, on which figures, that, however etiolate, were sufficiently substantial for one never to be able to forget them, moved to their own measure and were left striking the most unexpected attitudes against the mauve and lime-green horizon. Each book, as it appeared, was a new revelation of style, and of a wit that rippled the surface of every page without ever breaking it. The virtuosity of the author was able to net any situation, however crazy or occasionally even obscene, and let it loose in the realms of a harmless reality; while just as in the autumn the silver cobwebs lightly cover the trees with a thin mist of impalpable beauty, so a similar highly stylised but intangible loveliness hung over every page, while wit ran in, round and underneath each word.

However, alas, I am not here to write about these fascinating books . . . (how ably the very titles beckon to one—*Vainglory*, *Valmouth*, *The Flower Beneath the Foot*, *Caprice*, *Santal* and *Prancing Nigger*) . . . but, difficult enough task, to attempt to pin down upon this paper that unrivalled butterfly their author—a butterfly, indeed, which perhaps himself was the only writer who could have tackled successfully—and to record a little of him before it is forgotten, a little of a shy, charming, sad, comic and unusual personality.

This first novel, then, filled us with curiosity about its author. Who was he, where did he live? we wondered. But for a while our search went unrewarded. The first information that reached us was through an old friend of ours, now, alas, like the subject of our enquiry, dead. She told us that he was the son of the late Sir Thomas Firbank, a noted railway magnate. Lady Firbank, a charming and beautiful woman, was at the time still alive. Both parents, it seemed, were conventional enough, so that the education of their son had been planned on the ordinary school-university model. But, when travelling in Egypt as a small child, he had been struck down with sunstroke and proved in consequence too delicate to remain at a public school for more than one 'half'. Incidentally, it was the sunstroke which later saved him from the necessity of active service, for he showed my brother the military certificate with regard to his exemption. At the age of eighteen or nineteen he had, however, been strong enough to fulfil their ambitions for him by going up to Cambridge. There he became an aesthete, and was particularly interested in every society connected with the drama. He had already published a first book* and it was at the time understood that he was engaged on an absolute masterpiece of a second book, for, like all decent and intelligent undergraduates, he held very strongly the opinion that a man was finished at twenty-five. In due course he left Cambridge, but no tale appeared. Years fled by—years spent in drifting round Spain, Italy, North Africa and the Near East—and nothing more was heard of a second book until, some ten years later, suddenly, now unexpectedly even, it swung into the literary firmament, with, for a new writer, an extraordinary mastery, within its scope, of words and technique, and with its own quaint but unbiased view of a mad world. His long sojourns and travels abroad he broke, she told us, by visits to London. Here he would usually take furnished rooms in the neighbour-

---

* Firbank often in later years talked to me about his work, but never for one moment did he mention this book. He had always given me to understand that *Vainglory* was his first published volume. The title is *Odette d'Antrevernes* and it was issued in 1905 by Elkin Mathews. It contains also *A Study in Temperament*—and though the name of the author is given as Arthur Firbank, this tale is said to be prophetic in style of the Ronald Firbank who was to come. Grant Richards later republished *Odette*, but without including in it *A Study in Temperament*.

hood of Piccadilly. Since the war he was living in the country, but she was not sure where.

The next accurate information we obtained was from C. R. W. Nevinson, who had met him at luncheon with Grant Richards, Firbank's publisher. Nevinson had at once divined in him an amusing character. He described his appearance to us, I remember, and related how after the meal Firbank, rising willowly to his feet, observed, 'Now I must go to the Bank.' 'But they are all shut, you won't be able to get in,' objected Richards; to which Firbank, displaying his long unmuscular arms and thin fingers, replied anxiously, 'What? Not even with my crowbar?'

Soon we heard that Firbank was living at Oxford, and when, in the February after the war, I went there to see my brother, we decided to call on him. Only now was it that I realised who he was, this silent, nervous, absurd figure of theatre, concert-hall and gallery, only now did I discover the identity of him upon whom I had so often pondered at Aldershot. And his past phantomhood strengthened my feeling of friendliness for him. Moreover, this hitherto soundless spectre proved to be possessed of its own voice and accents, sharp and clear, with very much its own interpretation of the world it haunted: though the voice was, indeed, more practised and incisive on paper than in conversation. For at the time we first met him in Oxford, Ronald Firbank had, during two whole years, spoken to no one there except his charwoman and a guard on the train to London (upon this line he was, as we shall notice later, a well-known figure). He felt himself totally out of place in a war-mad, khaki-clad world, where there was no music, no gaiety, and in which one could no longer travel except on the business of death. He failed to summon up any enthusiasm whatever over the 'Great' War, protesting that for his part he had always found the Germans 'most polite'. In fact, 'that awful persecution' was one of the phrases which it was his wont to use in describing it in after years. It drove him to become more than ever a recluse, and deprived of all outside interest, *ennui* forced him to write the books about which he had talked for so many years. These volumes were, therefore, far more truly than any others in the English language, the product of the war. He was in the best, the least boring, sense a war writer.

Very seldom, then, would he go out, except occasionally, and rather unexpectedly, for a bicycle ride. Or again, he might journey to London to see his publisher or solicitor. Firbank occupied charming rooms opposite Magdalen Tower, and we were now to see there for the first time that small collection of *objets d'art* from which he was never parted. With these few, chosen belongings, indeed, he standardised each place wherein he dwelt, whether it was a tent in the desert, a palace in Portugal, a furnished flat in London, an old house in Constantinople or these rooms at Oxford. Everywhere they provided for him a sufficiently personal setting. Just as his mind made of every subject of which it treated something new and interesting, so these things spread over his room an indefinable and delightful atmosphere that made of the most trite surroundings something unexpected.

Chief amongst these objects, which we were afterwards to see so often, and in so many different places, were two drawings by Downman, a bronze bull (would it be Greek or Renaissance?), a Félicien Rops drawing, a pencil portrait of Firbank by Albert Rutherston, a little green-bronze Egyptian figure of some bearded god or pharaoh, standing rigidly above a miniature marble pedestal, all the latest novels, a number of the silliest illustrated weekly papers (which provided him with a constant source of amusement), several of his own published books and manuscripts bound in white vellum, a photograph of his mother in Court dress, mounted in a large silver frame, elaborate inkpots, coloured quill-pens, a vast tortoiseshell crucifix, and cubes of those large, blue, rectangular postcards upon which it was his habit to write. To this collection he subsequently added a fine drawing by Augustus John. There was always, too, a palm-tree near him, and in some way the author's personality was able to translate it back into a tropical and interesting plant, so that here it lacked that withered 1880 boarding-house air which it usually assumes in England. Moreover, on this occasion for our reception there was a veritable beacon of a fire and a profusion of orchids and peaches, gay cornucopia that banished the dim February light creeping in through the grey windows. It was, then, in this Oxford version of his habitual setting, which staged him so appropriately, that we first heard those delightful fits of deep, hoarse, helpless and ceaseless laughter, in such contrast to the perpetual struggle of his speech. For so nervous was he, that the effort required to produce his words shook his whole frame, and his voice, when at last it issued forth, was slow, muffled and low, but never perfectly in control. He suffered, I believe, from a nervous affection of the throat, which prevented him swallowing food easily. To this misfortune was due the fact that he drank so much more than the little he ate. On one occasion, for example, he went to dine with a friend of ours, who in his honour had ordered a magnificent dinner, and refused to eat anything except one green pea!

As for his laughter, to which we have just referred, it would often descend on him just as he was beginning work. Usually he wrote his novels upon those huge blue postcards, which we had noticed piled up on his desk, writing on each wide oblong side of them, though each blank face only gave room enough for a few —perhaps ten—words, so much space did his large regular handwriting take up. Thus at the moment when he would be starting to inscribe laboriously one more word on the card in front of him, the essential absurdity of the situation that he was with such care elaborating would overcome him, and he must quit work till the next day.

It was during this first acquaintance with him at Oxford that he read us portions of *Valmouth*, the book upon which he was at the time engaged. 'You have no idea how difficult it is,' I remember him saying, 'to keep up one's interest, when writing of a heroine who is over one hundred and twenty years of age—not that the other characters are meant to be any younger'. Perhaps he found in the end that youth, too, was merely relative, and that by presenting her companions as yet older, he could succeed in imparting a debutante quality to his heroine, for one of her friends is made to say, 'The last time I went to the play was with Charles the Second and Louise de Querouaille to see Betterton play Shylock.'

It was at Oxford, also, that we arranged for the publication of one chapter of *Valmouth*, under the title of 'Fantasia in A Sharp Minor', in *Art and Letters*. Of that now dormant periodical I was then an editor. The publication of this chapter, I think, helped to bring Firbank's work to the notice of a discriminating audience, though in the interests of truth it must be admitted that many of the people who now constitute his greatest admirers were at the time enraged by it beyond measure.

During the summers that were to follow in London, and during certain winters and springs (as, for example, that April and May when he had rented Bochlin's Villa in Florence, and when we would so often meet him in the Via Tornabuoni, staggering under the load of flowers he had bought, and looking round in a wild and helpless way for a cab to carry him home), we saw much of Firbank. Looking back over those years, let us face the truth; for the strange being of whom we write is interesting enough as writer and man to deserve such treatment. Let us admit, then, that there was about him something a little ridiculous, which blinded fools to his other remarkable and much more characteristic qualities, and which since his death, as during his lifetime, has made him the easy butt of vulgar journalists. As a talker he was most unequal; and if we are bound to say how extremely amusing he was for the first ten minutes of any meeting with him (always a deliriously funny period), we are also bound to add that, after a time, conversation became difficult—not but that every now and then he would not convulse one with laughter. Nevertheless, one was always surprised in talking with him, so vague and almost incoherent did he seem, at his love and knowledge of beautiful things. He was not, I think, a deeply read man, but his reading was very different from the rather blowsy pastures so well cropped by the ordinary 'literary man'. French novels, French poetry and eighteenth-century Memoirs of every European country composed the bulk of it, and in these matters he was excessively well-informed; yet often in his books there flashes out an allusion to some subject or another on which one would not have expected him to be an authority, but which this reference proved him to have mastered.

In addition, there is surely to be traced in all his books a marked love and understanding of the stage and its personalities. Just as virtuosity and manner were for him the chief merits of literature, so he demanded in his favourites of the footlights mastery, manner and, above all, established fame; for the effect of celebrity, through a decade or so, upon the temperamental nature essential to the executant artist delighted him; and thus among those he most adored in the theatre were to be numbered Pavlova, Isadora Duncan, and Mrs Patrick Campbell.

If it was his reading, as much as his own experience, which made the general sense of his books so cosmopolitan, yet it must be remembered that he had not only travelled, but had lived in various cities of Southern Europe and Northern Africa for quite considerable periods. He had spent nearly a year, for example, in Madrid, and asseverated that there he had become a mighty horseman. Moreover he always accused a then promising young diplomat (and a now promising young author) of having stolen his charger; an unlikely, indeed mythical, theft, but one which caused him to harbour the greatest resentment. It accounts for the rather unflattering portraits of young diplomats in *The Flower Beneath the Foot*, just as it accounts, also, for the rather unflattering portraits of eccentric writers in a certain book by a young diplomat. Otherwise Firbank pursued no feuds and treasured hardly a single hatred, though he was apt, as he said, 'to be disappointed' in his friends.

Occasionally, though, he would be angry, as, for instance, when he suddenly announced to everyone that I had said that the Firbank fortune had been founded on boot-buttons—a remark of which I had never been guilty. He was enraged about it, and would sit in the Café Royal for hours, practising what he was going to say in court, in the course of the libel action which he intended to bring against me. The great moment in it, he had determined, was to be when he lifted up his hands, which were beautifully shaped, and of which he was very proud, and would say to the Judge, 'Look at my hands, my lord! How could my father have made boot-buttons? No never! He made the most wonderful railways.' But within three weeks we were the best of friends again.

The first impression of him in conversation must always have been surprise that so frail, vague and extraordinary a creature could ever have arranged—let alone have created—a book. But there it was. He was a born as opposed to a self-made writer. This is, perhaps, the greatest gift that can descend upon authors, so many of whom will write because they are intelligent or clever and want to—not because they must—write. It was obvious as well, even at first sight, that Firbank's health was far from strong. But this delicacy at least was possessed of one advantage. It prevented him from being forced to waste his time in the Army. The constant callings-up and medical examinations had, though, further shattered his health, just as he, in his turn, must have somewhat shattered the health of the various military authorities with whom he came in contact. He told us, for example, that when, after a dozen or so examinations, the War Office finally rejected him as totally unfit for service (which anyone else could have told at a glance), and then, in their usual muddled way, at once called him up again, he replied to them through his lawyer with the threat of a libel action. The War Office, at a time when it governed the world, was so taken aback at this simple piece of individual initiative that it at once sent back to him a humble apology.

Wonderful as it was that a man, with apparently so tenuous a hold on life and its business, should be able to write novels, it was even more astonishing that so vague, delicate and careless a person—one, in addition, who ate almost nothing and usually drank a good deal—should survive travelling by himself in wild and distant countries. One would have taken him, the moment one saw him, as plainly destined to be defrauded or, if necessary, murdered, so weak and helpless did he appear; an obvious victim for guile and violence, if ever there was one. But his resistance towards the world was of an order more subtle than that of the average person, and it may be that swindler and murderer desisted because they felt the latent strength of his personality. Moreover, not only did his apparent helplessness fail to injure, it actually tended to protect him, both from danger and from boredom, for he was always able, by dint of it, to compel others to carry out for him the tedious things of life. Far from feeling it a moral duty, as we had been taught, to do something unpleasant every day, he conceived that it was his moral duty to find others who would on every occasion perform it by proxy. Thus, for example, there was his visit to Mr Augustus John. It was related that, torn between his desire for a drawing by that artist and his nervousness at having to meet him and express it, he drove round to John's studio in a taxi-cab, and decided, on the way, that the taxi-driver should introduce him to the great man and explain his business. The poor driver, therefore, was forced to act in the role of St John the Baptist, to take the strain of the ultimate emergence of Ronald upon himself. After a time our novelist appeared, much quieted, from the cab, and everything was arranged.

Here I should like to acknowledge my debt to Mr Augustus John for his great kindness. Remembering this story, and knowing of Firbank's tremendous admiration for him, I wrote to him, and received in reply a most interesting letter, some of which I quote below, while other anecdotes contained in it I have, for sake of context, incorporated elsewhere in this essay.

'Ronald Firbank,' he wrote, 'came to me to have his portrait drawn some while before the publication of *Vainglory*. As you have heard, he sent his taxi-man in to prepare the way, himself sitting in the taxi with averted face, the very picture of exquisite confusion.

'He came frequently afterwards, although always with the utmost diffidence, and I made various studies of him. When the strain of confronting me became unbearable, he would seek refuge in the lavatory, there to wash his hands. This manoeuvre occurred several times at each sitting.

'His mother once called and lamented the solitary life he led—a dear old lady, to whom Ronald was, I think, quite attached. Upon her death he for a moment, in my presence, hesitated on the brink of some almost Dickensian sentiment, but corrected himself just in time. . . . It's amazing how sometimes he struck, amidst his excellent persiflage, a chord of deep and heart-rending sentiment.'

All those who knew Firbank best, agree that under cover of this seeming futility in matters of the world he was a shrewd and capable man of affairs. 'He had,' writes John, 'in spite of appearances a practical side to his nature, carrying always in his trunk, as he did, a few good big blocks of Welsh anthracite.' And it is in accordance with this theory that he was certainly always coming to me to request that I would witness wills, deeds, sales of land and the like, so that there must have been a quite extensive business undercurrent to his life. One document I recall concerned his sale of a cemetery to a Welsh town, and seemed all that it could be of a morbid bargain.

But his ability as a traveller was not less marked, or more expected, than his talent for the affairs of life. Without doubt on meeting him for the first time one would have pronounced against his journeying alone, even for such a short distance as that from London to Oxford; but here, again, he had found someone to be responsible for him. It was his custom, during the two years he lived at Oxford, to travel back on the 'milk train', but owing to lateness of the hour, the difficult machinery of buying, and the unpleasantness of handling, tickets for himself, he had arranged a running account with the guard. This score he only settled once every two months. And then, on longer voyages, and ones on which his helplessness found no answer to its appeal, it at least led to the unexpected: and it was precisely in the unexpected that he most revelled. Moreover, his seeming incompetence furthered as much as it hindered his travelling. Thus as a very young man he went to France with some Cambridge friends. Their arrival in

Rheims happened to coincide with the local Wine Week, in which celebration they all joined with the due earnestness of their years. Ronald remembered little that took place after dinner . . . and woke up to find himself in Venice! It appeared that, once a fortnight, a train touched Rheims on its way to Venice, and that he had contrived to wander into the station and, with little money and no ticket, to catch this *rara avis* and remain undisturbed in it until his safe arrival at this distant but unintended destination the next day.

Rheims, however, is hardly dangerous except in a bacchic sense, but Ronald Firbank even managed to make a considerable stay in the Negro republic of Haiti (which, however incorrect the impression may be, does, nevertheless, sound wild and far to ordinary English ears) without any untoward incident occurring. The announcement of his intention to go there was very typical. Usually he would write to one in his large, regular handwriting, on a whole series of those enormous blue postcards that we have mentioned, and upon which he wrote his novels. These postcards, for the purposes of correspondence, were written upon on both sides, placed in an envelope, and posted. This was his usual method, seldom a letter. But on this occasion he sent us a simple postcard, simply posted, on which was written: 'Tomorrow I go to Haiti. They say the President is a *Perfect Dear*.'

All the same, there were occasions on which surprising events happened, events that were so like those that take place in his novels that they could only have happened to him. We have already suggested that there was something of the ecclesiastic in his appearance. After the war he spent a good deal of time in Rome; and we remember his being much alarmed because he declared that the priests had tried to kidnap him. He had descended the steps of his hotel one evening and had asked the concierge to call him a cab. A smart, black-painted brougham drove up immediately and he stepped into it. The door was closed at once and it drove off at a quick trot, before he had time even to tread on the toes of its occupants, for he found, to his bewilderment, that it was occupied by two priests, who quickly pulled him down between them, saying, 'You are one of us, aren't you!' Eventually, however, Ronald managed to escape.

After the war he had resumed his old method of life, the travelling and the returning to London for the season. But flying had recently come to his rescue, and now he often flew from

London to Rome or to Constantinople. While, in another respect, his life had altered, for in these later days he would always solemnly announce his arrival in London through the social columns of *The Times* or *Morning Post*. By this time he had found many admirers of his writings among painters and authors, though among the more purely intellectual of these there was to be found, joined to their admiration, a sort of contempt, wholly undeserved. This was caused, I think, by the perfection of Firbank's novels, and by their lack of striving earnestness in a time when nearly every author was setting out to air his inward struggles to an unwilling but awed public. His assured income may also have been a reason for envy, since it spared him the worries of forced journalism; while he, for his part, conscious of the income which separated him from most of the world, felt that many people were only nice for the sake of the meals and drinks which they could expect from him. He would reply by treating them with an almost childish hauteur, as though he were a Tsar among authors, in itself an amusing feat from so amiable and delicate a man. But nobody who understood him could be offended, for this affectation of proud eccentricity was only equalled by the genuine kindness he displayed at other times.

During these years just after the war he was once again constantly to be seen. No theatrical or musical performance of note passed without his attending it. Now we usually found him lunching, dining or having supper at the Eiffel Tower, though formerly he had frequented one of the 'Junior' political clubs, where his appearance and manner must have formed a strange contrast to that of the musty, bearded elders sitting all round him.

The genial and talented proprietor of the Eiffel Tower Restaurant, M. Stulik, was a great friend of Firbank, and used to take a deep interest in his welfare. He was, nevertheless, somewhat grieved at the smallness of this customer's appetite, and I remember once, when Firbank had just arrived from Rome by air, Stulik saying: 'Mr Firbank is much better. He is wonderful. What an appetite he has got now! Yesterday for dinner he ate a whole slice of toast with his caviare . . . how I love my customers!'

Augustus John gives the ensuing graphic account of a typical afternoon spent with Ronald, starting at this restaurant. 'I once presented him to the Marchesa C—— at the Eiffel Tower; and we lunched together, all three. He then proposed that we should go to his rooms in Brook Street, but on the way deposited us at

Claridge's and on some vague pretext disappeared himself. The Marchesa and I were becoming rather bored (it was "between hours") when Ronald reappeared with an enormous bundle, which he unfolded in his rooms, displaying a magnificent bunch of highly exotic lilies which he offered with many apologies to the lady. He also showed her, but did not give her, a complete edition of his works, luxuriously bound. Naturally she was enchanted, and proposed we should all go to America together without wasting a moment. The plan was agreed to, but somehow or other never came to pass.'

Often, too, Ronald was to be found at the old Café Royal, observing the odd life that centred there, the bookmakers in their bowler hats, the celebrities, the art-dealers, the painters, touts, financiers and sculptors. Indeed, it inspired several passages in his novels, notably that one in *Caprice*, where the daughter of a Rural Dean enters the Café for the first time. And it was the situation of it, as much as its habituals, that entertained him, since he was always impressed by the moral of the tombstone-shop opposite; for just across the road there was a large plate-glass window, in which the white marble spectres of all the Christian emblems, weeping females and modest, plain headpieces gleamed all ghostly under the primrose light of arc-lamps. Dark inscriptions could be read on them, expressive of morbid hopes or fears, while, after any riot at the Café, when one or two people had been forcibly requested by the giant in charge of such procedure to leave the premises, they could be seen ricocheting across the road towards these graveyard paraphernalia, or standing swearing in return at his uniformed figure against this ominous and inevitable background. 'It ought to be a warning to us all,' Ronald would remark as he watched such scenes.

Yet whenever one saw him, whether it was here, at the opera, in a concert room or theatre, he seemed, always, to be alone. This is not to say that very often he was not the centre of an appreciative crowd of friends; but even then he appeared lonely and by himself; a figure who, however kind and amusing, was hedged off from his fellows by his temperament, and must live in a world of his own seeing, different from that of others. Even his longing for friendship, which was strong in him, could seldom surmount the barriers of his own intense nervousness. It seemed to him that he must ever seek the affection of others to a greater extent than they sought his friendship. There was a pathetic instance of this unhappy outlook one day at lunch time in the Café Royal. Firbank entered and walked up to one of his friends, a young artist who was sitting at a table having a drink, and asked him to give him luncheon. The young man replied that he could not do so for he had no money; upon which Firbank took a pound-note out of his pocket, pressed it into the hand of his friend and, sinking at the same time into the seat opposite, exclaimed 'How wonderful to be a guest!'

Yet his summer visits were really a delight to all his friends and acquaintances, for he never disappointed them. First there would be the solemn heralding of his arrival in *The Times* or *Morning Post*, and then some fresh piece of grotesque fantasy was sure to mark each occasion. One year he rented a small flat in Sloane Square, and there set out the few objects that were the assertion and extension of himself, raising aloft once more the standard of his palm-tree. Accordingly, he arranged with a flower shop in the Square to send in a gardener twice a day to water and attend to it properly. Ronald was much pleased with this man, for he wore a green baize apron, and had a rustic way of speaking, so that it was 'just like being in the country'. When, therefore, after a fortnight, he decided to move to an apartment in Piccadilly, he insisted that, no matter what the cost, the same gardener should come twice a day to water the palm-tree. Further, he laid down, as a condition of his employment, that the man must walk the whole way, except in wet weather, from Sloane Square to Piccadilly and back again, wearing his green baize apron and carrying a miniature watering-can, painted green to match it. The proprietor of the shop made no objection, for by this time he knew his customer, money rained in on him for orchids, and the gardener found him 'Very nice-spoken', while it was worth it, from Firbank's point of view, for it added a touch of rural pageantry to the grey streets of London. We can still recall the joy it used to give us, as we sailed down the ugly desert of Sloane Street on the top of a then open motor omnibus, to see this solemn rather self-conscious procession of one, and to realise that a familiar, fantastic sense of humour was once more at play among us.

Towards the end of his life he was as much pleased with the select appreciation of his books as disappointed at the small range of it. He had been simple enough, perhaps, to expect for his work as large and wide an audience as that obtained by Miss Ethel M.

Dell or some such book as *Beau Tarzan*. He was especially gratified by the enthusiastic tone of Mr Carl Van Vechten, and would carry about his letters, together with various laudatory notices of his writings that had appeared recently in the American Press. He was also very elated at a letter sent to him by some transatlantic cinema magnate, asking for the film-rights of *Caprice*—the novel in which the heroine, who, as we have said, is the daughter of a Rural Dean, sets up in theatrical management, herself playing the chief part, and being too poor to rent a bedroom, has to sleep on the stage after an enthusiastic first-night, finally meeting her death by falling into a mousetrap that she had not observed in the darkness!

At this period he undoubtedly looked very ill. He knew how delicate he was, and as he sat there at the Café Royal showing one these documents, or as he lay, rather than sat, in the front row of the stalls at a theatre the sable angel of death ever hung over him. Moreover, he was much given to fortune-tellers, crystal-gazers and givers of Egyptian amulets, and the soothsayers, seeing him, ever prophesied evil. It may be that it was his intense relish and understanding of the silly and absurd side of modern life that made him consult them. But he was in many ways, I think, so near the things which he so beautifully skimmed and parodied that perhaps he was genuinely superstitious. Be that as it may, however, at the end of each summer for five or six years it was his habit to drive round in state and say good-bye to my brother and myself; and, each time, he would tell us that he knew there were but a few months more for him to live. These doleful tidings had invariably been conveyed to him either by a Syrian magician or by some wretched drunkard at the Café Royal. Whilst talking with us of it, he would keep his taxi-cab waiting outside, ominously ticking out the pence and minutes, and would then leave us in order to drive on and bid farewell to his other friends. So many times did these final scenes occur that when in truth he came to us for the last good-bye in our house, it conveyed little, being merely part of a regular and ordinary routine. But actually my final meeting with him was in the Café Royal, then undergoing at the same moment the dual, and apparently contradictory, process of being pulled down and rebuilt. And upon that occasion, owing to a sudden impulse, I had the pleasure of telling him how exquisite a writer I judged him to be, and how much, how infinitely, better than most of his contemporaries, many of whom were more highly esteemed. For Ronald suffered rather than gained from the fact that he was a true, born artist, with no propagandist axe to grind.

That winter he spent in Egypt, and then came back to Rome, where he had taken an apartment in the Palazzo Orsini for a term of years. But the change of climate from Cairo to Rome gave him a severe chill, which turned to pneumonia, and he died within a few days.

It was odd how slowly the news of his death travelled and it was several weeks before most of his friends heard of it. It was barely recorded in the Press and, at that, three weeks after it had taken place, while little or no mention was made of his books. The only friend of his who was in Rome at the time of his demise was Lord Berners. The latter saw him a day or two before the end, when he was already ill, and tells me that Firbank had no suspicion that he was dying. The doctor, too, appears at first to have treated the matter lightly, as an ordinary chill. So little did the dying man himself expect the end that only a few hours before it, feeling very much better, he discharged his nurse.

So he died: at the age of thirty-nine. He never saw forty, the thought of which he so much disliked. Growing older pained him, and would have pained him more, though he held, with one of the characters he created, that 'I suppose when there's no more room for another crow's-foot, one attains a sort of peace.'

In any case, his death could not have been long averted, even if he had not contracted that fatal chill. Apparently he had been examined by a doctor before leaving England, and though he did not inform his patient of it, lungs and heart were even then in such a bad state that it was obvious that any illness would finish fatally for him.

Even about his last resting-place there was an inconsequential, as well as a tragic, element. For, through a strange error, the Catholic Firbank rests—not far from, of all people, Keats and Shelley—in the Protestant Cemetery at Rome. One could always, even in his lifetime, see a miniature legend in attendance upon him, hovering round him, waiting like a bird of prey to batten on his dead body: and already, even now, they say—and write—in America that Firbank never in fact died; that he is alive, wandering round and observing in remote countries. And we, who knew him, are left to wish that this myth were the reality, and that again we might see that jaunty, sad and unique figure, or hear once more those sudden gusts of deep silly laughter which so convulsed and shook his frame, or those few unexpected remarks, wrenched out of himself with so much seeming effort; that we might again receive a sheaf of ridiculous postcards, with his large handwriting on them, and, above all, that we might have the joy of reading a new book from his pen, a book that would be so deliciously unlike any others in the world save his own. And many years after his death, whenever any particularly ludicrous situation arises, we are still forced to cry 'How I wish Ronald were here!' or 'How like Firbank!' Indeed, he ranks high as a prophet and diviner of the future, for everyday life resembles more and yet more the subtle intricacies and simplicities of his novels.

LORD BERNERS

My first meeting with Ronald Firbank was not exactly a felicitous one. It took place soon after the war at a performance of the Russian Ballet.

Firbank was not at his best in a theatre. The atmosphere of the Russian Ballet in particular seemed to go to his head, and his behaviour during the *entractes* and even during the performance itself was distinctly fantastic. One would become aware of a growing uneasiness in a certain portion of the audience, and after a time one discovered the cause of it to be the extraordinary antics of Ronald Firbank. One of his favourite postures seemed to entail sitting with his head nearly touching the floor and with his feet in the air.

It was at the Russian Ballet that an absurd incident occurred in which Firbank and Lady X (a well-known female eccentric) both loudly complained that the one had 'leered' at the other.

On encountering Firbank for the first time, I was a little disconcerted both by his appearance and his general demeanour, which seemed to be attracting a good deal of attention. His incoherence (which I attributed to intoxication) I found decidedly embarrassing: and in those days I was still young enough to resent being embarrassed.

A few days later I met him again in Piccadilly—inappropriately enough, outside the Naval and Military Club. I feared another difficult encounter, and so, shouting at him 'You are my favourite author!' I hurried on.

To become a friend of Firbank was no easy matter. One had to take a good deal of trouble. There was one's own shyness to be overcome as well as his. A lady who was one of Firbank's earliest friends and admirers told me that often when she used to visit him while he was living in Oxford (at his own invitation—there was no question of intrusion) she would find him in such a state of nervous diffidence that he would only talk to her with his back turned and looking out of the window.

A symbolical attitude perhaps! Many passages in his books seem as though written with his back turned and looking out of the window. And through that window there is no doubt that he saw some very curious things.

It was several years later, in Rome, that I came to know Firbank well—that is to say, as well as it was possible to know that strange, orchidaceous, incoherent, fantastic personality. Conversation with him was like playing tennis with an erratic tennis-player. You never knew in what direction his thoughts would fly. After a time a sort of technique could be acquired. It was no use, for instance, ever asking him a question, or, at all events, to expect a reasonable answer. He seemed to dread being pinned down to any positive assertion even of the most simple nature. 'Where does So-and-so live?' one might ask. 'Why should one live anywhere?' he would reply, and go off into peals of convulsive laughter generally ending in a paroxysm of coughing. The phrase 'I wonder!' was constantly on his lips, and uttered in a tone that seemed to evoke all the unsolved riddles of the universe.

The flashes of brilliance that animated his conversation and made his company so delightful are impossible to reconstruct. One might as well attempt to record the hovering of a humming-bird or portray the opalescence of a soap-bubble. There was an intriguing irrelevance, a delightful, fantastic silliness in all he said or did. (I have perhaps rather overdone the word 'fantastic', but, then, Ronald Firbank was an Arch-Fantastic.)

Considering his aloofness, his detachment, his apparent antipathy for all the practical aspects of life, it is surprising that he ever managed to get anywhere. Yet he travelled into all the quarters of the globe with the greatest ease. On one occasion, even, in the course of an expedition down the Nile on a dahabeah, he succeeded, single-handed, in quelling a mutiny.

When in Rome he would rent some huge and generally rather gloomy apartment, where he would live in absolute solitude. It was stipulated that he should never see the servants. They were to live out and only come in to execute their functions, such as tidying up and preparing his meals, at certain specified times when he was absent.

A man I knew who occupied rooms on the opposite side of the courtyard of a Palazzo where Firbank was living told me that sometimes in the depths of the night he would hear through the open windows the sound of chuckling and laughter coming from the lonely inmate of the apartment *vis-à-vis*. Like the Pope in *Cardinal Pirelli*, he 'often laughed when he was alone'.

He died in as strange and as aloof a fashion as that in which he had lived.

A few days before his death I motored out with him to Lake Nemi. Almost my last impression of him was seeing him ambling down the precipitous streets of Genzano followed by a crowd of children shouting 'Ridolini! Ridolini!' (Ridolini—not to be confused with Mussolini—is the name of a popular Italian comic film character.) From time to time Firbank would stop and scatter handfuls of nickel coins, a proceeding which only tended to aggravate the situation.

He did not seem to me on that last excursion to be in any worse health than usual. He coughed a good deal, but not more alarmingly than on other occasions.

For four or five days after that I heard nothing from him. Thinking that he was engaged in writing, I did not wish to disturb him.

One evening I got a telephone message from the Hotel Quirinale saying that Mr Firbank was very ill and had asked me to come and see him. The doctor was in the hotel, and I spoke to him on the telephone. He reassured me and said that his patient was feeling much better that evening and had even sent away the nurse who had been engaged for him. As it was then very late, I said that I would go round and see him the first thing in the morning.

But that night Ronald Firbank died.

Owing to his solitary way of living and his habitual reticence, it was extremely difficult to find out anything about him. I was his only friend in Rome at the time, and as to his domestic affairs I was as ignorant as anyone else. I knew he had a sister living, but her address was unknown. By the merest chance the name of his solicitor was discovered on a crumpled piece of paper.

I had never for a moment imagined that Firbank was a Roman Catholic. His attitude towards the Church of Rome both in his conversation and his writings was distinctly heretical. I believe that in his early youth he had thought of taking Holy Orders. But more than once he had said to me, 'The Church of Rome wouldn't have me and so I laugh at her.'

Thus he came to be buried in the Protestant Cemetery in Rome. It transpired later that he was a Roman Catholic. But, distasteful as this error may appear to Catholics, I cannot help thinking that he himself would prefer to lie in the shade of the Pyramid of Cestius, in the company of Keats and Shelley, than with a crowd of Italian bourgeois out at San Lorenzo.

The funeral took place on an early summer morning under a cloudless Italian sky, amid the cypresses and roses and the singing of the nightingales, whose vocal outpourings in Italy are not confined, as in northern countries, to moonlit groves. In fact, they sing more vigorously in the daytime than at night.

The nightingales that attended Ronald's funeral were presumably Papists, for they did their utmost to drown the voice of the officiating clergyman.

Part Two

OTHER REMINISCENCES

A. C. LANDSBERG

Firbank at Cambridge

UNDATED

My dear Mr Kyle Fulther

I am very sorry to have been so slow about answering your letter. I have been waiting for an opportunity to do so conscientiously. It is very difficult to answer your questions about Ronald Firbank, so I hope you will verify whatever facts—especially dates—I am about to give you. I am terribly vague and have a rotten memory. It is fifteen or sixteen years since I last saw Firbank. We lost touch with each other during the war.

You may well speak of 'the elusive charm of the man' as no one could be more full of contradictions than he was, being one of those people who are naturally 'artificial' and sincerely paradoxical. He often posed as being 'méchant' but was really most kind. In a way I used to think that he 'played to the gallery', but he was really too fastidious ever to be cheap unless it is cheap to be forever striving *not* to be so! He despised ordinary people and often lived 'like a hermit' (as he was fond of saying), yet I think he hated solitude really, and adored luxury and the world (though he was continually wounded by it through his over-selfconsciousness and sensitiveness).

His sensitiveness was such that it was obvious when one saw him what book he had last been reading—especially of course if it was something very strong like Hamlet or Volpone—when he would behave like Hamlet or Volpone and speak to one almost as if he were Hamlet or Volpone! 'Bruges la Morte' and Maeterlinck's and Huysmans' books I remember were great favourites of his at the time when I knew him. He hated poverty, but hated

---

Bertie Landsberg sent this long letter from Italy in answer to Ifan Kyrle Fletcher's request for information about Firbank. Although many details from it already appear in the Kyrle Fletcher *Memoir*, it is worth reading in full, and is reprinted here by permission of A. C. Landsberg's executors. The spelling, including the first line, is Landsberg's own.

vulgarity still more. He was tremendously 'spoilt', and yet could live alone with the greatest simplicity—'austerity' he liked to call it! But what saved all was his whimsicalness, humour and love of beauty—(though of course—being so strongly marked a personality—there were people who couldn't bear the sight of him).

I knew him in 1907 when I went to Cambridge and found him in my college, Trinity Hall, where he had been for at least a couple of years. His rooms were on the right (chapel) side of the entrance court of the college. I met him, I think, through E. Dent (the musical don, of King's—author of the 'Life of Mozart' etc. Probably you could get some interesting facts and impressions from him). Trinity Hall was then a very sporting college (with a long record of being 'head of the river' etc.). Apart from that it was also a 'law' college, so neither Firbank nor myself fitted into it particularly well. The great advantage of it for both of us was that one was not bothered too much about passing exams—especially as we were both supposed to be preparing ourselves for the Diplomatic Service. So lenient were they then that I only passed the 'Little-go' at the end of four years! (I apologise for speaking of myself, but it makes it easier to answer some of your questions).

As he was a little older than myself he seemed to me without age—for he gave one the impression both of being old, and of being under-developed in some ways. He and I were the only members of the college who took the least trouble about making our rooms beautiful, or who took any interest in 'Art' generally. Through him I was introduced to the 'Yellow Book', 'Savoy' and Wilde tastes, to d'Annunzio, Maeterlinck and to modern French poets & novelists such as Baudelaire, Mallarmé, Flaubert, Samain, Verlaine, Robert de Montesquiou, and Henri de Régnier, etc. As I was at the time fresh from Harrow and English coaches, & full of the usual schoolboy prejudices & mistrust of originality, I was both thrilled and a little suspicious (this is not quite the right word but it will have to do!) In my case in some ways I consider that I sympathised no less with the general college atmosphere than with him—especially at first. I both admired him and found him a little ridiculous—and even, sometimes, pathetic! You see, ours was such a very 'sporting' college that I was myself conscious of not being in my right element, and he was even less so, and looked *terribly* feminine, sophisticated, cosmopolitan and 'elegant'! Yet he could—often did—turn the tables on 'the mob' (as he called the average undergraduate) and make it seem very coarse and ordinary. Besides he was always very absorbed in whatever he was writing, (which at that time was like a sort of mosaic work of pretty touches and amusing details with scraps of over-heard conversations which he was always delighted to be able to put into the mouths of one of his characters).

In appearance he always reminded me of the portraits of society women by Boldini, as he was always writhing about, admiring his hands, etc. His clothes—although made by the best tailors—always looked a little foreign somehow—perhaps because he wore French ties from Doucet's & from Charvet's, & always had his hair waved in 'artistic disorder', besides often wearing either a Chinese green jade ring, or one of those Egyptian blue earthenware ones. He was very anxious to remain slim at that time & used to starve himself, go out for runs in all weathers, etc. He looked so absurd in his running togs that I believe he was once more or less mobbed by the rougher elements in the college (but that was before my time).

He was happiest in the curtained and shaded twi-light of his rooms, that were always full of flowers and lit by candles in carved & gilt Italian altar candle-sticks. There he would sit with his back to the light, surrounded by old silks & photographs of his mother in court dress and innumerable little tables covered with books & statuettes (reproductions for the most part of little religious Gothic figures & of Pompeian & Tanagra things). He often went to London for exhibitions or concerts & brought back sentences & scraps of phrases for his mosaic-work, books (such as Max Beerbohm's) &, once, an Egyptian bronze statuette which he spoilt by having an opal set into it 'as a propitiatory offering'. He gave little dinners in college at some of which I met Rupert Brooke (from King's—then in his last year), & Robert Ross & other people from London. By the way I think S. Cockerell (the director of the Fitzwilliam museum) also knew Firbank, & could tell you something about him, also Lord Leconfield who, I think was a relation of his mother's, who at that time had a house at Petworth.

Of his life before Cambridge I can't tell you much. I remember that he seemed to be very fond of his Mother & to admire her tremendously. I gathered that she was in every way a great and beautiful lady, only too good & fine for his Father whom he seemed to consider as rather a vulgarian. (*Please*, in your book, *do not quote me* as saying this, or anything!) Also—more vaguely—I think I remember that he had two brothers, an elder

—very normal—one who—to his Father's despair—died about the time when I met Firbank, & a younger one who—unless I am mixing him up with someone else!—made a foolish marriage, went to the colonies & was considered 'beyond the pale' by Ronald (but I remember all this so vaguely that you had better verify it. He may have had only *one* brother!) He also had a sister whom he was fond of, & whose debts he used often to pay. I gathered that she was terribly extravagant.

He 'went down' from Cambridge before me, & soon after had rooms somewhere near St James' St. where he was very pleased with a black carpet (He used a lot of black in his rooms always). At one time he had a house in Curzon St in which he had some very fine old English silver, & French 18th century furniture & prints (the remainder I believe of important collections that had belonged to his Father. I do not know what was the origin of his Father's fortune which at one time must have been considerable). He (his Father) had been at one time, I think, a conservative member of parliament.

When the war broke out, he was living at the Inner—or was the Middle?—Temple in nice old pannelled rooms with a view of trees & the river. There he showed me a drawing he had bought from Gordon Craig, who may possibly be able to tell you something about him. Another friend of his whom I have just remembered is Vivian Holland (Oscar Wilde's son) at present living in London, I'm told. In London Firbank belonged to several clubs—the Junior Constitutional was one of them.

In the Cambridge days he had—as far as I remember—only published 'Odette' which, I seem to remember, had some connection with his stay—after leaving Eton (I think) where he had only been a very short time—in some very beautiful & old French chateau in the Touraine, where he had been sent to learn French in a very French family whose memory always seemed to amuse him.

As for his religion I think that his mind was too comprehensive & subtle to take any one creed as being the only absolute truth (but I may be mistaken). He gave me the impression of merely flirting with the Roman Catholic church out of boredom, and it amused him to coquette intellectually with priests, also he would have liked to be able to believe in wickedness (as a means of adding color to life). But, as I have said before, I may be wrong about all this. In any case he was always going to the Roman

Catholic church in that long, ugly street that goes to the station. If the same Padre is still there (He was always talking about Father —— —unfortunately I can't remember his name) he ought to be useful to you. It must have been in 1907 or 8, and it was in that modern gothic building that he was received into the R. Catholic church. I seem to remember that he afterwards held, or intended to apply for some sort of position at the Vatican. Mr Evans Morgan (Lord Tredegar's son) who has lived a lot in Rome knew him I think & ought to be able to tell you something. Also Lord Berners (the composer, painter & collector) who lived in Rome and knew him. Already in the Cambridge days he spoke of having been somewhere for a retreat (as much for his looks and physical welfare as for that of his soul, he used to say). I *think* the Sitwells knew him in his later days, but I'm not sure.

Now I think I've told you about all that I can remember. It is only a vague rigmarole, I fear, but from some of the people I mention you ought to get more precise and interesting information. Roger Quilter (of 7 Montagu Street, Portman Square) knew him slightly I think. I wish I could give you an idea of Ronald Firbank's great charm, distinction & originality, but that I hope, will be done by yourself. I very much look forward to reading your book and wish you luck.

Yours truly,
A. C. Landsberg

P.S. I had the impression that after leaving Cambridge R.F. greatly improved intellectually, but 'went off' physically as he drank too much & became—for him—fattish, & rather red-faced. He *hated* growing older!

P.S. I *think* he was partly Irish on his mother's side.

P.S. I have lately returned from Paris where I looked for a photograph I had of a portrait-drawing in pastels of Firbank, done towards the end of his time at Cambridge by Charles Shannon. Possibly Charles Ricketts may have a copy of it—(he also knew him, by the way). Unfortunately I could not find mine or I would have sent it to you. A. John too, I think, did a drawing of him.

P.S. Jeanne Granier, the famous old Parisian 'comédienne' was one of his friends. You might write to her too?

HAROLD NICOLSON

'Lambert Orme'

I

It would be impossible, I feel, to actually be as decadent as Lambert looked. I split the infinitive deliberately, being in the first place no non-split diehard (oh, the admirable Mr Fowler!), and desiring secondly to emphasise what was in fact the dominant and immediate consideration which Lambert evoked. I have met many men with wobbly walks, but I have never met a walk more wobbly than that of Lambert Orme. It was more than sinuous, it did more than undulate: it rippled. At each step a wave was started which passed upwards through his body, convexing his buttocks, concaving the small of his back, convexing again his slightly rounded shoulders, and working itself out in a backward swaying of the neck and head. This final movement passed off more rapidly than the initial undulations, with the resulting impression of a face upturned generally, but bowing at rhythmic intervals, as if a tired royalty or a camel slouching heavily along the road to Isfahan. At each inclination the lock of red-gold hair which shrouded the lowness of his brow would flop, and rise again, and then again would flop. He was a tall young man and he would bend his right knee laterally, his right foot resting upon an inward-pointing toe. He had retreating shoulders, a retreating forehead, a retreating waist. The face itself was a curved face, a boneless face, a rather pink face, fleshy about the chin. His eyelashes were fair and fluttering; his lips were full. When he giggled, which he did with nervous frequency, his underlip would come to rest below his upper teeth. He held his cigarette between the index and the middle fingers, keeping them outstretched together with the gesture of a male impersonator puffing at a cigar. His hands, rather damp on their inner side, gave the impression on their outer side of being double-jointed. He dressed simply, wearing an opal pin, and a velours hat tilted angularly. He had a peculiar way of speaking: his sentences came in little splashing pounces; and then from time to time he would hang on to a word as if to steady himself: he would say 'Simplytooshattering FOR words', the phrase

Reprinted from *Some People* (1930) by permission of Constable and Co. Ltd.

being a slither with a wild clutch at the banister of 'for'. He was very shy.

I had not met nor noticed Lambert Orme during my first term at Oxford, but in the Easter vacation he came out to Madrid with a letter of introduction to my people. They asked him to luncheon. I eyed him with sullen disapproval. He stood for none of the things which I had learnt at Wellington. Clearly he was not my sort. He had the impudence to announce that he had resolved to devote himself to art, music and literature. 'Before I am twenty-one,' he said, 'I shall have painted a good picture, written a novel, and composed a waltz.' He pronounced it *valse*. My gorge rose within me. I refused during the whole course of luncheon to speak to Lambert Orme. And yet behind my indignation vibrated a little fibre of curiosity. Or was it more than curiosity? I hope that it was something more. Subsequently I was reproved by my mother for my behaviour. She said in the first place that I should have better manners. In the second place she said that I was little more than a Philistine. And in the third place she said that she was sure that poor boy wasn't very strong.

It interests me to recapture my own frame of mind at the time of this my first meeting with Lambert Orme. It amuses me to look back upon the block of intervening years in which I also aped aestheticism, toyed with the theory that I also could become an intellectual. Have I returned after all these garish wanderings to the mood which descended upon me that afternoon in the dark and damask dining-room at Madrid? No, I have not returned. It is true that some faint and tattered fibres of heartiness do still mingle with my ageing nerves. I *have* my Kipling side. But I can at least admit today that Orme was in several ways a serious person. And I have been told by people whose opinion I would not dare to disregard that such was indeed the case.

2

The immediate result of my mother's lecture was that I promised to take the fellow for a ride. At the back of my mind (but not I fear so very far at the back) was a desire to humiliate Lambert, a quite caddish desire on my part to show off. I sent the horses to the entrance of the Casa de Campo and drove down there with Lambert in a cab. He mounted his horse and remained there with surprising firmness, and, moreover, with an elegance which shamed the clumsiness of my own arrant style. His languid manner dropped from him; if his back curved slightly it was but with a hellenic curve, the forward-seat of some Panathenaic rider. I was at pains to readjust my conception of him to this altered angle. We rode out under the avenues to where the foothills look back to the façade of the palace chalk-white against the smoke above the town: in front, the ramparts of the Guadarrama were jagged with pinnacles of snow. The larks rose from clumps of broom and lavender: a thousand larks above us: a shrill overtone under the crisp spring sky; and from west to east a flock of April clouds trailed rapidly, pushing in front of them patches of scudding shade. The feeling of that afternoon is now upon me: I see no reason to become sentimental about it: even in our most intimate period Lambert Orme possessed for me no emotional significance: yet I recognise that on that afternoon the sap began to mount within me. That, and the summer evening in Doctor Pollock's garden, are my first two dates.

Not that Lambert said very much. I feel indeed that he was actually unconscious of my existence. He was thinking probably of Albert Samain and of Henri de Régnier, of how pleasant it was, that spring day, among the uplands of Castille. I said: 'Over there —you may see it if the sun strikes—is the Escorial.' He said, 'Yes, I see.' I said, 'And Aranjuez is over there,' pointing vaguely towards Toledo. He turned his head in the direction indicated. 'And Segovia?' he asked. I was not very certain about Segovia, but I nodded northwards. 'La Granja,' I added, 'is quite close to it—really only a few miles.' We turned our horses, and the wind and sun were behind us. The smoke of the town billowed into sharp layers, an upward layer of white smoke hanging against a sweep of grey smoke, in its turn backed by a crinkled curtain of black. The sun and snow-wind behind us lit and darkened this grisaille. 'Oh!' I exclaimed, 'What an El Greco sky!' It was an opening. He could have taken it had he wished. He merely said, 'Does the King live in the palace? Is he there now?' I answered that he was.

We crossed the Manzanares, where there were women washing white sheets. They beat them against the boulders. The palace above us was turning pink against the sunset. Lambert asked me to tea. I gave my horse to the groom and walked round with him to the rooms he had taken near the Opera House. It was some sort of pension, and he had characteristically caused the walls to be distempered with a light buff wash, and had arranged the room with red silk, and walnut furniture, and two large gilt candelabra from a church. He was very rich. Upon his writing-table lay a ruled sheet of music-manuscript, and upon another table some paintbrushes and tubes of water-colour. He had painted a little picture of an infanta in what I now realise to have been the manner of Brabazon. It was rather good. There were a great many cushions and several French books. He became artificial again when he entered his rooms and his voice slithered and he ordered tea in highly irritating French. There was a sheet of vellum lying near the fireplace on which, in an upright scribble, Lambert had written: 'Mon âme est une infante . . .' and then again. 'Mon âme est . . .' and then, very calligraphically, 'en robe de parade.' It was cold in his room and he lit the logs in the fire. He then threw incense on it, and a puff of scented smoke billowed beyond the grate. My antagonism returned to me.

Lambert thereafter became very foolish about the tea. He did hostess: his gestures were delicate: there was a tea-cloth which was obviously his own. I lit my pipe and said I must be going. He picked up a book at random: I really believe it was at random. He said, 'Would you like to take this?' I said I would. It was the *Jardin de Bérénice.* I suppose that, really, is what dates the occasion.

3

When I returned to Oxford I visited Lambert in his rooms at Magdalen, drawn by an attraction which I should have hesitated to admit. They were in the new buildings and looked out upon the deer park: as one sipped one's Malaga, one could hear the stags barking amorously underneath the trees. His sitting-room was exquisitely decorated. When I think of that room I am again convinced that there was something *cabotin* about Lambert Orme: people at the age of twenty should not have rooms like that. He had painted it a shiny black: there were grey sofas with petunia cushions: there was a Coromandel cabinet with blue china on the top and some hardstone stuff inside. It was not in the least like the room of an undergraduate: it made me at first rather ashamed of my own room with its extracts from 'the hundred best pictures', its photograph of the charioteer of Delphi, and its kettle-holder with the Balliol arms: it made me, in the end, like my own room very much indeed. And yet inevitably I was entranced by that little *gîte* (I use the correct word) at

Magdalen: by the firelight flickering upon the yellow books: by the Manet reproductions, by the Sobranye cigarettes in their china box. Lambert possessed even in those days a collection of curious literature, and I would sit there after dinner reading *Justine*, or the novels of M. Achille d'Essebac, or even *Under the Hill*. All this, I feel sure, was admirable training. My early oats I find were singularly tame. But they were oats none the less. Lambert at the time was writing his novel *Désiré de St. Aldegonde*. He would read me passages which I failed entirely to understand. They were in the style, curiously enough, of M. Maeterlinck: a style which, in English, tastes like bananas and cream. The book was published some time in 1910 by the Bodley Head. It attracted no attention whatever. And when Lambert, under the influence of M. Guillaume Apollinaire, came to adopt his second manner, he bought up the remaining copies of *Désiré* and burnt them on the rocks at Polperro.

It was all very pleasant and seductive my dropping down like that to Magdalen; but it became a little awkward when Lambert, in his velours hat, would climb the hill to visit me at Balliol. In any case I never learnt to cope with Balliol until after I had left it: my real Oxford friends were only made when I met them again in after life. The effect of Balliol upon my development was salutary and overpowering. But it didn't work at the time. On looking back at Balliol I realise that during those three years I was wholly abominable. That Balliol should have shared this opinion indicates its admirable sense. But although I had at that time but little conception of what Balliol was thinking, yet I realised quite definitely that they would not, that they did not, approve of Lambert at all. I cannot therefore say that I relished his visits. My sitting-room with its grained wood walls looked somewhat squalid at his entry: the rep sofa, the brass reading lamp with its torn red shade, that other light hanging naked but for a glass reflector: the inadequate books: Stubbs' charters, Smith's classical dictionary, Liddell and Scott—none of that crystalline glitter of those rooms at Magdalen. My scout would burst in with his cap on, and bang the chipped plates beside the fire: the tin covers rattled. The kettle also rattled internally when one poured it out. There was always a little coal inside the kettle. The spout of the teapot spouted diagonally owing to a slight abrasion. The cloth was stained and bore in place of embroidery my name in marking ink. There were buttered buns and anchovy toast. Lambert ate them gingerly.

'I wish,' I said to him, being incensed by the refinement of his attitude, 'that you wouldn't wear a hat.'

'But if I didn't,' he giggled, 'I might be taken for an undergraduate.'

'But at least not that hat, and at least not at that angle.'

'Now don't be tahsome.'

There were moments when I hated Lambert. It is a mystery to me how Magdalen tolerated him for so long. The end came, as was inevitable, after a bump supper. I never knew what they did to Lambert: I know only that he escaped in his Daimler never to return. I missed him for a bit, and then I was glad of his departure. I realised that I had been tarred a little by his brush. I mentioned the matter, rather tentatively, to Sligger Urquhart. He seemed to have no particular feeling for Lambert, either for or against: he pouted for a moment, and then said that he had found him 'absurdly childish'. I do not suppose that that remark was intended to be very penetrating: I know only that it penetrated me like a lance. The angle from which I had began to regard Lambert Orme was shifted suddenly: it ceased to be an ascending angle and became in the space of a few seconds a descending angle: I had begun, in a way, to look up to Lambert: I now, quite suddenly and in every way, found myself looking down. A few days later Sligger, most subtle of dons, presented me with a copy of *Marius the Epicurean*. I found it on my table when I came back from the river: there was a note inside saying, 'I think you had better read this': and on the fly-leaf he had written 'H.N. from F.F.U'. By this homoeopathic treatment I was quickly cured. And yet this false start, if it was a false start, left me troubled and uncertain. I remained uncertain for several months.

4

As so often in such cases, my ensuing reaction against the eighteen-nineties took the form of a virulent loathing which I have never since been able to shake off. I am assured by reliable people that it was a serious movement of revolt and liberation: I can see for myself that the Yellow Book group were all extremely kind and made jokes which, at the time, were found amusing: I am prepared to respect, but I cannot like them. The whole business is too reminiscent of those puzzled and uncertain months at Oxford. It takes me straight back to that room at Magdalen: 'Now listen to this, it's too too wonderful: it's really toomuchfun.' I have a sense of many little wheels revolving brightly but devoid of cogs. I have a sense predominantly of the early Lambert Orme.

I did not see him again for some five years. He went round the world and sent me a postcard from Yokohama. He was immensely impressed by the beauty of American cities, and it was from them, I think, that he first learnt to see life as a system of correlated planes. It was several years, however, before his very real and original talent for association was able finally to cast the slough of symbolism. When I next met him he was still intensively concerned with the relation between things and himself: it was only in his final period that he became predominantly interested in the relation of things towards each other. His talent, which though singularly receptive was not very muscular, had failed to extract any interesting synthesis from the confrontation of the universe with his own twitching heart: he had tried, and he had failed, to interpret conscious cognition by a single simple emotion. But in his later period he did in fact succeed in conveying an original analysis, implicit rather than expressed, of the diversity and interrelation of external phenomena: he was able to suggest a mood of subconscious perplexity sensitive to unapparent affinities. The conception of life as a repetition of self-contained and finite entities can be integrated only by the pressure of a compelling imagination: Lambert's imagination though mobile was not compelling: I suspect indeed that less power is required to disintegrate such entities, to suggest a world of atoms fortuitously whirling into certain shapes, to indicate a tremendous unknown, quivering below the crust of our convention. His later poetry succeeded because of its reference to this unapparent reality. I am now assured that some of his later poems were very respectable.

Meanwhile, however, Lambert Orme continued to represent for me something 'absurdly childish'; his attitude of mind struck me as undeveloped and out of date. He was obsessed by false claims. He was no longer, not in any sense, a guide: he was just someone who rather uninterestingly had wandered off. The circumstances of our meeting, five years after he had escaped from Magdalen, confirmed me in this opinion. It made me very angry with Lambert Orme, and when I think of it today I become angry again.

He came to Constantinople on his way back from Egypt. He left a note saying that he had 'descended' at the Pera Palace and would like to see me. I was interested to hear from him again, and told him to come to the Embassy at 9.30 the next morning and I would take him sailing up the Bosphorus. I had a sailing boat in those days, a perilous little affair, which I called the *Elkovan*. I had bought it in a moment of optimism, imagining that I would sail daily out into the Marmora, and that on Sundays I would go for longer expeditions to Ismid and Eregli and the Gulf of Cyzikos. But in practice the thing became a bore. The current which streamed out from the Black Sea permitted no such liberty of movement. I ascertained that if I followed the current I should be unable, when the wind fell at sunset, to return. So I would tack painfully against the stream, gaining but a mile or so in as many hours, and then I would swing round and float back rapidly while the minarets showed their black pencils against the setting sun. This pastime became monotonous; it was only on those rare occasions when the south wind blew strongly that one derived the impression of sailing at all. The Sunday on which I had invited Lambert Orme to accompany me was one of these occasions. A spring day opened before me, enlivened by warm gusts of the Bithynian wind—the wind which the Byzantines to this day call *vóros*: I ordered a large and excellent luncheon; with luck we should get out beyond Kavak and into the Black Sea. We might bathe even. I looked forward to my day with pleasure.

I waited for Lambert Orme. At 10.00 a man brought me a note in his neat hellenic writing. 'Today is too wonderful,' he wrote, 'it is the most wonderful day that ever happened: it would be too much for me: let us keep today as something marvellous that did not occur.' I dashed furiously round to his hotel, but he had already left with his courier to visit the churches. I scribbled 'Silly ass' on my card and left it for him. I then sailed up the Bosphorus indignant and alone. When I returned my servant met me with a grin: my sitting-room was banked with Madonna lilies. 'C'est un Monsieur,' he said, 'qui vous a apporté tout ça.' 'Quel Monsieur?' 'Un Monsieur qui porte le chapeau de travers.'

5

I thereafter and for many years dismissed Lambert from my mind. As a person he really did not seem worth the bother, as an intellect he was absurdly childish—he represented the rotted rose-leaves of the Yellow Book. I came to be more and more ashamed of the period when I also had dabbled in aestheticism, a feeling of nausea came over me when I thought of the Malaga and cigarettes in that expensive room at Magdalen. Lambert represented a lapse.

I do not today regard him as a lapse. He was inconvenient doubtless and did me external harm. But he represented my first contact with the literary mind. I see now that my untutored self required some such stimulant: that it should have been Grand Marnier and not some decent brandy is immaterial: he provided an impetus at the very moment when the wheels hesitated to revolve. Balliol was all very well, and Sligger Urquhart at least understood and assisted, but my palate was, in fact, too insensitive for so matured a vintage. I therefore look on Lambert, in retrospect, as a short-cut. What I failed to realise was the possibility that Lambert also might grow up. His later method, that obtuse angle from which he came to regard life, would, had I realised it, have been an even shorter cut and to more interesting objectives. But once I had discarded him, I did so with no reservations. I thought that any resumption of his influence would entail a retrogression: I failed in my stupidity to see that he had once again sprung ahead of me: and while I dabbled in Bakst and Flecker, Lambert had already reached the van.

As I write of this period, its atmosphere of diffident uncertainty descends upon me. I wish to convey some sharp outline of Lambert Orme, but it all results in a fuzz of words. I am still quite unaware whether I regard Lambert as ridiculous, as tragic, or as something legendary. A section of me is prepared to take him seriously, to read with admiration those of his poems which I am told are good. Another, and less reputable section, wishes to deride Lambert, to hold him up to obloquy. And yet another section feels rather soppy about him, simply because he died in the war. Which is, of course, absurd. Physically he is definite enough. I can see him again, as at our next meeting, sinuously descending the steps of the National Gallery. A day in late October with the cement around the fountains glistening from the damp of fog. A stream of traffic past Morley's Hotel, another stream past the shop of Mr Dent, a river of traffic down Whitehall. And in the centre, that ungainly polygon, doves and urchins and orange-peel, and a sense of uncloistered quiet. It was the autumn of 1913: he had abandoned his velours, which since our Oxford days had become the headgear of the proletariate: he wore instead a black Borsalino which he had purchased while studying baroque at Ancona. But still he wilted: he wilted when I accosted him: he entered the Café Royal with a peculiarly selfconscious undulation which made me shy.

He still employed the old vocabulary (he said that I had been 'very tahsome' at Constantinople), but his whole angle had shifted. The former avid subjectivity was leaving him, he was far less excited: his interest in life was no less passionate but had come under some form of control: predominantly he was interested in the sort of things that had never interested him before. He was in love with the wife of the Rumanian Military Attaché at Brussels. He talked about it quite simply as if he had always been a sensualist. He had decided to live in Paris, and had, in fact, already bought a house at Neuilly: he would write and collect pictures, and see to his own education: once a month he would go to Brussels for love and inspiration. He had evolved a not uninteresting theory of the necessity of living in a mechanical framework: at Neuilly the externals of his life were to be organised according to the strictest time-table: every day was in all material respects to be identical with every other day: this rhythmic repetition would in the end produce a background of symmetry against which all new experience would acquire a more intense significance, would assume the proportions of a physical displacement. The eighteen-nineties and the nineteen-hundreds (he spoke of them in a detached and objective manner) had failed because they dissipated their emotions: they were unable either to concentrate or to select. Their system of life was garish and dispersed: his own system, out at Neuilly, would be a monochrome and concentric: he would limit his emotions: he would achieve a pattern rather than an arabesque. I suggested that so artificial a system of detachment might in itself be limiting. He was unexpectedly sensible about it all: he said that he realised that his system could only be an experiment, that even if successful it might be suitable only for himself. But he was quite determined. And ten months later, in July of 1914, he published *Lay Figures*, which, with his book of war poems, places him in a perfectly definite position. There is something very mean in me which resents this position. I am not myself very convinced by it. But it is recognised by people whose judgement I am honestly quite unable to ignore.

6

At moments, in the roar and rattle of the early stages of the war, I would reflect a little grimly on the collapse of Lambert's symmetry, on those cobweb time-tables swept aside unnoticed in the onrush of the maddened beast. He sent me a copy of *Lay Figures* which reached me in the early days of August and which remained unopened for many years. Until the spring of 1916 he stayed at Paris, justifying his existence by a little hospital work, writing those poems which figure as 'mes hôpitaux' in his war volume. And then in March he crossed over to England and joined the army. He came to see me before he left for France. He did not look as odd in his uniform as I had expected: he talked voraciously about the new movements in French literature and in a way which I failed entirely to understand: of his training down at Salisbury he said little, giggling feebly when I asked him about it, telling me 'not to be morbid' when I pressed for details. I could see no signs of any alteration in his physique: a little fatter in the face, perhaps, a little more fleshy round the jaw; but he still wilted, and his walk was as self-conscious as ever. I asked him if he was afraid of Flanders, whether the prospect of the trenches alarmed him as much as it alarmed me. He said that he dreaded the rats and was afraid of mines. 'You see,' he said, 'it is the inevitable or the wholly unexpected that is horrible. The rest is largely mechanical. It becomes a question of masochism. I certainly shall not mind the rest.' I thought at the time he was being optimistic, but I have since met a man in the Anglo-Persian Oil Company who was with Lambert both in France and Mesopotamia. 'Oh, no,' this man said to me, 'he was a quiet sort of fellow, Orme. And he had a violent temper. But he was rather a good regimental officer: he put up a good show, I remember, at Sheikh Sa'ad. A very good show. We liked him on the whole.'

Sheikh Sa'ad and Magdalen, that Coromandel cabinet, those bleached and ochre flats—Lambert himself would have savoured these contrasts: it was the sort of thing by which his rather dulled sense of humour would have been aroused. Was it aroused, I wondered, as he lay in the hospital ship at Basrah dying of dysentery? I like to think that it may perhaps have been aroused. He had dignity and courage: I expect he giggled slightly when they told him that he was unlikely to survive.

I heard of his death as I was running, late from luncheon, down the Duke of York's steps. I met a man coming up the steps who had been at Oxford with us. 'You have heard,' he said, 'that Orme has died in Mesopotamia?' I walked on towards the Foreign Office feeling very unheroic, very small. I had no sense, at the moment, of wastage—that sorrow which oppresses us today when we think back upon the war. I had no sense of pity even, feeling, as I have said, that so startling an incongruity would have illumined Lambert's courage with a spasm of amusement. I merely felt exhausted by this further appeal to the emotions: a sense of blank despair that such announcements should have ceased to evoke any creditable emotional response: a sense of the injustice of my sheltered lot: a sense of numbed dissatisfaction: a revolting sense of relief that it hadn't been me.

7

In the summer of 1925 I went to a party in Bloomsbury. I went with much diffidence, alarmed at entering the Areopagus of British culture. They treated me with distant but not unfriendly courtesy. The fact that, through no fault of my own, I was in evening dress increased the gulf between us. I sidled to the back of the room, hoping to remain unobserved. There was a curious picture on the wall which I studied attentively, trying to extract some meaning from its doubtless significant contours. My host came up to me. 'What,' I asked, 'is that supposed to represent?' Had I been less unstrung I should not, of course, have asked that question. My host winced slightly and moved away. I turned towards the bookshelves, searching in vain for the friendly bindings of one of mine own books. They were all talking about a sculptor called Brancousi. I pulled out a copy of Hugh Faussett's *Tennyson* and began to read. An untidy man came up to me and glanced over my shoulder. He had eyes of great kindness and penetration, and he adopted towards me a manner which suggested that I either had said, or was about to say, something extremely interesting. I asked him whether he had read the book and he answered that he had, and that he felt it was so far more intelligent than the other one that had been published simultaneously. I agreed that it was, it was. He then moved away, and I put the book back tidily in its place. On the shelf above it were some volumes of poetry, and among them Lambert Orme's *Lay*

Figures, which I had never read. I opened it with suddenly awakened interest and began to turn the pages. My eye was arrested by a heading: 'Constantinople: April 1912'. I sat down on the floor at that and began to read. 'Thera' I read:

Thera, if it indeed be you
That are Santorin,
There wander in
The furtive steamers of the Khedivial Mail Company,
Rusted, barnacled,
And from the bridge the second officer
Shouts demotic to the Company's agent
Bobbing alpaca in a shore boat.

Thera, if it indeed be you,
That are Santorin,
You will fully understand
This my cleansing—
At which he leant forward and pulled a rope towards him,
And the yacht sidled cross-ways,
At an angle,
'That,' he said (he was a man of obtuse sensibilities)
'Is Bebek.'

It went on like this through several stanzas, and conveyed in its final effect a not unconvincing picture of the poet sailing somewhat absent-mindedly up the Bosphorus in a little white boat, accompanied, as he so often repeated, by a man of obtuse sensibilities. I was a little wounded by this posthumous revelation, and put the book down for a moment while I thought. After all, I thought, Lambert didn't come. If he had come he mightn't have found me in the least obtuse. I should never have said 'That is Bebek'. I should have waited till he asked. And surely, coming back at sunset, and I so silent—surely if he *had* come, the poem would have been a little less personal. My host was searching in the bookcase behind me, and the rest of the room were in suspense about something, evidently waiting for him to illustrate his discourse. 'I know,' he said, 'it's here somewhere—I was only reading it last night. They want to do a new edition of both books together—both *Lay Figures* and the *War Poems*.' I held the book up to him and he took it from me, a little curtly perhaps, anxious to regain his seat and to continue the discussion. 'You see,' he continued, 'there is no doubt that Orme was a real pioneer in his way. Of course his stuff was crude enough and he had little sense of balance. But take this, for instance——' He began to turn the pages. 'Yes. Here it is. Now this is written in 1912. It describes him sailing up the river at Constantinople with some local bore: there's really something in it. There really is.' At this he adjusted the light behind him, jerked himself back into his cushion, and began. 'Thera,' he began,

> Thera, if it indeed be you
> That are Santorin....

He read the whole poem, and when it was finished they made him read it again. They then discussed the thing with appreciation, but with that avoidance of superlatives which so distinguishes their culture. The untidy man leant forward and knocked his pipe against the grate. 'Yes, there is no doubt,' he said, 'that Orme, had he lived, would have been important. It is a pity in a way. He must have been an interesting man. Did you ever meet him?' He was addressing my host: he was not addressing me.

'No,' my host answered; 'he lived in Paris I believe. I've never met anyone who knew him.'

The lady, whom, from a distance, I had so much admired, was sitting in the chair in front of me. She turned round and, for the first time, spoke to me. 'Mr Nicholls,' she said, 'would you mind opening one of the windows? It is getting hot in here.'

I did as I was told.

COLERIDGE KENNARD

Introduction to The Artificial Princess

So much has been written about Ronald Firbank that I do not propose—although at one period, when I lived in London, he

First printed as the introduction to *The Artificial Princess* published posthumously by Gerald Duckworth and Co. Ltd. in 1934.

used to come to see me frequently—to add anything to the minute descriptions already extant of his mannerisms and eccentricities. I hold that all that is essential about a writer is to be found in his works. Firbank expressed himself completely in his books. Moreover, he was excessively shy; he would be horrified if he could know how he has been stared at. . . .

To understand the writer and his development it is necessary, I think, to realise the prestige enjoyed by the craft and practice of letters in what I suppose I must now call a bygone age. The circle in which we moved may have been small but it was enthusiastic; we all dreamed of writing books; our lives were aimed at authorship, though what we were going to write books about and be authors of I don't think any of us knew. I fancy Firbank at first had no precise idea himself either. But he had, as Mr V. B. Holland has well emphasised, had a book *published* even before he went up to Cambridge. It was, as a matter of fact, only a poor pastiche of a story by Francis Jammes but in those days we did not know that, and the fact that *Odette d'Antrevernes* did exist and was even given to friends with inscriptions from the author surrounded Firbank with a halo. Indeed I think that his nervous habit of clawing at his head, on which all his biographers have laid such stress, was really a definite effort on his part to keep that object in its place. Briefly, he had no difficulties to contend with. The few friends he made at Cambridge burned incense around him; in later years he had the opportunities and the surroundings in which continuously to burn it round himself. For him no wearisome and protracted disputes with publishers who think only in terms of an author's 'public' and £.s.d. He had adequate private means; Mr Grant Richards accepted his books with alacrity.

In those early days (1906–9) Firbank had the habit of writing down on long strips of paper any phrase that particularly struck him and hoarding these strips in his desk. There were already several hundreds of them when I was first allowed to share the secret. At that moment they were destined to be fitted in, mosaic-wise, to make a play but the pitfalls of construction were baffling him; it was 'such a bore'. He never mastered, nor, I think, seriously attempted to master, the technique of the theatre but these carefully chosen and jealously preserved phrases were to form at last 'the subtle intricacies and simplicities'—to use Osbert Sitwell's felicitous expression—of his first novels. Behind the seemingly incoherent pages of his prose were months of toil, of conscientious selection and revision carefully hidden from every eye. It is only necessary to examine the text of the present story to find evidence of his manner of work. What, I suppose, might be called 'echoes' are scattered here and there but they are only individual phrases; the treasured strip of paper has been taken out of the drawer and placed here and there like a piece of velvet or brocade; the context is always different.

> Overhead the sky was so pale that it appeared to have been powdered all over with *poudre de riz.*

occurs in *The Artificial Princess* in a description of the Wellan hills. With 'all over' changed to 'completely' it happens in *Vainglory* over Vigo Street in London (p. 140).

> . . . A pause just long enough for an Angel to pass, flying slowly

occurs in *Vainglory* (p. 94) apparently at Totterdown junction.

> From the mantelpiece came a sudden 'whirr' from an unconcerned Sèvres shepherdess; a coquettish silence, followed by the florid chiming of a clock.

occurs in *Vainglory* in Miss Compostella's bedroom. Likewise the paragraph beginning 'Her secret lay simply in her untidiness', (*Vainglory*: p. 52) and the verses beginning 'I am disgusted with Love' attributed here to 'a Court Poet', in *Vainglory* to Mrs Cresswell.

The Artificial Princess though slightly prior to *Vainglory* is a mature and typical work. In it the faint, shadowy Court, the Conder-like figures, the ceremonial, the stifled twilights and whispered innuendos that were to form the background of his later books are sketched for the first time. Firbank's world is already peopled; even Cardinal Pirelli first peeps at us under the traits of Monsignor Parr (to be developed in *Vainglory*). Wit and artistry play on every page. Who else, past, present or future, could have penned such absurdities as

> The Queen had a passion for motoring. She would motor

> for hours and hours with her crown on; it was quite impossible to mistake her . . .

or this on dramatic critics:

> They had been presented with diamond scarf pins by the Mistress of the Robes as soon as they arrived so they knew just what to say . . . Nature by some mechanical process . . . can produce dew, but it takes Art to produce tears.

As I have said, *The Artificial Princess* was written just prior to *Vainglory* (1915); put away amongst old papers in England before its author started on one of his numerous travels, forgotten and only remembered and retrieved during Firbank's last visit to London. At the time of his death he was deliberating whether to publish it or not. He realised that he had drawn on it, from memory, in his later books and sent the story to Lord Berners, who was in Rome, for his opinion. Lord Berners was presumably too busy to offer the advice asked for and a few months later gave me the MS together with Firbank's last letters to him, to do what I liked with. The last letter Firbank wrote before his death is characteristic. In it he excuses himself from seeing his friend at the hotel, not on account of his illness but because the wallpaper in his bedroom was so dreadful. The MS has been in my keeping ever since and has been seen by none. By the kind offices of Messrs Duckworth and the Centaur Press it appears now as, I think, Firbank would have wished, in their beautiful edition of his *Collected Works*. (In his Introduction to this edition, Arthur Waley writing of *Sorrow in Sunlight* remarks that Firbank 'was becoming famous and only famous people are allowed to write short books'. I have often wondered if this was the reason why *The Artificial Princess* was discarded at the time in favour of *Vainglory*.)

I cannot, even after so many and varied years have passed, take leave here of a delightful friend without paying tribute to the charm and magnetism of an unique personality. Firbank lived in a fantastic and solitary world of his own but a word of sympathy or understanding would always cause him to pause, unlock its gates and let one, if only for a few seconds, glimpse at it. I remember well the first time I met him. I had motored down to Cambridge with Vyvyan Holland, we were received in those rooms at Trinity Hall which only Miss Compostella's Sumph could, I think, adequately describe. The flowers, I know, reminded me of the wreaths stacked in the Windsor Castle courtyards after the death of Queen Victoria. Wine flowed, conversation became wild; we left, bemused and completely under Ronald's influence, much later than we had intended. For some reason I had taken an old family butler with me. Dreaming of all the things we were so certainly going to write I missed the road and ran into a village duckpond, where the car, fixed firmly in the mud, refused to move. There was nothing to do but wait for help. It was a fine night and the stars shone brightly so, perforce, we gazed at them.

'Isn't that there the Milky Way!' the butler ventured at last.

'The Milky Way!' we replied, 'Certainly not. That is the dust falling from the feet of Saint Rose de Lima as she rises to Heaven!'

As the old man's feet were dangling in the water I do not know whether he appreciated this reflection of Ronald Firbank's spell.

GRANT RICHARDS

Ronald Firbank

How Ronald Firbank first appeared on my horizon I cannot now recall. Did he sway and wave his fragile body up my St Martin's Street stairs, carrying the typescript of *Vainglory* in his hand, or did he send it to me by post? I think he must have come himself, for otherwise I do not suppose I should have read far into even so slight a manuscript. I must have had some personal motive. Firbank's personality would have supplied it. His was not a figure that you could easily forget—and yet, as far as the beginning is concerned at least, I have allowed much to fade. I am not going to attempt to estimate the value of Firbank's queer talent here or ever, but I have never been quite sure in my secret mind that he

From *Author Hunting* by Grant Richards first published by Hamish Hamilton in 1934, reissued by the Unicorn Press in 1964. Reprinted by permission of the Garnstone Press.

really deserved the appreciation that he secured both here and in America—but especially in America. No line that Firbank wrote was like the work of any other writer. One thing I do remember and that is that I felt that *Vainglory* was intensely individual and also not a little mad. Its perversity and that of its several successors did not strike me particularly. Perhaps I hardly noticed it. Certainly those of my friends who had read any of the books would rally me for my blindness and simplicity. It is true that now and again I was brought up suddenly by some ambiguous phrase in one of the stories, and that I suspected that a schoolboy naughtiness had gone to the coining of the names of some of his characters. Then I would say to Firbank: 'Come, this won't do, you know: you must alter this phrase and this name'; but when I did he would look so shocked or would answer me so ingenuously that I had great difficulty in persisting. Perhaps even I did not persist. I felt about Firbank that like a child he could take liberties, and that I, as one of his elders, must not take them seriously. It was just his way.

Vainglory when I had read it through had some curious fascination for me. I took it for granted that the extraordinary punctuation or lack of punctuation was a mere carelessness of an uninstructed copyist, and that the printer would, if the book came to be produced, follow the usual custom and supply the deficiencies and correct the errors of the author. But first I refused the book. Firbank came down to see me about it and undulated shyly about the room. What was the matter with his story? Surely it was better than most stories. He had attempted to do somehing like Beardsley had done in the illustrations to *The Rape of the Lock*. Was I an admirer of Beardsley? Did I like Félicien Rops's work? So I knew Beardsley . . . ! Surely I would bring his child into the world. I could not be so unkind as to turn it from my door. It was my impression that the book was so slight and unusual that there was little chance of selling more than a few copies. Well, he would of course like it to sell, but it wouldn't matter so very much if it didn't. But it would matter to me. Yes, he supposed it would. Supposing he paid for the cost of production, would that make any difference? He was not rich; really he was very poor although perhaps I didn't think so. It didn't do to look poor; besides he loved clothes. And he waved himself a little more sinuously. How much would it cost to produce his book in a small edition, but beautifully—yes, beautifully?

I felt as if I were dealing with a child.

And after a while we came to terms and Firbank waved himself down my stairs. But first he had promised to bring me a little Rops painting of a girl. It was so charmingly corrupt. Could it not go on the wrapper of *Vainglory*? And as a frontispiece too? Well, he would bring it to me tomorrow. Colour printing was expensive? He was very poor, 'but we can talk of that tomorrow. I am so happy you are going to do my book, so happy . . .'.

Although I say it who shouldn't, I did make a very attractive, if simple-looking, book of *Vainglory*—but no, Rops's young woman does debar me from the use of the word 'simple'! Firbank was delighted with the result. I think now that his ideal was to have a thing look very simple and unadorned and yet to be in very fact as corrupt and as depraved as art could make it. I was hardly his accomplice. Perhaps I was his dupe.

Ronald Firbank was the most nervous man I have had dealings with, and in some ways he was both cunning and suspicious. But he had a curious wayward charm which, however, slowly lessened even in the short period of our association. I could never be sure of his age. His face and his figure too in some way seemed, towards the end, to be going the same way as did the picture of Dorian Gray. Or was it fancy on my part?

His nervousness? He had a definite reason for nervousness in those war years: he had an idea, very unlikely on the face of it, that he would be roped in for the army. A less reasonable fear was that someone with whom he was in more or less daily contact had acquired a mastery over him and his soul and that if he were not careful he would be destroyed. Poor Firbank had dealings with wizards, crystal-gazers, astrologers and soothsayers, and it was an acolyte or practitioner of those sciences who in some unholy way was to finish him off. I struggled to the best of my ability with this notion. After a year or less it died down of itself, but not before he had suffered considerably. He was during that period a man who either actually or metaphorically was always looking over his shoulder lest his persecutor should steal up behind him. . . .

One day he came to me and said, as if he expected me to be astonished, that on the previous morning, before leaving me, he had had a strong impulse to ask me to lunch.

'But why? Why didn't you ask me? I couldn't have come, but I should have appreciated the gesture.'

'Would you have come? Would you really have come?' He waved himself about the room. I waited for some fresh pronouncement.

'Will you come to lunch with me today? To the Savoy? I want to go to the Savoy. Will you come?'

'Yes, of course I will. But I hope it's to the Grill Room you're going. I don't like the restaurant at lunch. I don't want music.'

He looked disappointed. 'Are you sure?' There was a pause, and then: 'Very well, we will go to the Grill Room.'

We started out in a taxi. As we passed the Cecil he looked at me seriously: 'Are you sure you couldn't stand the music? It's very good. It would be so kind of you to go to the restaurant.'

There was nothing for it but assent. We entered and were given a table in the middle of the large room. The maitre d'hôtel tendered the carte.

'You must have what you like—everything you like. I shall only have strawberries and Chablis. But I insist that you have all you want. I eat nothing but strawberries.'

'Chablis is good. I approve of that, my dear Firbank. But I'm afraid strawberries wouldn't stay my hunger. You see I live in the country and breakfast early.' I looked at the menu of the lunch of the day. 'I'll have smoked salmon, and khebab, and then I'll have strawberries.'

Firbank was satisfied. After a minute, however, he became restless, looking about him as if he feared something untoward would happen: 'Would you mind if we changed our table? I can't stand this table. I want to be on the balcony.'

'But you've ordered your meal here. . . .'

'I don't care—I can't stop here; I can't stop. I won't. The waiter must find us'; and before I could let anyone know of our intention we were half-way across the room and, in a moment, were seated on the balcony behind a pillar. The waiter did not find us, and soon Firbank was querulously demanding attention. . . . When at last the knot was unravelled and when, after we had drunk a double cocktail apiece, the food and the wine did arrive, Firbank regarded the wine-waiter with ire. 'I don't want Chablis now. You have spoilt my pleasure in the idea of Chablis. I won't have Chablis. Give it away. Bring me a bottle of ——' and he named the most fashionable and costly brand of Champagne. We were by now attracting a deal of attention. . . .

Some months later he appealed—yes, that is the word—to me

to lunch with him again. But would I mind the Café Royal? He liked the Café Royal. Was I sure I wouldn't mind? At that time the Café Royal had a very mixed clientele. Firbank evidently had a vogue of his own in that gilded saloon, the domino room or café itself. Our entry was much observed. We found a table. Cocktails of course. No, the ordinary lunch wasn't good enough for us. While our special food was being cooked we sat and looked on at the curious medley of painters, young officers, models and daughters of joy. C. R. W. Nevinson drifted by, nodding to me as he passed. He returned: 'You haven't seen John, have you—Augustus John? I'm lunching with him here.'

I had not. He stood for a minute and I introduced him to Firbank. 'I don't like that fellow,' my host said, as Nevinson left us; 'I think he's sinister.'

In a few minutes Nevinson, who had been roaming about like a lost spirit, returned: 'I don't think John's coming. Can I have my lunch at your table, Grant?'

I assented with rather a poor grace, indicating that Firbank, as my host, was really the man to ask. After all, I was in a difficulty, since my host had said he didn't like Nevinson. Nor did Firbank help. He glared. I said something that implied that Nevinson had been a soldier, that he had been invalided out and that he was not anxious to return to any kind of battlefield now or at any time. Firbank's face brightened. Evidently the painter was a fellow sufferer fearing the same enemy. Nevinson must have a cocktail. The waiter must bring double martinis for all three of us. Nevinson must be his guest.... Painter and writer became as thick as thieves, bosom friends in the twinkling of an eye. Left alone with Nevinson for a minute, I told him who Firbank was, indicating that he was a possible patron as he was interested in the arts. Later, Firbank insisted on knowing where his guest was going. To the New English Art Club show. Could he come too? 'Yes, do go,' I broke in, 'and buy one of Nevinson's paintings.' Firbank looked, unsteadily, at his watch. Good God! Was it really half-past three? He must get to Coutts' to cash a cheque. He'd break the door down with a hatchet rather than be balked. I had time to tell Nevinson to look after him a bit. 'He's got to get back to Oxford,' I added, for Firbank was then living in Oxford, occupying, I believe, a whole large house at the bottom of the High, where he hoped that the military authorities had lost sight of him.

A day or two afterwards I saw Nevinson. What had happened? 'Well, I took him to a party in the Temple after he'd failed to get into Coutts' and we'd looked at the Show. He got tighter and tighter, proclaiming all the time that he must catch the 6.05 to Oxford. . . . But he wouldn't start. You told me to look after him so I thought I'd better see that he did catch the train. I got a cab and pushed him into it and, while I was telling the driver where to go and to hurry, Firbank opened the door and got out on the other side. Then, looking at us, he smiled jauntily and remarked that he could very well look after himself, that anyhow he'd changed his mind about Oxford and that he was going to see St Paul's. That's the last I saw of him.'

I was not myself at the luncheon at the large, round corner table at the Junior Carlton Club when, having entertained Osbert and Sacheverell Sitwell, Firbank got under the table at the end of the meal rather than face the head-waiter, but I had been invited and the story was told to me afterwards as a solemn fact and as an example of what I had missed. Firbank's behaviour on another occasion does not lead me to doubt its truth. I had received a formal invitation from him to luncheon—again at the Junior Carlton. We were to be a party. The only man to turn up, however, was Michel Sevier, the young Russian painter, who with his amiability is a host in himself. We started with cocktails of course—double cocktails. The same large corner table had been reserved for us upstairs. There was a magnum of an old Champagne at its side. Sedate and more mature members saw us come in, I thought, with a certain distaste—and that reminds me: On leaving home that morning I had told my wife that I was lunching with Firbank and could not lunch with her, although she was to be in town. Forgetting this, she turned up at the office at one o'clock. Firbank had come to fetch me. I introduced them and, later, went down with her to the door. Women generally do not like men with the peculiarities of manner and bearing that my novelist affected, and she was not an exception: 'Your Firbank may be all the reviewers say he is, but I don't like the idea of your lunching with him. Well, it can't be helped: don't stop too long over the meal; I'll look for you on the 4.50 train.' The fact that I was to walk and lunch with so strange a creature did really distress her.

To go back to Pall Mall. Yes, the crusted members of the Club did look towards our corner with a certain resentment. I formed an idea of the reason. Here was this young fellow, whom they didn't like the look of any way, both outraging their ideas of the right ways to behave and drinking up all their best wines. . . . As the meal approached its end a rare vintage port made its appearance. I believe it too was no ordinary bottle but a magnum. I am not sure. I don't myself drink port after champagne for choice, and did little more than sip at my glass, and after a while we went down to the smoking room. The brandy of the Junior Carlton is very good. The waiter brought us double portions. Soon, having smoked a large cigar, I went out to the fresh air of Pall Mall and walked towards Waterloo Place. By the time I reached the Carlton Hotel I began to feel a little sleepy; I felt that I had better postpone my return to the office. No, no, I wasn't drunk: I have never been drunk—not what you'd call drunk; the nearest I was to it was in December 1895 when, lured by its classic name, I drank a whole bottle of Falerno all by myself in a cellar-restaurant in the Corso and did not thereafter walk too straightly to the Pincian, where I slept the afternoon away on a seat. Well, on this occasion too I went to sleep. Indeed I went to sleep in the little drawing-room just inside the Carlton door. I slept there for hours. Indeed I slept until the attendants, who knew me, made a noise in order to wake me up. I looked at my watch. It was after six. I caught the 6.50. And I had promised to meet my wife by the 4.50! There was a certain coolness at Cookham Dean. . . . It must have seemed to my wife that her worst fears were realised.

I am afraid that Firbank could never make up his mind that he liked me. On one occasion he told me that he had meant to bring with him that day a jade elephant which he greatly liked and which he wished to give me as a mascot. He promised that I should have it on his next visit. Now it happened that I was anxious to have an elephant, and if it were jade it would be so much the better, so when he did next come I asked him quizzically if he had remembered my quadruped. He writhed; I had never seen him more annoyed. 'I am taking great care of the elephant for you. You shall certainly have it.' I heard no more about it.

All the same, my relations with Firbank were invariably cordial. We never differed, although he was unable to accept the fact that the 500 copies I used to print of his books were, even after allowing for fifty copies going out for review and for free copies, more than sufficient to meet the demand. In spite of his having slowly attained a small but precious reputation, of its having become fashionable in certain circles to discuss his improprieties, and of young and highbrow reviewers often bestowing upon him too warm if rather equivocal praise, the various books sold in single copies rather than in dozens. Even after America discovered him 500 copies of a book sufficed. I am told that smart young hostesses in New York would give parties at which each guest would be presented with a copy of the same Firbank book and that one who could discover most improprieties therein after an hour's reading would get a prize. Indeed American adulation almost ended my relations with Firbank. That tall and solid imp of mischief, Carl Van Vechten, wrote an article about him in one of the New York dailies, in which in detail, and with an apparently serious pen, he described how on mail days the traffic would be suspended owing to the crowds of people who were trying to get to the Holliday Bookshop in order to make sure of their copies of the new Firbank out of that week's consignment. And so on. . . . Firbank took it all at the foot of the letter, and it took me a long time to convince him that all together the Holliday Bookshop importation of that particular book had hardly exceeded a score or so of copies. I wrote to Van Vechten, whose *Peter Whiffle* I had had a great deal of pleasure in publishing, and remonstrated with him. Of course it didn't cure him of his joke. And Firbank wrote to him and received a reply to the effect that if he would go to New York many thousands would flock to his lectures and many scores would meet him at the pier. And, Van Vechten added, if he would but publish his books in America he would sell thousands and thousands and thousands. . . .

It had happened indeed that for a year or two before this American publishers had been writing to me or dropping in and asking for a set of Firbank books to be sent to them in order that they might consider issuing them in New York. This occurred several times. Then invariably they would write from America and declare their great admiration for the books, but—well, they wouldn't 'dare'. . . . Dare what? *I* couldn't see it. Van Vechten's advocacy, however, made a difference: Firbank offered his next story to Brentano and it did sell many more in America alone than I had succeeded in selling of any one of his books in the two countries. By then, of course, the ground had been well prepared. . . . It was not unnatural that the sale should increase. But it annoyed me, especially as Brentano's London house published it here.

However, Firbank came back to me. He came up my stairs a little sheepishly. Might he return? Would I publish his next story? My books were so very much more distinguished in their appearance than the American had been. He professed contrition; he felt, he said, 'like a lamb returned to the fold'. He did not add that he had been doing his best to get C. S. Evans of Heinemann's interested in his work! I discovered that fact from a clue in Dulau's catalogue. One of the Firbank letters they have for sale is to Evans: he asks him to consider *Sorrow in Sunlight* which he describes as 'purposely a little "primitive", rather like a Gauguin in painting—extremely gay'.*

One other anecdote: I had suggested to Firbank that he should follow the Rops of *Vainglory* with similar decorations by painters of distinction on and in each of its successors. He agreed: in one case a drawing by Augustus John was used; Albert Rutherston, Albert Bührer and C. R. W. Nevinson were pressed into service. In the case of Nevinson I suggested—it was not long after the Café Royal episode—that as he knew Nevinson he should take the proofs of the story up to Steele's Studios and discuss the matter with the painter. He assented, but by the time he had reached the Sir Richard Steele public-house all his courage had oozed away. He was too shy to ring the bell. Ultimately he flung the packet through an open window and took to his heels. Nevinson told me he found it on his bed.

I have remarked that the young intelligentsia did Firbank more than justice. The practice continued. Here is the *New Statesman* of 24 August 1929, about *Concerning the Eccentricities of Cardinal Pirelli*: 'In a universe crowded with talent, uncomfortably overflowing with brilliance, his was not a gift which can be entirely ignored.' The whole article should be sought for by the Firbank fan. And there was Arnold Bennett in the *Evening Standard* of 19 September 1929: 'For a dozen years I have been hearing, from the young, of the work of Ronald Firbank; and during all that time I refrained from reading him because of a suspicion in my wrong-head that he belonged to the confraternity of the precious. I gathered that he was in revolt against current ideals of imaginative literature, and I like and sympathise with literary rebels—but on the sole condition that they are not precious. I admit that I have listened to praise of

* I realise at this moment that it may not have been C. S. Evans of Heinemann, but Mr A. W. Evans of Elkin Mathews.

him from young men who had done good things themselves and whose opinions, therefore, I valued.... The whole thing' [he is discussing *Caprice*] 'is lit with the refracting light that never was on sea or land. It is a lark, a joke, a satire, accomplished in a manner rather distinguished, mainly by dialogue and in brief paragraphs. It is brief, but it is homogeneous. It can be read easily, and without shame or humiliation. Whether it is worth reading I cannot quite decide, even in the privacy of my wrong-head. I have a notion that it isn't.... At the same time, I should not be surprised if the Firbank cult grew. I can foresee young men and maidens at large in King's Road, Chelsea, stating plainly to the uninstructed that Firbank is the sole modern author worthy of attention from the elect. However, I am not of the elect and never shall be. And I should regard Firbank more seriously if he showed strong imaginative power. He does not show it. To me he is an elegant weakling.'

Both these critics were writing rather after the fair: Firbank had been some time dead. Later still, on 11 May of this very year, Harold Nicolson wrote of him in connection with a post-humous work, The *Artificial Princess*, for which Coleridge Kennard wrote an introduction ('Anything which can tempt Sir Coleridge into print had fulfilled its function', Mr Nicolson says. The phrase reminds me of how 'The Sphinx' loved her Coleridge Kennard!): 'Ronald Firbank is an arresting figure. Most people who were born before 1900 belong to a bygone age. The odd thing about Ronald Firbank was that he belonged to two bygone ages. Emotionally he belonged to the Beardsley period, whereas intellectually he belonged to the Sitwell period.... Firbank possessed a talent at the same time undulating and incisive. Being a shy man with acute instincts, he indulged in innuendo. It was not the demure innuendo of Samuel Butler, nor yet the hearty innuendo of Norman Douglas; it was a baroque type of innuendo. He dealt in porcelain hints. The timidity inseparable from such epicene giggling has discouraged me from becoming an admirer of Ronald Firbank. Yet, in his own medium, he was almost a supreme artist.... A certain immortality always attaches to writers who are inspired by one period and forecast another. Ronald Firbank, even today, is regarded in America as one of our important literary figures. I question whether such a reputation will prove durable. As a specimen of all that is most delicate and witty in Ronald Firbank this *Artificial Princess* could scarcely be surpassed. Yet would any serious reader, however fascinated he may momentarily be by the cachinnations of Ronald Firbank, contend that he is anything more than a literary curiosity? Had he lived longer he would certainly have written something of lasting value; his talent, however variable, was authentic and unexpectedly wise; yet he died while still in his experimental period; he achieved several brilliant improvisations on the theme of Beardsley in plus-fours; and brilliance is an evanescent quality.'

I myself should have been much surprised if Firbank had written something of lasting value. The Nicolson tribute is generous. Let me quote again from that *New Statesman* review: 'Firbank's satirical portraits are too spiteful to be always very amusing; but when a distinguished diplomat and essayist tried to turn the tables and gave us his version of "Lambert Orme", we were left with the impression that, in the various encounters he narrated, it was the diplomat, and not the novelist, who had always had the worst of it. The diplomat was brilliant and talented, but Firbank had an additional, undefinable spark. . . .' One knows one's Firbank better when one has read Harold Nicolson's admirable reconstruction in *Some People.*

Not long ago Charles Graves, who is generally right, described the Hon Evan Morgan as having been Firbank's greatest friend. I wonder. Certainly a Firbank of the middle period was to have been dedicated to Evan Morgan. He heard of it and called at my office to protest. He was very angry, and he was angrier still when I told him that I had no power to interfere, that Firbank was free to dedicate his little story to anyone he pleased except perhaps the King, the Queen and the Prince of Wales, and that all I could do was to promise to represent his views to the author, who would no doubt attach great importance to them. Evan Morgan went away threatening to invoke the law. Indeed he did invoke the law in the person of an Officer of the Court, his solicitor, who threatened—well, I don't quite remember what he did threaten. Was it an application for an injunction? I did tell Firbank what a hornets' nest he was raising. Naturally I added that he could do what he pleased. He would, he said: it pleased him to keep the dedication. He would keep it. It was well perhaps that before the book went to press he thought better of his resolve. The dedication was taken out. What would have happened if he had remained obdurate? I wonder. . . .

NANCY CUNARD

Thoughts about Ronald Firbank

You will see that I knew him relatively little. And none of his books is left me, not one. And none of his letters, which all disappeared during the war from my house in Normandy. It is detestable to have to rely on memory alone!

There are two impressions of Ronald Firbank in my mind—two opposing ones. The former is rather of the surface values; the last, of the inner being, of a deeper personality which was a most valuable one and to be cherished—come to through discovery of what was beneath the exoticism of the exterior, behind the sort of public personality that had evolved or been made about him and whose *leitmotif* was 'fabulous'. By then, too, his books were proof that he was more than the errant voice of fantasy, which, at first, because of all its *précieux*, might have flourished in the days of *The Yellow Book*. Maybe this connection is nonsense! His wit, his kind of inventiveness have really almost nothing in common with that particular season. Why does it occur to me—had I his books again, should I perhaps find the reason?

By 1919 he was already legendary. As was the case for me with Norman Douglas, he had been 'edited' by the Sitwells who were very appreciative of him, and they remain foremost in memory as those who thought him 'fabulous'. Swift-moving, flitting, unseizable, aloof, a solitary—and, luckily, well-off. That is exactly all I know about his background: he was independent, well-off and had been to Cambridge University.

Was it not *Valmouth* that first made him known? It was termed decadent and dilettante by some, acclaimed as a sparkling fountain by others; its humour and writing so new and different that it nonplussed many. *The Flower beneath the Foot* is more than fantasy, for it contains fair measure of satire and among its delights is a portable, collapsible altar. The owner of this in the book was inspired by The Hon Evan Morgan, who could certainly lay claim to that same word 'fabulous', judged by his own generous brand of 'milordisme'.

Written in 1954 at the request of Miriam Benkovitz, and first published 1971 in a limited edition by the Albondocani Press, New York. Reprinted here by permission of Nancy Cunard's representative.

Maybe I first met Ronald Firbank in the Eiffel Tower Restaurant in London in its authentic art days, as yet uncommercialised by fashion, a little place of writers, painters, musicians and sympathetic bohemians. He would be about thirty by then, or a little more, in 1919. In one corner you might find Augustus John and Mark Gertler; upstairs the *avant-garde* artist, Roberts, would be about finishing his decorations; the Wyndham Lewis room was already done. Famous indeed became this little restaurant to which I went first with Iris Tree and Alvaro Guevara, the Chilean painter, in 1915. They too, like Augustus John who has drawn him, were great appreciators of Firbank. Its patron, Austrian Rudolf Stulik, who, up to a point, inspired Wyndham Lewis's *The Ideal Giant* and, in a very different field, Michael Arlen's first book, *The London Venture*, had a flair for genius, encouraged and helped the painters, delighted in personalities and was himself a very great delight to all of us. He had told me for a long time about Firbank. He had very much good to say of Mr Firbank —whose fare, incidentally, was reputed to be *only* strawberries and champagne....

Why just these? Well, said some of those who knew him, he maintains it is all he can consume! Ronald is really ill. And he is also highly nervous.... The strawberries cum champagne fitted perfectly into the fable.

Tall, thin, narrow, erect, with a most sensitive, intelligent, aquiline face and cheeks rather high in colour, a townsman—such was the impression he gave me—probably more of a noctambule (even in London) than to be met with regularly at literary functions or opening-days in art galleries. That he was most sensitively perceptive to art, to life, to people and situations was instantaneously clear. How lengthily consumptive he was before his death, I do not know, but it seemed already an understood thing. In good form he was extremely witty, of particular quickness, and it seems to me I always saw him in good form. If he was really ill, then he was brave and adroit indeed, for one noticed nothing of the kind, save, at moments, a sort of asthmatic conflict between words, breathing and laughter as his quips popped into the conversation. A few times have I seen him really paroxysmal, as if savouring some private joke, about—or no—to tell it. Then might come that unique and characteristic gesture: one hand flying up to clasp the opposite shoulder, drawing it inwards; thus, as it were cupped within himself, some astonishing point would be made which had everyone immediately rocking. The next thing you knew would often be that he had disappeared. The contrabandist's leap back into the dark is no quicker—gone!

Sudden appearances: that was the style of him then. I suppose there is a caricatural self in nearly everyone (perceptible, or no, to its owner). In such exits and entrances, Firbank could appear enchantingly caricatural, as if everything about him were heightened in tone. So light the touch, so deft the *glissando* . . . he seemed a walking-talking Max Beerbohm version of himself.

For all his fantastic progressions he could not be considered the sport of conventional man, and the memory of one ineffable occasion arises, this time in the Eiffel Tower for certain, in June 1922. A charming, but at that moment insufferably drunk, young man was with me and we were about to have dinner. Noisily and lengthily captious at the menu's many suggestions, he had finally reached the point of announcing 'I'll have . . . I'll have a . . .' while the waiter stood by looking more than weary. At that moment Firbank swept in, ecstatic, and came dancingly towards us. As I tried to introduce them my companion scowled at him, muttered something about 'fairies' and reached the end of his thought: 'A beefsteak'. 'And what with, sir?' asked the waiter. 'What with, what *with*?' groaned the angry man, 'with . . .' Firbank stood poised above us. With a swoop over the table and an ingratiating giggle he suggested clearly and winningly: '*Try violets!*' Then with a cackle of delight at the effect he swept off among the potted palms and other aspidistral embellishments of the place. My escort was pricked, deflated, collapsed as the laughter rang out loud and long. Had this . . . this incredible apparition, he asked now almost humbly, meant to make a fool of *him*? May all tipsy, bullying, gross 'he-men' meet with such a neat little swipe as that dealt by Firbank!

He was like a dipping strand of willow with a nerve of steel, and that 'something' floating, bending but unbreakable in him is, of course, the integrity of the good artist. There are touches in his books that seem to evoke a branch tapping, unexpected and teasing, against the window. He is full of surprises. At the very end of one of his novels is that vision of St Laura de Nazianzi pressing her hands in passion against the glass shards embedded on the top of a wall. Not many are the books that have an ending of such sudden poignancy.

For all his aloofness, or solitariness, he had many friends who found as much delight in his ways as a growing number of readers extracted from his writings. He was a good deal in France and Italy and would settle down to work, refusing to be interrupted. I think it was in Italy that Osbert and Sacheverell Sitwell looked for him once in his chosen solitude to fetch him to lunch or dinner. Perhaps they took him by surprise. He could not come with them, no, no. Not just then! I suppose they must have pressed him until—the tale continues—he found something insurmountable that clinched the matter. With an ecstatic swoop of his long, fine hands, he announced that to go out was quite impossible, because, because . . . NO BUTTONS! That being interpreted meant that his clothes—that is to say, his suit—had not yet been gone over by the landlady. So many buttons were off, and—look—not back in place!

Such graces were his fortifications. And the 'button-story' being fresh in mind, it was with some trepidation that I too went to look for him one dripping January day in Bordighera in 1923. On the way there from Ventimiglia, the American painter Curtis Moffat and I decided that Ronald might fob us off with equal ease—and no offence—if he did not want to see us. It was impossible to warn him of our coming, his exact address being unknown. After several enquiries for the *signore inglese che scrive molto* in wan-looking *pensiones* along this or that alley that would soon be filled with happy mimosa, transformed into a feathery little pleasaunce, we reached the right house. He was there, alone. I remember a drenched magnolia and some draughty, unhappy stairs and damp rooms as that particular background. He seemed glad to see us. He was working a lot, fairly well, liked Bordighera and did not mind the seasonal discomfort. The lunch that followed, full of agreeable talk and cheering wine, lasted till nearly tea-time and there was a glow to it that made us forget January. He was a very good talker—this came out yet better that day *à trois*—with individual ideas about art and writing and sudden offshoots, now and again, into fancy. We left him amid the dank palm-trees, and he impressed me that day as spiritually at ease and full of vitality, mainly perhaps because he was working hard.

Later on I may have sent him some poems. I think I must have, because in memory there is a vague connection between several letters from him during the next two years and some poems of mine. Those letters of his—a few words to a line, in beautiful, spaced, strong handwriting which is as clear and purposeful, almost, as if it were done with a brush! Short letters, maybe, most of them, and notes about where we should meet, but affectionate—and that was, of course, reciprocal. No definite, precise occasion can I recall after this, although I know we met again in Paris and, I think, in London; no definite occasion except one. It was months since I had seen him and there he was, suddenly, in the street, in Montparnasse. Would that have been in 1925 or 1926? I think it was the last time I saw him.

We entered Le Dôme and sat down in a surprisingly empty stretch of it, the more unusual as it was noon. And here we had a long and very peaceful talk. How consecutive he was. A new personality was revealed, an entirely new personality. I have thought of him ever since as he was that day. Some kind of silent confidence appeared to develop between us, then and there. Thinking of it a little later, that talk seemed to me as good and long and all-of-a-piece as if we had been walking together in some fine, fresh place—perhaps over the great cliff scenery around Varengeville or Berneval in Normandy on either side of Dieppe. A long, long walk, at any rate. The effect of his conversation was as stimulating as the wind over the rough cliff-grass, with the spray at the rocks below and a few gulls on the wind. It showed me the vitality of his being beneath all the 'fantasia-fantasia'. He was a very sympathetic human soul and I hoped I should see more of him thus, *à deux*. Maybe he said he would be coming to Normandy; it was at the time of one of my summers there, and the gratuitous-sounding link between him and the conversation-walk may have been inspired by wishful thinking! What is certain is that something concrete about his personality came into being that day: he could never be 'the legend' to me any more. There were further letters, I know—but never the continuation of that long talk at noon.

This is all I can find in my memory about Ronald Firbank that will go into words. Of course he was 'a friend'. But I scruple and hesitate, somehow, in using the word: so many other people have known him well, so many have known him far better and more fully and uninterruptedly than myself. *How* well, how unintermittently do you know someone before such a hesitation leaves you?

In Toulouse, where I now am, I cannot procure his books and they might have recalled other things. You are welcome to the little I can tell you; I only wish it were very much more.

SEWELL STOKES

Reminiscences of Ronald Firbank

Ronald Firbank—like his novels—was elusive and enchanting; but, to be perfectly frank, there were occasions when it was difficult not to find him somewhat ridiculous and slightly exasperating.

Not that I was a very intimate friend of his. I believe very few people were. The reason why he walked so much by himself may well have been that in some respects he was an embarrassing person to be with. Embarrassing in the sense that unless one was attuned to him, and prepared to accept his eccentricities, his companionship could prove alarming. I wasn't alone in finding his behaviour odd, or in fearing to be made conspicuous when seen in his company. Lord Berners, who knew him much better than I did, confessed that once, to avoid the embarrassment of a conversation in public with Firbank, he shouted at him: 'You are my favourite author!'—and then quickly hurried away.

In his appearance, and in his manner, Firbank was disconcerting. A description of what he looked like has been given by Cyril Beaumont, the ballet critic: 'He was tall and slender in figure; his physique was almost feminine in its delicacy; he had the wasp waist affected by Victorian exquisites . . . his face was oval in shape, the eyebrows thin and arched, the nose long, the chin weak; his complexion was fresh, with a rosy blush on the cheek-bones. His hands were white and very well kept, his nails long and polished, and what was unusual in a man is that they were stained a deep carmine.' Now that description precisely fits Firbank as I remember him, though I would add, with regard to the 'rosy blush on the cheek-bones', that on days when this was not naturally in evidence he carefully made good the deficiency on his own account.

His fluttering movements, the contortions that his sinuous body seemed always to be getting into—like a child who can't keep still—are almost impossible to describe; but astonishingly accurate is the impression of it given by the late Eddie Marsh, who saw him at the Russian Ballet: 'A strange figure pirouetting about the corridor and making little faces to itself.' Firbank did make little

---

From material originally published in *Pilloried* by Sewell Stokes (Richards Press, 1928). Revised and extended by the author for this book.

faces, so constantly that anyone watching him for the first time might easily have thought he suffered from some nervous twitch; though on acquaintance these little grimaces suggested that their owner was, in fact, merely holding a silent conversation with himself.

Firbank had inherited considerable wealth, which enabled him to lead a life of graceful leisure, to indulge his expensive tastes. It also enabled him to pay for the publication of most of his books, which no publisher, however much he might admire them, could possibly afford to take a risk on. They were far too unlike anything that had been written up to that time, to attract more than a handful of discerning readers.

It was at the Café Royal—it must have been 1922, I think—that a mutual friend introduced me to Firbank. In those days it was as much a café as a restaurant; and because he drank a great deal, but ate very little, Firbank used often to go there. He would join us, but only to watch. As we ordered food, he ordered more drinks. The reason he ate so little was the absolute dread he had of losing his slim figure. At least, that was the excuse he made, always with a sly chuckle. I do recollect him toying with a small sandwich sometimes—a chicken or *paté* sandwich—and describing it as a 'positive feast'. He would waft in and out of the Café (dressed invariably in a black suit, but with a bright necktie) just as he would waft in and out of exhibitions of modern paintings, concerts, theatres and the Russian Ballet. There were times when he failed to turn up for weeks on end. And then, from the picture-postcards he sent us, we knew that he had wafted as far as Italy and Spain—even as far as South America.

By a number of his friends he was likened to a butterfly. Personally, I always thought of him as a dragon-fly, hovering brilliantly above the surface of things, rather than flitting from place to place. However, it was as a butterfly, I remember, that he once referred to himself, he drinking his endless double-brandies, and I with my glass of orange juice that he used to say it made him ill to look at! I told him how thrilled I was at the thought of being taken the following day to meet Siegfried Sassoon. And rather wistfully he inferred that I seemed more impressed by Sassoon's name than by his own.

'Siegfried,' he said, 'is Tolstoy in goloshes, digging for worms, deep, deep . . . I am only a butterfly, waiting to catch caterpillars as they drop from the leaves.'

My love of contrast led me to take him one day into a Lyons teashop—not even a 'Maison Lyons'. There, in an atmosphere of tobacco smoke, eggs-on-toast-twice, coffee-with-a-dash, thick cups and strong tea, he wilted like an orchid too long worn. When I asked him what I should order he replied: 'Ask for herons' eggs whipped with wine into an amber foam.' I lacked the courage to give this order, so we left the shop. Though it was an absurdly short distance from the shop to his club, he insisted on taking a taxi. When the taxi man claimed more than his actual fare, pleading that his clock was out of order, Firbank did not bother to argue with him. 'I couldn't argue,' he explained, 'with a man who had such a *bad* complexion.'

Because his own work was appreciated by so few, he was not unnaturally a little jealous of those of his contemporaries who enjoyed fame. Suddenly, for no apparent reason, he would exclaim: 'Rupert Brooke is *not* as clever as I am.' Why poor Rupert Brooke was cited as a rival, I cannot think. They had known one another at Cambridge and, I believe, had been friends.

After many of his seemingly disconcerting utterances, Firbank would clutch the right lapel of his jacket, bury his face in it, and laugh hysterically, for what seemed quite a long time. I once told him that his was the most sinister laugh I had ever heard, and apparently he never forgot that remark of mine. Augustus John, with wonderful precision, recalls not only the laugh itself, but also the gesture that often went with it: '. . . A long hollow laugh about nothing in particular, a laugh like a clock suddenly running down, accompanied by a fluttering of the hands (not the clock's hands), which he would then proceed to wash with the furtive precipitation of a murderer evading pursuit.'

One does realise, of course, that the anecdotes told by his friends about Firbank are apt to sound trivial to those who never knew him. But since, apart from his work, these anecdotes are the only material left out of which to build his statuette, a certain importance has to be accorded them. Once, for instance, after lunching in his company—I doubt if he partook of more than a shrimp himself—I said that I had to return to Fleet Street.

'Where is Fleet Street?' he asked.

I told him. 'Oh,' he said, 'I've often thought I'd go exploring one day, and discover what does happen after the Haymarket comes to an end.'

Now if Oscar Wilde had said the same thing—and he very

nearly did—I imagine one would have felt that he was being affected on purpose. It wasn't so with Firbank. He convinced you, somehow, that his knowledge of London actually was limited to the small space in which he moved, between the Café Royal and Knightsbridge. Although I did venture with him once as far as the wilds of Chelsea.

'Let us,' he said, 'go and watch the *funny women*.'

I hadn't an idea what he meant, and said so.

'All women are funny,' was his reply. It was a conviction of his, which he never ceased to elaborate in his novels. The way that women behaved, when they thought no one was observing them, sent him off into fits of that uncontrollable laughter. It amused him enormously to watch them running for a bus, diving earnestly into their handbags, making up their faces with the aid of a pocket mirror, adjusting their hats. And he must always have been studying them, for his pages are filled with the results of his shrewd observation.

That afternoon I suggested that we should go to Chelsea in a bus. I knew that for him walking would be out of the question. But so, apparently, was the bus. He looked at me in utter astonishment, then shuddered at the awfulness of such an idea. He said he'd never been in a bus in his life, and thought it must be a nerve-racking experience. For him a taxi was the normal means of conveyance, and the sight of him either gingerly alighting from one on arrival at a party, or, in a limp state, being gently assisted into one when the party was over, was very familiar indeed.

So we took a taxi to Chelsea Embankment, got out near Cheyne Walk, and kept the taxi waiting some time while we sat facing the river. Presently a woman who was passing stopped and leant against the stone wall a few feet from us. She made an elaborate pretence of watching the river, but the real purpose of her pause became obvious when surreptitiously she took a comb from her handbag and began slowly scraping away at her 'bobbed' hair. At this distance in time I cannot remember anything about the woman except the fact that she combed her hair, and afterwards went on her way. But I shall never forget the paroxysm of helpless laughter to which Firbank was instantly reduced by this commonplace action of hers. He was still laughing when we got back into the taxi. But no explanation was forthcoming. He wasn't the kind of person you asked to explain things. You accepted his point of view, and left it at that.

Any woman who happened not to be one of his goddesses was likely to strike him as comic. Five of his goddesses were Duse, Mrs Patrick Campbell, Marie Tempest, Isadora Duncan and Florence Mills. Isadora, I later came to know quite well. Now if she had been on the Chelsea Embankment that afternoon, and felt so inclined, I'm sure nothing would have prevented her from washing her red hair in the Thames and dancing about until it was dry. And I'm sure, too, that such behaviour on her part would not have seemed in the least out-of-place to Firbank. It was the little, everyday actions he found so intensely funny; never the flamboyant gestures of the artist. And because he saw humour in little everyday actions, he was able to make those actions wildly amusing in his books.

It is difficult to believe that he ever seriously noticed what a human being was up to. He never appeared to look at anything, save the glass of brandy in front of him, or the face of the person he was talking to. Yet few of our habits and conceits escaped him. Into the purple ink he always used went his pen; and in his clear handwriting—only a very few words to each page—he told the human race how delicious and ridiculous he thought it.

His manuscripts were never much larger than a roll of music, for all his novels are short. I once saw him with one, neatly done up in brown paper, and hanging from his gloved finger by a loop of string. 'You think, I suppose,' he said, holding it up, 'I've been shopping at Swan and Edgar's.' Then twisting his head in denial, he added, 'But this is a masterpiece—on its way to the typist.'

I would not have called him a conceited person, though he certainly liked to hear his work praised. And he was pathetically grateful when a good review of a novel of his, written by what he called 'an understanding critic', appeared. He would cut it out and cherish it, even carry it about with him, like a provincial actress with her press-cuttings. He took one from his pocket-case to show me, I remember; a notice that had recently been written by Carl Van Vechten. Van Vechten, in New York, was doing all he could to gain new readers for Firbank in America.

'You must be immensely gratified by such an encouraging notice,' I said, returning it to him.

'Isn't it wonderful?' he replied, squirming selfconsciously. 'It's enough to give one wings for a week . . .'

'Wings for a week'—I mention it particularly as being the only phrase I heard him use in conversation that also appears in one of his books, *Caprice*. It occurs when, coming up to London from the country to seek an engagement on the stage, Miss Sinquier, arriving at Euston Station, is confronted by the poster of an already famous actress: 'On a hoarding, as if to welcome her, a dramatic poster of Fan Fisher warmed her heart; it was almost like being met. . . . Miss Sinquier tingled. A thing like that was enough to give one wings for a week.'

Firbank never mentioned other people's novels to me. Anyway, not unless I started the subject. And then it seemed he was surprisingly familiar with certain best-sellers. I remember admitting to him that at school I'd read everything written by Marie Corelli.

'You, of course, wouldn't have read a line of hers,' I added, a little on the defensive.

'Oh, I've glanced at her,' he said. 'Miss Corelli has style. Only it's the wrong style. Ouida was *much* better. She *knew* her world.'

Of Firbank's own novels, I'm afraid there is little that can usefully be said. I would claim, however, that the writer who comes nearest to explaining Firbank's work to the uninitiated is Arthur Waley. The point Waley insisted on, is that Firbank is the first Impressionist in English fiction, the earliest writer to exclude that crushing load of unnecessary words under which so many stories are buried. And for that reason he was not surprised at the comparatively small number of Firbank's readers; though he believed it would steadily increase. At one time, he reminds us, people looked askance at the pictures of the Impressionists. Publishers, he suggests, might be well advised to buy manuscripts by Impressionist authors, as an investment for the future. Waley made this suggestion in 1929, and he has been partly justified. In a subtle way, Firbank's special technique has influenced a number of modern writers. None of them has successfully imitated him, though. That would be quite impossible.

In 1953, the news that one of Firbank's novels was to be adapted for broadcasting came as something of a shock to his earliest admirers. To them, the transposition of a single word of his artful prose seemed unwise. Firbank, in the words of V. S. Pritchett, 'discovered the fact of hysterical private humour—the joke the mind makes but does not communicate'.

But I am certain that Firbank himself would have welcomed the new medium. I can imagine how he would have listened to the broadcast—sitting alone, in a darkened room, sipping his brandy; and as a favourite phrase came over the air, twisting his slim body into an agony of delight, and laughing immoderately.

I last saw Ronald Firbank on the evening of an unusually warm Easter Monday in London. Although, as he stood on the pavement just outside the Café Royal, he spoke to me, I think he no longer had any idea who I was. We had driven the short distance from Pall Mall where we had dined late, and all the way Firbank had kept repeating the name of a famous journalist whom he detested. The journalist was Hannen Swaffer, who, having read one of Firbank's novels, wrote in his Sunday paper: 'It is a piece of decadence which I am surprised to see published. What the censor of books can have been thinking about when he let this pass, I do not know. With pleasure I will show my copy to any policeman who cares to call at the office and see it.'

We had talked about Swaffer during dinner, and though I several times tried to change the subject, Ronald kept returning to it. Impatiently—for it is a weakness of mine to be impatient with those who have wined too well—I looked away to where a white moon floated over the roof of the Piccadilly Hotel. I was hoping that instead of entering the Café Firbank would decide to return home to bed. When suddenly I felt myself pushed, very gently, into the gutter.

Turning, I saw Firbank gazing at me with a kind of blurred contempt; as he repeated Swaffer's name once more, at me this time, not to me, I realised he now believed I *was* Swaffer. Before him he saw, not my slightly surprised self, but the man who had abused his work. Once again he hissed the hated name at me, then turned abruptly away; but as I turned up Regent Street in the opposite direction, I knew that his pathetic gesture of scornful aloofness was already at an end. I heard him fighting down his ominous cough. And much as I felt like turning back, I deemed it wiser not to.

Firbank's last words to me came in a letter from Rome shortly before he died: 'Have you forgotten a certain laugh? It is becoming rarer and rarer now. . . .'

VIVA KING

Ronald Firbank

I knew Ronald only towards the end of his life, in about 1923, when I was working as a student with C. R. W. Nevinson, in whose studio off the Hampstead Road Ronald was a frequent visitor. As his flat in Upper Brook Street, on the corner of Grosvenor Square, lay on my way home to South Kensington, we often made the journey together and he would ask me in for a talk. It was a dark place, the one piece of colour a pot plant with red leaves with which he was very pleased.

For some reason not quite clear to me today he was endlessly kind and generous to me, a mere student whose acquaintance could be of no particular use to him; he would at the end of the day often find me a taxi and give the driver ten shillings to take me on to South Kensington. Such was my poverty that sometimes at the end of the journey I would nerve myself to ask the driver for the change from the ten shillings; but I never got it!

I don't think I ever heard him laugh, but honest indignation was certainly within his range; I remember his fury at the low prices Sotheby's got him for the silver he was selling through them.

In all the many times our paths crossed—with the Nevinsons, at Wigmore Hall concerts, at Stulik's Eiffel Tower restaurant—I never saw him (even at the restaurant) accompanied by anyone; he was always alone. I remember his characteristic walk as he strode down the aisle of the Wigmore Hall, half pouter pigeon, half marionette—more perhaps of the latter, as if his limbs were all disconnected and being manipulated by a puppeteer. I remember too his high colour—doctors call it a 'malar flush', I believe—which made me sure he had a bad heart condition; and I am fairly sure that he died in the end of starvation, so little solid food was he ever seen to eat. When I diffidently ventured this opinion in public at a party soon after his death, it was thought to be the height of paradoxical wit; but I have little doubt I am right. One does not have to live in a garret to starve.

He gave me an inscribed set of all his novels in the Grant

Written by Viva King for this book. See also her autobiography, *The Weeping & the Laughter* (1976).

Richards editions, which I later sold, needing the money. I was unsophisticated enough to hope, at our various meetings, that he would sometimes talk in the brilliant manner of the characters in his novels, but this never happened. He did once, however, coin a new word in my hearing: 'I feel so *tiredful*—yes, I like that.'

I think the best likeness of him is the picture of him done by Wyndham Lewis which appeared on the title page of the Kyrle Fletcher memoir in 1930; and at the time I knew him this was his favourite too.

THOMAS J. FIRBANK

Uncle Ronald

I have been asked to write some recollections of my late Uncle Ronald, but find that I can offer impressions rather than facts. He died just half a century ago, and it is a little longer than that since I last saw him. His family contemporaries were unable to explain Uncle Ronald to me; so as a very young prep school boy I could no more comprehend him than the logarithms of which I had dimly heard.

All I understood was that he was good for tea and cakes and a ten bob tip at our meetings, which were rare because his visits to Britain did not often coincide with my holidays from boarding school. Had he visited me there, it is probable that he would have been provoked into one of his most satiric works, and no doubt the school authorities would have requested my removal when the penny dropped.

Our last meeting was at the Grosvenor Hotel, near Victoria station. It was perversely typical of him to select this venue, rather than Gunters. The Grosvenor's clientele of worthy dowdiness contrasted diametrically with the frothy brightness of the Gunter ambience which he knew so well.

My only positive memory of this occasion is that Uncle would not be enticed into conversation. Between cakes, I really tried to

---

Written for this book by Ronald Firbank's nephew, author of *I Bought a Mountain*, etc.

get the party rolling. The gallant efforts at last foundered after I had favoured him with a sophisticated description of a recent soccer match in which I had assisted my school to decimate a rival gang of young hellions. When I had done, Uncle put his head between his knees and murmured: 'I wonder.'

In retrospect the oblique comment may have had depth and validity, being his query about the value of the practicalities. Some might say that he saw only the superficial flesh over the bones, but it may be argued that he also saw through the bones to their marrow.

Certainly Uncle Ronald was among the first to caricature in words the pomposity residual from the late Victorian period, and he must have probed quite deeply to pick out the pieces which form his airy lattice-work. Did he get through to the marrow and make a soufflé of it? I wonder.

My hazy direct recollections are supplemented by memories of Uncle Ronald's mother and his sister Heather, respectively my grandmother and aunt, who lived at this time in what grandmother considered to be the genteel poverty of widowhood and spinsterhood.

The house was in the then semi-rural London suburb of Richmond, and was named Denbigh Cottage to underline Granny's penury. To underscore the state even more deeply, she had taken to doing her own shopping if the weather was clement.

I would accompany her, when staying at the Cottage during part of boarding-school holidays. Even at that young age I noticed that these excursions were more ceremonial than practical. We would set off, followed at a proper distance by Granny's personal maid, Hallett, who carried a basket. Purchases were few, since Grandmother was horrified at the cost of necessities, such as hothouse peaches.

Nevertheless, these tours were gracious experiences, the tradesmen doffing their caps, bowing and exclaiming: 'Good morning your ladyship! May I help you, my lady?' They could afford the courtesies because the housekeeper had made the rounds earlier, expense no object.

Aunt Heather also went shopping. Her economy took the form of buying identical articles in lots of one dozen, with the prudent intent of a squirrel storing nuts against winter. Prudence also dictated quality, and suspect nuts would not do; just umbrellas—

by the dozen—from Briggs, leather goods from Swaine and Adeney, and haberdashery from Harrods.

During my visits to Grandmother, communications would very frequently reach her from Ronald, often by postcard from Egypt or Italy, usually with no message to follow. There would be intense speculation between my grandmother and aunt about his health, his immediate acquaintances, the progress of his current writing, and his innocence in a world of villainous publishers. These messages arrived at breakfast time.

I digress about breakfast at Denbigh Cottage. I had confided to Hallett that my school occasionally served kippers at that meal. She corrected me discreetly by admitting that she had heard of kippered herring. I confirmed that I had become addicted, and the subject lapsed. However, the roe had been sown, and during my next school term Hallett must have sought the favourable moment to mention my desire to Grandmother. I assume that consultations later were held with the housekeeper, the cook and possibly the parlourmaid, who would be required to transport the things to table. Anyway, on the first day of my next visit kippers appeared, and I consumed them happily, oblivious to the discomfort of Grandmother and Aunt. During the afternoon, workmen arrived to insulate us from the cooking odour by fitting an airlock formed by two green baize-covered doors in the passage which led to the kitchen and servants' hall.

In addition to postcards, Uncle would sometimes send Grandmother letters, beginning 'My Dearest Baba', usually about the family properties in South Wales. Following one of these, Granny would retire to her private sitting-room to reply with anxious advice, writing on thick and creamy Truslove and Hanson notepaper. Still economising, not only did she write to 'Darling Artie' on both sides of the sheets, but she would turn the completed pages sideways and superimpose at right-angles. The result was surprisingly clear, though rather like a new form of acrostic.

I think Grandmother was utterly confused by Ronald, as is a fond hen who has hatched a duck egg, and sees the duckling perform in ways no chicken would dream of.

It would be interesting if Ronald were alive today. He would see a human society standing on opposite edges of a mental crevasse: on the one side those who move stage by stage with the build-up of ancestral experience from the first anthropoid—the reactionaries—and on the opposite lip the extremists of right and left shouting that history begins now, and all that has gone before should be denied if not destroyed—the anarchists.

The hard cores of both factions are humourless: dough without the yeast.

Perhaps Ronald could have poked enough self-revealing fun into them to leaven the dough with some smiles, introducing an insidious touch of the humanities—tongue in cheek, of course.

We wonder.

MAURICE SANDOZ

A Fantastic Young Englishman

I was having dinner in a restaurant in Rome which discreetly conceals itself in a tangle of small streets not far from the Piazza di Spagna.

On this particular evening the guests were few and far between, but even had there been a crowd, the arrival of the hero of this story could hardly have passed unnoticed.

He entered in sections. By which I mean that the first thing one saw appearing from behind the half-opened door was a lock of disordered hair. This lock seemed to be dragging after it, by an invisible hand, a head that looked as though it were feeling the effort it had made to get to an opening which was too narrow for it.

Two eyes darted inquisitive glances to right and left. Then the owner of the head, obviously reassured, introduced a pair of extremely long arms into the dining-room. Finally there appeared in due course a pair of even longer legs.

But what astonished me still more was the extreme thinness of the new arrival. He might have been an animated silhouette. I hardly knew what to compare him to, unless it were to those figures cut out in leather which Javanese showmen manipulate in their shadow theatres.

Like those figures, he appeared to be absolutely disjointed; and

From Maurice Sandoz, *The Crystal Salt Cellar* (Guilford Press, 1954). Reprinted by permission of the publishers.

his walk, like theirs, had something jumpy and jerky about it which was amusing and at the same time rather disquieting. This singular apparition also reminded me of the prints one sees of Paganini.

He sat down at a table close to mine and, speaking in what appeared to be perfectly correct Italian, ordered a bottle of Monte Fiascone.

The waiter bowed, disappeared and returned, a moment after, not carrying the bottle as I expected he would be but accompanied by the proprietor of the restaurant, who with a charming smile and exquisite courtesy, under which one could detect signs of firmness, turned to his new client and said:

'I regret, sir, that I am not able to serve you wine by itself. This establishment is a restaurant, not a café.'

My neighbour did not seem to be in the least put out. He replied quite simply, but with a touch of haughtiness: 'Then bring me a bottle of Monte Fiascone and a couple of roast chickens.'

The proprietor, dissolved in obsequious salaams, withdrew, anxious to do the honours for so remarkable an appetite. The bottle was brought at once, and the newcomer sipped the wine in little mouthfuls with his eyes closed. Then, as he was obviously satisfied, a smile flickered across his face.

As to the two solid chickens which were placed on the table a little later, he had them put one on his right hand, the other on his left, and completely ignored them.

When he had settled the bill this strange creature withdrew, as he had arrived, a section at a time.

I then inquired about his name and learnt that my neighbour at dinner was the well-known novelist Ronald Firbank. I knew his books and had been charmed by their originality. They are fluid, subtle, elusive creations, sweet, or bitter, always with a flavour of their own, but carefully worked out, woven as one might say round certain recognised landmarks which are sufficiently stable to give definite shape to the whole work. Rather like the wax hexagons of the comb which imprisons the honey. But Ronald Firbank's work can hardly be compared to a comb of wild honey. His honey was gathered by domesticated bees from not wholly innocuous flowers in the gardens of a royal palace.

The next day I read *Prancing Nigger*, which increased the

desire I had felt the day before to get to know the writer. A publisher in Rome gave me his address.

He had taken a year's lease of what was a largish residence, consisting of the entire first floor, the *piano nobile* as the Italians call it, of the Palazzo Mattei. Five o'clock in the afternoon found me ringing at his door, which had a marble surround.

I waited for half a minute, but waited in vain. I rang again.

This time I seemed to hear muffled groans coming from an inner room, and then the sound of furtive footsteps shuffling along the corridor. The door was held ajar. The hair, the head and the neck of the writer appeared, in that order. This time he did not materialise any further.

'Mr Ronald Firbank?' I asked with a smile in which I tried to mingle shyness, admiration and an expression of respectfully proffered friendship.

I suppose that my smile can actually have expressed nothing of the sort. The writer rolled a pair of frightened eyes and replied curtly: 'I never give my autograph', after which he shut the door again.

I found myself in the most idiotic situation imaginable. But I must privately confess that it served me right if I was disappointed. A word of introduction, the favour of a moment's audience, are things which could be easily obtained. I had supposed that with so extraordinary an individual the usual procedure would be the least likely to succeed. I realised my mistake.

Suddenly I noticed an interesting detail. When this fashionable author came to open the door, I heard him approaching, but once the door was closed, I did not hear him go away. Ronald Firbank was staying there, behind the door, ready, I was convinced, to open it should I reappear. Possibly he was even hoping that, if the bell were rung a second time, he would have a fresh excuse for saying something sharp.

I rang again. It was a loud, prolonged ring, meant to indicate my unshakeable resolve if not to be admitted, at least to meet with a better reception than last time.

The door was reopened, the emaciated face appeared again.

'Listen, my man,' I then said to this apparition, while my heart was beating rather more violently than usual. 'Kindly tell your master that an importunate visitor absolutely insists on seeing him, and that you don't know how to get rid of him.'

Ronald Firbank burst out laughing. 'Come in, come in, importunate visitor, if you are not afraid of spiders, dust, and an old man's conversation.'

I grasped the hand of the make-believe old man in such a way as to give him to understand that I had never really taken him for his manservant.

He led the way into a sitting-room which was on too large a scale for me to attempt to describe it here, pushed me into an armchair, threw himself on to a sofa, and at once began: 'I'm afraid that at the moment I'm out of glasses that aren't damaged. But if you look under your chair you will probably find a bottle of quite tolerable Monte Fiascone.'

Determined not to be surprised at anything, I rummaged under the fringe of my armchair and triumphantly fished out a bottle of Monte Fiascone, while my host on his side did the same. We both of us sipped the delicious pale-coloured wine from slightly chipped Murano goblets.

After a moment Firbank started talking again and explained to me the ingenious method he employed so as to be able to do without servants: 'Tyrants, that's what they are, tyrants,' he said solemnly.

'Well, this is what I do to be quit of them. I rent a palace in Italy, or some other country; a single floor of one sometimes suffices, provided it contains at least ten furnished bedrooms, all ready for sleeping in.

'When the room in which I have spent several days becomes too sordid, when the bed is tousled and the general aspect of things too chaotic, I move into the next room. Transferring a toothbrush, pyjamas and my slippers takes practically no time and demands only a minimum of effort. When the last of the rooms needs a thorough cleaning, I look for another house to rent.

'That is freedom, or rather would be freedom, if it were not for the dust that seeps in everywhere. The dust compels me to open the flat on occasions to admit a chorus of ancient females, armed with feather dusters, who simply transfer it straight back into the street.'

One of the singular effects of wine is to confer the gift of genius on those who drink it. Do not misunderstand me; this genius is, of course, conditional; its subtleties and depths only last as long as the effect of the nectar. After that, the phrase which seemed so brilliant becomes what it doubtless always was: just noise and spurious glitter; and the daring hypothesis which seemed so fertile is nothing more than daring.

I shall not attempt, then, in this place to report our conversation. When I had finished exchanging immortal thoughts with my host, and the last word in criticism, I noticed, as I was about to take my leave, a goldfish, sad and solitary, turning in the traditional bowl.

'Is he dangerous?' I asked, as I slipped on my overcoat.

'Not when I'm there,' replied the writer quite seriously, looking with affection at the creature, who resembled a carrot in a jar of pickles. 'I prefer him to a canary. He's less noisy. Moreover,' he added confidentially and with a touch of mystery, 'this animal never drinks the water.'

Amused, I inquired what he ate.

'Pearls. He costs me a fortune.'

'Have you tried him with artificial pearls?' I suggested, keeping up the game.

'He spits them out,' replied my host in a tone of despair.

I took my leave.

In a tiny village in the province of Naples, they are ready to show tourists—what won't people show for money?—a tree in which the Madonna appeared to a little boy.

I was talking one day to the local clergyman, an excellent man, proud of his church, proud of his hens, and above all proud of his miraculous peach tree.

'Frankly,' the good man confided to me, 'I must admit that at first I was sceptical about what the little Remo had told us, for he is not a very truthful child, or particularly trustworthy. But he stuck to his story and maintained that if the Holy Virgin had not actually spoken to him, he had at any rate seen her eat of the fruit of the tree. Well, my dear sir, I went to have a look at the tree and, sure enough, on the ground I found . . . a peach stone! After that, I ask you, could anyone have any doubts?'

Just as I was leaving Ronald Firbank, my foot slipped on something hard and round, so suddenly that I nearly broke my leg. After looking about for a moment, I found what had caused my misadventure.

It was an artificial pearl. It cost me a fall, but it convinced me that the novelist had spoken the truth!

When I returned to Rome six months later, the body of Ronald

Firbank had been laid to rest for eighty days close to the monument of Caius Sestius, in the shadow of an immense cypress.

From the beginning of his illness, he had kept to his bed, but without suspecting that death was at hand, for I was told that he refused to have a nurse, as a friend suggested he should.

'A nurse! For a cold in the head! What are you thinking of?'

Those, were, I believe, his last words.

Another three months went by without my having visited the tomb of the friend I had known so well, though for so short a time. The nights became mild, then warm. It was time for me to get back to my native lakes, to the Alps and their little mountain railways, and I reproached myself for having put off my visit to the English cemetery for three months. At last, on the day before I was due to leave, I firmly resolved to go there.

It was seven o'clock in the evening when at sunset, under a wild sky, I arrived at the pyramid of Caius Sestius. If one wishes to obtain entry into the sacred enclosure, one has to conform to an ancient tradition which enjoins that one should hang on to the chain of an enormous bell. As I detest loud noises, I was much afraid I might start a clamour fit to rouse the dead.

But the bell gave out a thin, cracked note which reassured me. The dead were certainly not going to wake for anything so trumpery.

After a moment the woman custodian of the cemetery appeared. To look at her you might have thought she was one of the three Fates who had come down a bit in the world. She ran her eye over me from the top of my head to the soles of my shoes. Having done this, she looked me over again in the reverse direction. That took time as I measure six feet and a few inches. After that she put this extraordinary question to me:

'You have come, sir, I presume, for Mr Firbank?'

'What's that you say?' I snapped, speaking with such animation that I was myself surprised at the tone I took.

'I was asking, sir, whether you had not come to see Mr Firbank?'

I felt something give way inside me—my presence of mind, I imagine—and I sheepishly answered 'Yes'. I did not even think of cross-questioning this Fate who was endowed with second sight.

'Have the kindness to follow me,' she replied, without seeming to be in the least aware of my astonishment.

For the benefit of those readers who are unfamiliar with Rome,

I may explain that many thousands of dead lie at rest in the Protestant cemetery in the shadow of cypress trees linked with garlands of roses. I followed my guide mechanically in the maze of alleys. As I went along, I read from time to time a familiar name on a tombstone, Emile David, Keats, Shelley, among hundreds of others.

I had been told that Firbank was buried among the cypresses, at the foot of the wall that encircles the cemetery. But instead of taking that direction my guide marched ahead of me without looking back, and led me to the chapel. She preceded me inside, drew my attention to a solitary coffin draped in a black flag, by pointing to it, and simply said: 'Mr Firbank'.

I felt there must be some sort of misunderstanding. 'There's evidently some mistake, my good woman,' I said to her. 'I am looking for the tomb of Ronald Firbank, the writer. I know that he was buried in the cemetery about six months ago.'

The custodian tapped the lid of the coffin with her first finger, like a second-hand dealer guaranteeing the authenticity of a chest of drawers.

'This is Mr Firbank, right enough,' she said. Then she added: 'You are the English consul, are you not, sir?'

I undeceived her and explanations followed. It had just been discovered that Ronald Firbank had been converted to Catholicism, and it was decided that he would rest more quietly in a Catholic cemetery than amongst Huguenots who might be feeling annoyed at his conversion.

As luck would have it, my tardy visit took place the same day and the very same hour that they were expecting a consular representative who would have to supervise the transfer of the body. At the very first glance at me the woman had rightly decided that I was a foreigner, took me for the person who was expected, and asked me the question by which I had so naturally been taken aback.

It must be admitted that, apart from any sort of mystery, it is slightly unusual to be able to be present at the burial of a friend, as I was a few minutes later, six months after his funeral.

RAISLEY MOORSOM

Reminiscences of Ronald Firbank

Letter received from RF:

16th June—22 Junior Carlton Club
Pall Mall S.W.1.

Dear Moorsom,

How charming of you to remember me. I should adore to come to tea next week, but Wednesday is the day of the Prince of Wales return, and the streets may be amusing! So shall it be Friday? at 4.30—but couldn't we, perhaps, meet before? I have only just got back, but quite lately was in Venice, and occupied your wonderful room on the Canal —so exquisite, and I thought of you with gratitude—! Till soon, and Friday, anyway,

Ronald Firbank

It was in the spring of 1921 when I was staying on the peninsula of Sorrento that I met Ronald Firbank. Going out on to the terrace of the hotel on a cliff overlooking the sea, after breakfast, I saw an ageless-looking, elegantly dressed man walking about in a self-conscious way. I noticed particularly his flushed, high cheekbones and his small mouth as he circled round me several times. I had heard about Ronald Firbank from Herbert Read so, by a premonition, I said, 'You must be Ronald Firbank.' When I said I'd enjoyed reading his books, he disappeared into the hotel and reappeared at once with a small case, saying, 'My books—here they are. *They're my children.*'

During our subsequent conversation I said I thought the setting of the black republic of Haiti would make an exotic background for a future book and he was immediately intrigued by this. He told me that he'd recently come from Carthage where the young men bathing in the sea 'wore diamonds in their navels flashing in the sun'.

I ran across him again later in the day on the outskirts of the town, and we agreed to share an open horse-cab back to the hotel. As we drove along in the twilight, he looked up at the moon and said, rather archly, 'I want the moon, I want the moon. *You're my moon.*' I felt embarrassed.

Making my way up Italy towards the north, I accidentally came across him again in Florence and Venice. Once I found him sitting on some steps, looking dishevelled and vulnerable, scattering rose leaves over himself. He said that he had been robbed of everything and thrown out into the street. Though dirty and torn he still looked elegant, his clothes clinging to him like the bark of a peeling tree. He was one of those people towards whom you could not help feeling protective. Although he had no money, he seemed to have no difficulty in obtaining credit for his needs. He once said to me, 'I'm not rich, I can't afford a yacht or to entertain or to buy pictures. *I've just enough for myself.*'

The next year I saw a notice in *The Times* announcing that Mr Ronald Firbank had returned to London, so I wrote reminding him of our meeting in Italy. He came to tea with me at the Travellers and I went to see him at the Junior Carlton Club once, in the morning, when we drank champagne. Soon afterwards, I believe, he went to Haiti, which became the setting for *Prancing Nigger.* I never saw him again, but he was someone whose eccentric charm was unforgettable.

FALLEN PETALS

FORREST REID

It is hard to tell, of course, but I cannot help thinking that my years at Cambridge must have coincided with a particularly unliterary period. Indeed, one of the things that most struck me was the almost total absence of any genuine interest in literature, either early or contemporary. It was an object of study, but for neither dons nor undergraduates was it a living thing. I am talking of English and French literature: on the classical side there was probably more sensitiveness. As for actual writing—well, at King's there was Osbert Burdett, who was working on an extremely bad novel, which I read, finding only one good sentence in it. (I conscientiously pointed out this sentence to the author.) To King's also, in my last year, came Rupert Brooke, and to Trinity Hall, Ronald Firbank. But upon these swallows alone depended whatever summer there might be, and they were as yet far from fully-fledged. Somehow I didn't believe they ever would be swallows that mattered much; in fact I doubted if Firbank were a swallow at all. Brooke I thought would achieve something; Burdett I thought would become the Burdett he actually became; but Firbank left me in the dark. He was so bad that he might easily become much better than either of the other two, for he had the conscience and determination of an artist: on the other hand, he might still more easily fizzle out. Yet it was of him I saw most, though nobody, I should think, can ever have been less of my kind. I liked him up to a point. That is to say, he never bored me, on the contrary he interested me—but he struck me as extraordinarily feline and sophisticated. Lord Alfred Douglas had given him two or three books to review for a paper called, I think, *The Academy*; and I can remember his fitful and half-comical struggles with a volume on Memlinc. He wanted to condemn the book, which he felt instinctively to be a bad book, yet he did not know enough about the subject to do so with safely. His short stories were produced with equal difficulty, and their psychology, or rather the psychology of their author, I could not fathom, nor can I, I confess, fathom it today. Firbank seemed to me unreal. I had never before met anybody in the least like him, and the polished surface was not merely protective but extremely baffling. The only time I ever saw the mask drop was on one winter evening, when, coming out of my sitting-room into the dimly-lit hall, he barked his shins on a coal-scuttle left there by my landlady. Then he said 'damn' quite savagely and naturally—as he might have at the age of fourteen—but a moment later the mask was resumed.

I expect he really thought me half-civilised. The first time I dined with him in his rooms at Trinity Hall the table was strewn with orchids and he himself was in evening dress. I unfortunately was not (after all I knew there were to be only the two of us), so he hastily donned a blazer, for at least he had excellent manners. Nevertheless, I felt that I had been guilty of a solecism and was annoyed. I said I had come straight on from a lecture, which alas! was not true, and moreover not even conceivable. But Firbank never expected the truth. 'The worst of this place,' he replied charmingly, 'is that sometimes people dress and sometimes they don't, so one never knows what to do.' I hastened to agree with him, and the matter was dismissed.

The dinner was elaborate—with a waiter—or he may have been a gyp; in which case he was a gyp of superior variety—in attendance. On its conclusion Firbank sat on the hearthrug and smoked 'drugged cigarettes'; I sat in an armchair and smoked a pipe. To me it was a strange evening, and I shouldn't have been surprised if Dorian Gray had dropped in. Somebody called Brocklehurst, as a matter of fact, did drop in for a minute or two, but I was not introduced to him—an omission Firbank explained later, on the grounds that it seemed silly to introduce people when it was only a matter of saying 'How do you do?' The excuse was quite reasonable; yet I suspected its veracity.

Firbank had been staying in Paris with M. de Max, the actor. He had met, or at any rate seen, various celebrities. He talked of Catulle Mendès and Pierre Louÿs. Occasionally there was a sentence in French, which he spoke beautifully. He read me a story he had written about a woman who decides to go into a convent, and then, for an equally frivolous reason, decides to come out again. He was gay, restless, elaborate. And suddenly, beneath it all, I divined that he was intensely nervous. But why?

I could not make it out. Why on earth should he be nervous with *me*? Nevertheless he was.

I don't know what sort of time Firbank had at Cambridge. He was a member of the Pitt, which was extremely exclusive. Members of the Pitt were difficult to get to know, and Firbank, as I have hinted, evidently had decided not to introduce me to his other friends. Once, at least, his rooms were ragged, and once, on a foggy November evening, I saw him in the grip of an intoxicated undergraduate, who was shaking him slowly backwards and forwards beneath a lamp in Trinity Street, and at the same time summing up a view of his character in realistic and unprintable terms. I myself find him difficult to sum up. He had the air of being witty without really being witty. It was the manner more than anything else; his good things would not bear repetition, and his range was extremely limited. Yet he must have been genuine after his fashion, for he never deviated from his course, his later books show only a development of what had been there from the beginning. E. M. Forster, in *Abinger Harvest*, says he had genius, but he hadn't—not a glimmer of it. He was fastidious, and he had a streak of talent, but he never wrote anything that had not before been better done by somebody else. He was a decadent of the school of Oscar Wilde, but lacking Wilde's intellect. I see him hovering between Wilde and Norman Douglas. There is nothing in his books that is not in the *The Importance of Being Earnest* and *South Wind*.

From his autobiography, *Private Road* (1940). Reprinted by permission of Faber and Faber Ltd.

Shane Leslie

Before he left Cambridge, Robert Hugh Benson could not help sketching his friends in his novels. Jack Collins was the hero of *None Other Gods*, and *The Conventionalists* enshrined a strange apparition from our midst: Ronald Firbank, who was an undergraduate at Trinity Hall. By birth Firbank should have been a railway manager or contractor. He was a delicate and precious romanticist. He was utterly extreme in all his aspects and amusingly perverse. In a rowing college like the Hall he resembled a goldfish at the common fishmonger's. His rooms were beautifully furnished and always redolent of flowers. His slim figure and exquisite mannerisms made him a creature apart. Catholicism was not enough for him, but he must needs be an ecstatic. Benson persuaded him or imposed as a penance sitting in a rowing eight. The iciness of the weather and the heat of the coaches combined nearly to kill him. But he showed pluck and endurance and later chose an unusual profession by joining the Papal Guard. It was amusing to think of Trinity Hall as the training school for a janissary of the Vatican. He wrote a number of orchidaceous books, whose style and texture grew more and more like himself. He was a harmless and pathetic being, and died like a lily which had always been trying to break its window-box.

From his autobiography, *The Film of Memory* (1938). Reprinted by permission of Michael Joseph Ltd.

Siegfried Sassoon

Osbert Sitwell was often in Oxford to visit his brother, and this led to my oddest experience there. One afternoon in February they took me to see Ronald Firbank, who was living in a house opposite All Souls. None of us had met him before, but his impressionist novels had led us to expect a somewhat peculiar person, so we weren't surprised when he received us in a closely-curtained room lighted by numerous candles and filled with a profusion of exotic flowers. A large table was elaborately set out with a banquet of rich confectionery and hothouse fruits. Firbank, whose appearance was as orchidaceous as his fictional fantasies, behaved so strangely that all attempts at ordinary conversation became farcical. His murmured remarks were almost inaudible, and he was too nervous to sit still for more than half a minute at a time. The only coherent information he gave me was when I heavily inquired where his wonderful fruit came from. 'Blenheim,' he exclaimed with an hysterical giggle, and then darted away to put a picture-frame straight, leaving me wondering how peaches were grown at Blenheim in mid-winter. The Sitwells were more successful in mitigating his helpless discomposure, but even Osbert's suavely reassuring manner failed to elicit anything except the disconnected utterances which were his method of evading direct explanations. For instance, when Sacheverell spoke appreciatively of his latest novel, *Caprice*, he turned his head away, and remarked, in a choking voice, 'I can't bear calceolarias! Can you?' Could this have any bearing on the book, I speculated, from the other side of the table, where I was now a mere cake and fruit consumer. There was an enormous fire, and the warmth of the flower-scented room made me drowsy while Firbank, who was shedding some of his agonised shyness and its attendant affectations, confided in the Sitwells that he had no servants in the house and lived almost entirely on cold chicken. Watching him through the jungle of orchids, I found it hard to believe that this strange being could have any relationship with the outer world. He was as unreal and anomalous as his writings, and the room—with its exquisite refinements and virtuosities of taste—seemed a pathetically contrived refuge. I afterwards discovered that he had travelled widely, and was much more business-like than he made himself out to be. But when I once ventured to ask what was his favourite country, he could only answer 'Lotus land, of course!' He had a horror of particularities, and my more literal-minded approach to life was too great a strain on him.

A few days later I invited him to tea, for I was curious to observe how he shaped by daylight and away from his 'highly stylised' surroundings. Rather to my surprise he accepted. Anxious to entertain him appropriately, I bought a monumental bunch of grapes, and a glutinous chocolate cake. Powdered, ninetyish, and insuperably shy, he sat with eyes averted from me and my well-meaning repast. His most rational response to my attempts at drawing him out about literature and art was 'I adore italics, don't you?' His cup of tea remained untasted, and he quailed when I drew his attention to my large and cosy pile of crumpets. As a gesture of politeness he slowly absorbed a single grape. In subsequent years I met him at intervals—mostly intervals at the Russian Ballet—and he sent me copies of his books, wittily inscribed in violet ink in his bold, feminine handwriting. The last time I talked to him he happened to be in a communicative mood. 'I am Pavlova, chasing butterflies,' he exclaimed; and then added with mock seriousness, 'You are Tolstoy, digging for worms.' His earlier books had amused me, but I regarded them as the elegant triflings of a talented amateur. Misled by their apparent lack of construction, I failed to see that he had a deliberate technique of his own. I was often charmed by his sensitive and diverting word-play, and in his later works I found a sort of opulent beauty and decadent gaiety. Firbank's writings, though leaving a superficial impression of exquisite accomplishment, never achieved the tenuous mastery which he aimed at. His chicness is too pervasive, and his improper innuendoes seem to me tittering and tiresome. Nevertheless he ranks high among nonsensical novelists, and might be described as having a genius for subtle silliness.

From *Siegfried's Journey 1916–1920* (1945). Reprinted by permission of Faber and Faber Ltd.

Vivian de Sola Pinto

The most memorable of the parties that I attended at the Golden Cross was a dinner given in February 1919 by the Sitwells and Siegfried in honour of Ronald Firbank. Sir Osbert Sitwell has described this party so vividly in his *Noble Essences* that any other comment on it must seem a feeble anticlimax. I remember that we assembled in the dining-room at the Golden Cross on that bleak February evening at about eight o'clock and, after waiting some time for Firbank, started to consume a good, solid English dinner, washed down by copious draughts of an excellent hock, of which Osbert was very fond. At last, when we had almost finished, Firbank arrived. He was a thin, stooping, frail-looking young man with fine eyes and what Sir Osbert has described as an 'aquiline, somewhat chinless face', dressed in dark, almost clerical-looking clothes. He refused to eat anything but consented to drink a glass of port. Sitting sideways on a chair and clutching sometimes nervously at his tie with his beautiful white hands, he began to read to us an extract from a work which he afterwards published under the title *Valmouth.* He did not read well but there was, nevertheless, a peculiar charm in his hesitant manner and low voice, and we were entranced by the quality of his writing. For nearly an hour we were living in a strange, fantastic world inhabited by the Negress Mrs Yajñavalkya and her centenarian patients, Lady Parvula de Panzoust and Mrs Hurstpierpoint. It was a creation as original as a fantasy of Watteau or Goya.

From *The City that Shone: an Autobiography* (1969). Reproduced by permission of The Hutchinson Publishing Group Ltd.

P. Wyndham Lewis

Ronald Firbank—the very *genius loci* of the 'post-war', and the reincarnation of all the nineties—Oscar Wilde, Pater, Beardsley, Dawson [*sic*] all rolled into one, and served up with a *sauce créole.*

It was almost impossible to do a portrait of Ronald Firbank, he was so interested in what I was doing. He wanted to look over my shoulder while I was drawing him. I pointed out that this was impossible.

We started off by my getting him up on the model's throne, an operation demanding a certain tact. He was afraid he might fall off. He fluttered at the thought of so much self-exposure. But I got him up. I stood in front of him for a little, to see he stayed put. I knew him well. I did not expect it to be easy.

He rolled his eyes and frothed at the mouth. He said that I ought to see him the first thing in the morning. I said I wished I could. The young day, he told me, gave him, fresh from sleep, a new face. It only lasted an hour or two. Breakfast was apparently the last straw. It was breakfast that started the débacle. To put the matter shortly—*Bacon and eggs!* Having soiled himself irretrievably with breakfast, he got through the rest of the day as best he could. *Until the night came.* With the night, things began to look up again—that is his face did. His beauty returned to him, the artificial light helping things out. But it was never quite the same as the first hour of the young morning. That was *really* the time to see him!

I am, myself, a late riser. I told him he must have confidence in me; that I should never see him as I *should* see him—that I should hate him anyway if I had to rise so early to look at him. But that I could well imagine what it was like and would endeavour to get into what I was about to do something of this immaculate daybreak beauty. Then I sat down and began work.

He writhed about on his chair, clasped and unclasped his hands. But I was not unaccustomed to hitting moving targets in the sitter line. I selected a position to which I noticed he always returned, however much he twisted and tossed. I disregarded the other positions he successively took up.

I fixed my eye upon his mouth. He gasped, as he saw me do this. Firbank was what is called 'toothy' and he foamed rather easily. A lather would collect upon his prominent muzzle. He leapt off the throne all of a sudden and rushed over to my side and looked down at the paper on which I was drawing.

'I *had* to look!' he exclaimed.

'Well?'

'Oh, I don't know! You are *cruel*,' he gasped.

'Don't you like it?'

'Oh, I don't know! It's lovely!' he stood writhing at my side.

I stood up.

'Return at once to that throne,' I said sternly. 'Or I shall probably beat you with that mahlstick.'

Shuddering and screaming he rushed back, barked a knee upon the edge of the throne and reoccupied the chair.

But he got worse and worse. His stomach began rumbling and he flushed so much at this and then went so pale, I was afraid he might faint. At last he bounded off again and came gibbering round behind me.

'I *had* to see what you were doing. I couldn't bear it any longer. I just had to have a look!' he panted in my ear, clawing at his arms and knees.

I got him back but it became quite impossible after that. He jumped on and off the throne every second minute. Also he had remarked how I had selected a certain position out of all those he presented me with, and he avoided it deliberately.

Again I stood up. I had to get a head of him done—it was for some publication and I was being paid for it. I dragged a table near my easel and I made him sit upon the corner of it, within reach of my foot. To say that he now remained quiet would be untrue. But he seemed more able to keep still this way than in a chair. And I was able to correct him from time to time with a warning kick.

I got my head, *tant bien que mal*. I consider it the best head that was ever done of him. Augustus John was as usual a little too flourishing and juicily skilful. For you can suggest too much juice with a pencil just as much as you can with a brush. Mr David Low the caricaturist does that, for instance. He has a juicy line very like a John line. How I managed it I don't quite know—some process of deduction rather than of mere sight. But I got him, and he even seemed to like it himself, after it was all over.

Firbank is buried in Rome next to the grave of John Keats. I shouldn't like to have a grave next to his. If there's one place where one may, I suppose, expect a little rest it is in the grave. And Firbank in his winding-sheet upon a moonlit night would be a problem for the least fussy of corpses in the same part of the cemetery, 'Thou still unravished bride of quietness!' I can imagine him hissing at Keats, 'come forth and let us seek out the tomb of Heliogabalus together shall us!' If there were only a Keats Society, I'd get up an agitation to have his grave moved.

From this you must not gather that I objected to Firbank. On the contrary. He seemed to me a pretty good clown—of the 'impersonator' type. Facially, he closely resembled Nellie Wallace. He seemed to like me—I had such relations with him as one might have with a talking gazelle, afflicted with some nervous disorder.

In Stulik's one night I had dinner with him and a young American 'college-boy' who was stopping at the Eiffel Tower Hotel. The presence of the fawning and attentive Firbank put the little American out of countenance. He called the waiter.

'I guess I'll have something *t'eat*!' he announced aggressively.

'What will you have, sir?' asked the waiter.

'I guess I'll have—oh—a *rump steak*.'

He pored over the menu: it was evident he felt that a rump steak would disinfect the atmosphere.

'Yessur.'

'Carrots,' he rasped out defiantly.

'Yessir. Carrots, sir.'

'Boiled pertaters.'

'Yessir.'

'What? Oh and er . . .'

But with gushing insinuation Firbank burst excitedly in at this point.

'Oh and *vi-o-lets*!' he frothed obsequiously.

Reacting darkly to the smiles of the onlookers the college-boy exclaimed, but without looking at his cringing 'fan'—

'There seem to be a lot of *fairies* round here!'

And he sniffed the air as if he could detect the impalpable aroma of an elf.

From *Blasting and Bombardiering* (Eyre and Spottiswoode, 1937). Reprinted by permission of Calder and Boyars Ltd.

Harold Acton

Reggie [Turner] was never allowed to slip demurely into middle age. He was continually being embarrassed. One day as he was walking down the Via Tornabuoni, Ronald Firbank, whose mere voice made Reggie wince, rushed upon him from a flower-shop and covered him from head to foot with lilies.

Though Firbank led an isolated life, maintaining no more than a jerky acquaintance with a few choice relics of the nineties who did not know what to make of him, nobody has conveyed the aroma of Florentine gossip better than he. He endeared himself to the waiters at Betti's by his handsome tips. Having carefully ordered fruit that was out of season, he would sit and contemplate it like an El Greco saint in ecstasy. Muscat grapes in mid-winter he would dangle against the light, eyeing the clusters caressingly as he sipped glass after glass of wine. At the food he merely picked and jabbed as if it repelled him.

Reggie cared as little for Firbank as for his writings. He complained that his laugh made him uncomfortable, and laughter had never made Reggie uncomfortable before. He had courted it all his life. Besides, Firbank sprawled over the furniture and his head was apt to fall on the dinner-table with grisly effect. Reggie infinitely preferred P. G. Wodehouse. But in spite of his efforts to keep up to date he never escaped from the nineties altogether. . . .

From *Memoirs of an Aesthete* (1948). Reprinted by permission of Eyre Methuen Ltd.

Martin Secker

When Firbank had finished *Vainglory* in 1915, he took it first to Martin Secker, who read it but could make very little of it and thought its prospects negligible. He recommended the author to show it to 'my friend Grant Richards in St Martins Street'. A month or so later, after Grant Richards had accepted the book and come to an arrangement to publish it at Firbank's own expense, Firbank revisited Secker at No. 5 John Street one afternoon, put his head coyly round the door and announced to no one in particular: 'Grant Richards has taken my novel—so there!' He then vanished.

In conversation.

Ernst Goldschmidt

Anthony Hobson once asked his friend Ernst P. Goldschmidt, who had been at Cambridge with Firbank, what he was like. Goldschmidt thought for a moment and replied: 'Like cold boiled veal.'

Communicated by Anthony Hobson.

John Steegman

FIRBANK: Where would you like to dine?

STEEGMAN: I have never been to the St James's Club and seen the dilettanti portraits.

FIRBANK: I expect I am a member.

They take a taxi to the St James's Club.

FIRBANK (*to the porter*): Is Mr Ronald Firbank in the club?

PORTER: No, sir. We have a member of that name, but I have never seen him.

FIRBANK (*falsetto*): that's me.

Communicated by Sir Ellis Waterhouse.

Part Three

CRITIQUES

CARL VAN VECHTEN

Ronald Firbank

Valmouth . . . a young man at an evening party caught my attention. Valmouth, he repeated and, after a significant pause, added, I will send it down to you.

Ignorant as to whether Valmouth was a liqueur or a new variety of dog, with some curiosity I awaited Stuart Rose's gift which, when it arrived, exhibited qualities inherent in both these surmises . . . and, yet it was neither. *Valmouth* was a book. The wrapper, probably with justification, was fashioned of a paper that resembled oil-cloth and displayed a quaint design in colour by Augustus John, together with the author's name, Ronald Firbank. I sat down to peruse a page or two. I rose an hour later, having read the book through, a reading interrupted here and there by spasms of merriment or nods of astonishment. *Valmouth*, indeed, with its lusty, impatient peacocks and parties, its portrait of the always surprising Mrs Hurstpierpoint, Lady Parvula de Panzoust and her pursuit of the josephian shepherd, and, above all, that ripping old coon, Mrs Yajñavalkya, procuress and masseuse, who, in the midst of the most utter nigger jargon, casually inserts such phrases as 'plein air!' The opus concludes with an amazing wedding, as smartly attended as that of the Princess Mary, in which the two chief rôles are enacted by a juvenile English naval officer and the young Negro woman, Niri-Esther. Just before this coda, the composer of this jazz concerto has indicated an opportunity for a superb cadenza.

Arthur Annesley Ronald Firbank, the second and only surviving son of the late Major Sir (Joseph) Thomas Firbank, M.P., and Jane Harriette, daughter of the late Reverend James Perkins Garret of Kilgarron County, Carlow, was born in London in 1886.

From Carl Van Vechten, *Excavations*, published by Alfred A. Knopf Inc. in 1924. Reprinted by arrangement with Donald Gallup, literary trustee of Carl Van Vechten, copyright 1926 by Alfred A. Knopf assigned to the author 1942 and renewed by the author 1954.

He was educated 'abroad' and at Trinity Hall, Cambridge. He has travelled extensively.

Elkin Mathews issued Firbank's first book, *Odette d'Antrevernes*, in 1905. This slender volume of forty-five pages, bound in grey wrappers, stamped in gold, also contains *A Study in Temperament*, suggestive in manner of his later work. Of *Odette*, there was also a tall paper edition, limited to *ten copies*, bound in vellum, from which *A Study in Temperament* was omitted. This story was also excluded from Grant Richards's reprint of *Odette* (wrappers) in 1916. Firbank's other books, published by Richards, are: *Vainglory* (1915), *Inclinations* (1916), *Caprice* (1917), *Valmouth* (1919), *The Princess Zoubaroff* (a comedy in three acts; 1920), *Santal* (wrappers; 1921), and *The Flower Beneath the Foot* (1923). *Prancing Nigger* was published by Brentano's in New York in 1924. These volumes are embellished with designs by Félicien Rops, Albert Rutherston, Augustus John, Michel Sevier, Albert Bührer, C. R. Nevinson, Wyndham Lewis and Robert E. Locher.

Sophisticated virgins and demi-puceaux will adore these romances. Married or unmarried persons over thirty will find them either shocking or tiresome, according to the individual temperament of the reader. I have a suspicion that a few delightful old ladies will enjoy a quiet closet-laugh on the sly. These novels are not suitable for public libraries and Brander Matthews and William Lyon Phelps will never review them.

To be 1890 in 1890 might be considered almost normal. To be 1890 in 1922 might be considered almost queer. There is a difference, however. The colour is magenta. Oscar's hue was green. The fun is warmer; the vice is more léger. Soon or late, one hears a good deal about the light touch in literature. It might be believed, forsooth, that this was no rare quality, so frequently do reviewers apply this ready epithet to writing which has no touch at all. Speaking for myself, I may say that Ronald Firbank is the only authentic master of the light touch I have discovered. His touch is so light, indeed, that after reading one of his books I find even Max Beerbohm a trifle studied, a little composed. Confronted by *Prancing Nigger*, Aldous Huxley might almost be regarded as an earnest fellow.

Firbank is, perhaps, the only purely Greek writer that we possess today. There is no sentimentality or irony in his work;

hardly even cynicism. There is, indeed, a baffling quality about Firbank's very lucidity, his gay, firm grasp of his trivial peccancies. His ellipses serve the same purpose as the descending curtain at the close of the first act of *Die Walküre*. His form arranges itself for the most part in a diagram of dialogue . . . and such dialogue! No matter how many ancient clouds of glory he trails behind him, and there is Greek, Firbank is more than up-to-date. He is the Pierrot of the minute. Félicien Rops on a merry-go-round. Aubrey Beardsley in a Rolls-Royce. Ronald in Lesbosland. Puck celebrating the Black Mass. Sacher-Masoch in Mayfair. *A Rebours* à la mode. Aretino in Piccadilly. Jean Cocteau at the Savoy. The Oxford tradition with steam from the Paris bains de vapeur. The cubists are remembered. Firbank plays Picasso's violin. The decorations serve more than their purpose. Flippant, impertinent symbols are the tools of his impudicity. Fruits, flowers, bees, and even mice play eccentric rôles in these concentric comedies. Roses and nightingales impose their furtive intentions. Cathedral towers and organ recitals are to be noted among the minor gems in a by no means despicable collection. At last, apparently, Tinker Bell's life is no longer in danger. Can it be possible that this impudent young man is satirising D. H. Lawrence, or is this the true picture of English life?

Quotations would serve no purpose—can one quote from a tapestry?—and they would be unseemly, but I may permit myself to bring forward a short passage from *Vainglory*, in which this jaunty, intrepid, if somewhat pale, original, referring ostensibly to Harvester's *Vaindreams*, sums up, perhaps, himself:

> 'He has such a strange, peculiar style. His work calls to mind a frieze with figures of varying heights trotting all the same way. If one should by chance turn about it's usually merely to stare or to sneer or to make a grimace. Only occasionally his figures care to beckon. And they seldom really touch.'
>
> 'He's too cold. Too classic, I suppose.'
>
> 'Classic! In the Encyclopaedia Britannica his style is described as *odd spelling, brilliant and vicious*.'

To such affairs of the world as those for which he has no taste he is utterly indifferent. He does not satirise the things he hates. He flits airily about, arranging with skilful fingers the things he loves. Make no mistake: what he wants to do he does, and is a master of the doing of. The delicate tranquillity of his prose, shot through with icy stabs of wit and shimmering gleams of sophistication, is very rare and very original. When you compare him with other authors, logically you can go no further than the binding. His utterly own manner alienates him completely from the possibility of any other form of estimate. He is unique, a glittering dragon-fly skimming over the sunlit literary garden, where almost all the other creatures crawl.

I own a special fondness for *The Flower Beneath the Foot*, although *Caprice* is a great favourite of mine, and *Valmouth* is *hors de concours*, like the Cathedral at Chartres or a gown designed by Madame Vionnet. The scenario is extraordinarily telling, the characters vividly droll, the flash of wit coruscating, the insinuations incredible. I have read *The Flower* three times and each time I have dug new worms from under the stones.

The chapter of my choice, possibly, is that which recounts the death of the Archduchess who, as she lies dying, gazes rapturously at the new model for one of her cloacal charities, placed conveniently on the coverlet before her, the while she mutters strange sagas. The Queen, at a desk in the death chamber, occupied in dispatching telegrams announcing the sad eventuality, annoyed by the interruptions, bids the Archduchess to hold her tongue. The form chosen for these wires, after a good deal of careful consideration, is 'Lizzie has ceased articulating'.

The Archduchess and the Queen, however, are but two in this rich gallery of ripe, rude figures. There is the Flower herself, who learned to read swiftly on the 'screens at cinemas' and who conquered her Ego in her eighteenth year, whom we leave in the tragic conclusion beating her fragile palms against the broken glass atop the convent wall, as she watches Prince Yousef enter the Cathedral to wed another. This is, indeed, her book, for the title page tells us that *The Flower* is 'a record of the early life of St Laura de Nazianzi and the times in which she lived'. Some times!

Further, there are the Tunisian Bachir and his group of flower-boys, and the Hon 'Eddy' Monteith, who dies of fright at the sight of a jackal while composing a sonnet before the excavations of Chedorlahomor. There is Mrs Wetme who desires to 'climb' from the Café Cleopatra to a royal drawing-room through the purchased aid of the impecunious Duchess of Varna. There is Count Cabinet who makes a curious discovery on the lake, through the telescope of his observatory, just before the sudden tropic night shuts out the view; there are the Nuns of the Flaming Hood and Their Majesties of Dateland, King Jotifa and Queen Thleeanouhee. On the whole, however, I laugh most permanently at the implication of the passage followed by a footnote on page 133.*

Ronald Firbank visited Havana in August 1922. The following month found him in the British West Indies where he wrote the first sketches of *Prancing Nigger*. He completed the book in Bordighera during the ensuing winter. The novel is typical of his talent. The tropical nights and dawns . . . how many brilliant passages they have evoked! . . . the trumpet-flowers and jasmines, the sapphire and emerald sea, the exotic birds, seem to have inspired him to write his best. There is possibly more beauty in this book than in any other by this author, and certainly no less humour.

Firbank's treatment of the Negro is his own; he owes nothing, it may be said, to such forerunners as Mrs Harriet Beecher Stowe, Octavus Roy Cohen, E. K. Means, Waldo Frank, or T. S. Stribling. The Mouth family, whose social advances and amorous adventures form the woof of this tapestry, are as decorative and fantastic as Firbank's more familiar English duchesses. Perhaps, indeed, he moves even more freely in this, to him, esoteric milieu. *Prancing Nigger* hovers delightfully between a Freudian dream and a drawing by Alastair, set to music by George Gershwin.

* The reference is to the English edition (p. 565 of *The Complete Firbank*).

ARTHUR WALEY

Introduction to Limited Edition

The chief charge against Firbank is that he was silly. The critics, in their natural fear of being hoaxed, have invented what they consider to be an infallible method of self-protection; they will admit no one who does not carry the passport of solemnity, countersigned by two octogenarians. Strangely, it has never occurred to them that a solemn aspect, so far from being a guarantee of good faith, has always been an essential element in the impostor's outfit. Captain Koepenick, who deceived the Prussian Guard, did not caper irresponsibly, a jaunty Autolycus, through the streets of Potsdam, but swept majestic to his hoax wrapped in all the ponderous casings of Tweedledee.

Indeed, the amount of silliness that can be smuggled in under the cloak of pomposity and despite the most solid credentials is proved each week by a well-known literary journal; and I could point to passages in such respectable works as the *Cambridge Ancient History* and *History of India* that for sheer silliness surpass the most dithering pages of *Transition.* Had Firbank's silliness been of the monumental kind, had he hidden it under a cloak of learning, respectability or even decency, the professional critics would long ago have occupied themselves with his name. But as he is singularly deficient in all these attributes, it has been left to irresponsible people, young, often American, occupied with literature more as a pleasure than as a duty, and in many other ways debarred from forming serious judgements, to appreciate Firbank's books.

There comes a moment in the history of every art when those very powers of minute observation and convincing mimicry, upon the increase of which all its progress has hitherto depended, begin to silt up the path of advance, to crush the artist under a complexity of detail that he can no longer arrange or control. Such was

This essay was the general introduction to the limited edition of Ronald Firbank's *Collected Works* published jointly by Duckworth and Brentano in 1929.

the fate, synchronous and perhaps connected with the rise of photography, that overtook nineteenth-century painting in England and indeed academic art all over Europe. A similar disaster befell the English novel early in the twentieth century, and it has not recovered. It seems as though, following upon the discovery of the camera, some parallel inward change took place. Just as those accidents and trivialities, which the hand of the painter had instinctively excluded, were to the camera no less important than the rest of the picture, so in the psychic apparatus of the writer some mechanism which previously excluded the trivial and unessential had begun to break down. And indeed to the modern mind nothing is trivial or insignificant. A door-knob, an umbrella, a match-box are all fraught with equally profound and sinister meaning.

Again, we attach importance to our sensations in proportion as they are peculiar to ourselves; the old writers regarded as interesting only what they felt to belong to the general experience of mankind. Thus the modern novelist is left with a host of facts so diverse and vast that there is small hope of weaving it together into any unity of material. In order to realise how great the change has been, take any chapter of a serious, ambitious novel, such as Rosamund Lehmann's *Dusty Answer*, and you will find that of the things she says Jane Austen's 'lens' would have cut out at least half as trivial, and a good deal of the rest (for example, discourse about the hair on the hero's knees) as indecent. Even such inhibitions as we possess do not help us, for they are directed chiefly against romanticism, the one impetus which might tend, without further ramifying our material, to infuse its parts with a uniform life and glow.

Art in the nineteenth century made two attempts to rescue itself from its predicament, the first of which, but not the second, subsequently had its exact parallel in literature. The pre-Raphaelites made a desperate attempt to see naïvely, primitively, and at the same time to utilise the English genius for poetry by raising the illustrative, literary side of their art from the anecdotic to the lyrical. This movement has found a parallel in recent English fiction.

David Garnett, Sylvia Townsend-Warner, Edith Olivier are our pre-Raphaelites; deliberate primitives, who achieve their simplification by persistently looking at life through a fictitious mind that is much less complicated and sophisticated than their own.

The Impressionist movement in painting, the second of the two attempts I have named, sought its simplification not in make-belief, not in a resolution to see primitively, but in a conscious and deliberate choice. To this movement there has been no parallel in literature. Except for the Neo-primitive School described above and Mrs Woolf, who stands entirely alone, the English novel is still in the Chantrey Bequest stage.

Firbank, then, is important because he is the first and almost the only Impressionist in English fiction, the earliest writer to discard the load of realistic lumber under which the modern story is interred—to do in writing what Cézanne, Matisse, Renoir did in painting. The first essential in an art-revolutionary is patience; for most people are as easily put off the scent by the slightest change in an art's outward forms as are children at Christmas, who gaze in terror and blank astonishment at a figure that differs from their own father only in the fact that he wears a white beard. English writers are only too familiar with this characteristic of their audience. At every moment they are haunted by the idea that they are becoming eclectic, allusive, obscure; and fearing that the crowd will melt away, they snatch up the megaphone and begin bawling comments and explanations in words of one syllable.

Firbank probably desired success—that is to say, a large audience—as much as anyone. But his natural diffidence was such that he could never conceive of more than a handful of his own friends wanting to read his books. He is therefore never haunted by this fear that one must *lecture* in order to be understood. He does not, in introducing us to a character, find it necessary to write treatises on the Public School tradition, the cramping influences of a Baptist upbringing, or what-not; he knows that he has only got to make his characters speak, either singly ('I always intended to visit Walt Whitman, didn't I, Lizzie? Poor old Walt. . . . I wrote: "Expect me, and my maid. . . . I'm coming!" I said. . . . It was the very Spring he died,' and there you have Mrs Hurstpierpoint complete), or in gangs (the Private View, *Inclinations*, p. 30), for us to know instantaneously and exactly what company we are in.

But though Firbank was encouraged to take many short-cuts and venture upon some meteoric transitions by the conviction that he was addressing not Trafalgar Square but a row or two at most in the stalls at the Russian Ballet, he was far too good an artist to speak in the language of a coterie, or assume in his reader interests that were merely parochial.

It has been said that Firbank's subject-matter was monotonously narrow. But it is certainly not more restricted than that of a writer such as Henry James. He treats of Mayfair at home and abroad, with excursions across the King's Road; Anglican country-life under the shadow of the minster's 'contented towers'; the plantations of Havana, the sacristies of Spain. But his vision was so strangely constituted that even if life had continued to pile experiences upon him, the stream of his art would never have lost its thin diluted purity. His mind seems as though endowed with a kind of inverted X-ray, which enabled him, not to penetrate into the unseen, but, on the contrary, continually to hover, as it were, an inch or two above the surface of things. Much slips through the gap, leaving a material almost too tenuous and clarified.

Firbank's reviewers had the odd idea that he was a satirist. But satire implies disapproval, and there is no sign that he disapproved of or in any way condemned the vapid society that he depicts. Only once is there anything that could possibly be called an attack. The Hon Mrs Harold Chilleywater (in *The Flower Beneath the Foot*), 'whose description of a cornfield makes one *feel* England', had evidently managed in some way to wound his feelings very deeply. His detachment breaks down, and slipping into the world of tiresome everyday discord, to which he does not properly belong, Firbank becomes positively ill-mannered.

The first published work was *Odette d'Antrevernes* (1905, Elkin Mathews), a thin paper-bound volume, containing the title-piece and another story called 'A Study in Temperament'. The author appears inside the cover as 'Arthur Firbank'. *Odette* ('A Fairy Tale for Weary People') is very ninetyish; but there are already hints of the writer to come. His genius for names is there (for example, Mrs Fortune as the name of an old nurse); it is seen again in the second story (Lobelia, for the young lady who said 'Oh no! I am not very musical but Mama is'). The name of Hester Q. Tail (an American poetess) is adequate, but rather obvious. She makes up for it, however, by a super-silliness ('But tell me, *dear* Mrs Corba, are you *the* Mrs Corba?') that anticipates Firbank's maturer absurdities.

What happened to him between 1905 and 1915 I leave to his biographer to disclose. He wrote, or at any rate published, nothing.

When *Vainglory* came out at the latter date (this time with Grant Richards, as was henceforth the case with all his books except *Sorrow in Sunlight*) he was already Ronald Firbank, and capable of far more sustained flights. I am so fond, for example, of this description that I cannot forbear quoting it:

> Mrs Henedge, the widow of that injudicious man the Bishop of Ashringford, was considered, by those who knew her, to be Sympathy itself. His lordship, rumour reported, had fallen in love with her at first sight one morning while officiating at a friend's cathedral, when she had put him in mind of a startled deer. She was really only appropriating a hymn-book, as she afterwards explained. Their marriage had been called a romance. Towards the end, however, the Bishop had become too fe-fi-fo-fum-Jack-in-the-Beanstalk altogether.

Next came *Inclinations* (1916), which he must have written when in very high spirits. The trouvail of this book is Miss Dawson, the Australian girl who is looking everywhere for her parents:

> 'And have you never found any trace?'
>
> 'At Palermo, once . . . I was wandering in the Public Gardens before the hotel, amid blown bus tickets and autumn leaves, when I thought I saw them. Father, anyway. He was standing at an open window of an eau-de-Nil greenhouse. He looked much younger.

She it is, too, who sings the very convincing Japanese folk-song:

> That which flies yonder,
> Wild goose is it, swan is it?
> Wild goose if it be . . . etc.

Caprice (1917) marks the entry of Chelsea, the Café Royal, the Stage; and there is a frontispiece by Augustus John. The opening, in which the stage-struck daughter of a Canon day-dreams and rehearses on Sunday evening in a cathedral town, is a good example of Firbank's Impressionist rapidity. In the brief pages that follow (his books were growing shorter and shorter) we see Miss Sinquier shoot to fame amid a breathless glitter of excitement, only to vanish, meteor-like indeed, but somewhat too pointlessly.

In 1919 came *Valmouth*, the first book to contain the black element henceforward to figure so prominently. Mrs Yajñavalkya, the masseuse, though very much at home on the west coast of England, seems to be at the same time a Mohammedan, Fetishist and Buddhist, and to emanate indifferently from India, Africa, and Asia. But bizarre as Mrs Yaj and her 'relative' Esther-Niri may appear in the setting of an English watering-place, they are not more exotic than Firbank himself. The blacks, indeed, henceforward become his chorus, and under cover of the *naïveté* with which Orientals are supposed to be endowed, he is able to vent his most hilarodiac fancies.

Has anyone tried to act *The Princess Zoubaroff* (1920)? It would need to be played very artificially, with full weight given to the smooth and punctilious cadence of the dialogue. The swiftness with which the characters take shape is amazing. For example, the entry of Lady Rocktower:

LADY ROCKTOWER [*hand extended, advancing to Nadine*]: I wrote to you about a week ago asking you to dinner, and having received no answer I thought I would ascertain . . .
NADINE [*retaining Lady Rocktower's hand*]: Did I *never* answer?

Or this introduction:

NADINE: My husband.
BLANCHE [*genially*]: I think we've slept together once?
ADRIAN: I don't remember.
BLANCHE: At the opera. During *Bérénice.*

There is precision and style in every sentence that is spoken; but a complete lack of climax or situation. The piece is so unreal as to be farcical. Yet it is doubtful whether on the stage it could ever raise more than a smile, and farce does not work unless it produces laughter. It is, however, despite its tenuous structure, so adroit in actual language that very exceptional actors might conceivably make it a success.

For *Santal* (1921) I cannot see that there is anything to be said.

Here we find Mrs Yajñavalkya and her 'niece' (or persons indistinguishable from them) transplanted to Algiers, where they figure as local inhabitants. They seem to miss the stimulus of English seaside air. After a brief and rather timid innings they give place to Cherif, a sentimentalised Arab-boy, who is altogether too waifish and wistful. Fortunately all is over in forty pages.

The Flower Beneath the Foot was already being written in 1921, but did not appear till 1923. With the exception of the early *Vainglory*, it is the longest book, and perhaps the best. The scene is laid at a semi-Asiatic Court, a sort of cross between Byzantium and Belgravia. The book contains some of Firbank's most amusing passages, for example, the description of Mrs Bedley, the 'mother' of the English colony, who keeps 'a circulating library and a tea-room combined', and 'gives information to tourists':

> 'What is the Embassy there for but to be hospitable?' Mrs Barleymoon demanded from the summit of a ladder, where she was choosing herself a book.
>
> 'You're showing your petticoat, dear—excuse me telling you,' Mrs Bedley observed.
>
> 'When will you have something new, Mrs Bedley?'
>
> 'Soon, dear . . . soon.'
>
> 'Are you looking for anything, Bessie, in particular?' a girl, with loose blue eyes that did not seem quite firm in her head and a literary face, enquired.
>
> 'No, only something,' Mrs Barleymoon replied, 'I've not had before and before and before.'
>
> 'By the way, Miss Hopkins,' Mrs Bedley said, 'I've to fine you for pouring tea over *My Stormy Past* . . .'

and so on.

There are charming small touches, such as the pair of venerable politicians who, after a dinner-party, 'were helping each other along with little touches and pats . . .' or the English governess who makes the young prince decline the present of the verb 'to be a Political Hostess . . .'

> 'Very good, dear, and only one mistake. "He is a Political Hostess.' Can you correct yourself? The error is so slight . . .'

In *Sorrow in Sunlight* (1925) he returns to extreme brevity.

He was becoming famous, and only famous people are allowed to write short books. And here I may be permitted a short digression. If fiction is to become an art instead of being a commodity it cannot continue to be distributed through the same channels as the ordinary commercial novel. To those who are not prepared for it, the Impressionist novel will be as incomprehensible as was the Impressionist picture in the nineteenth century. Some publisher must buy up manuscripts with a view to later publication just as a few dealers at Paris bought pictures for which the market lay wholly in the future. Years hence the greater public will take to a new kind of fiction as readily as it has taken to Matisse.

That, however, in parenthesis.

Sorrow in Sunlight is Firbank's one all-black novel, whites figuring quite subordinately. It is, and deserves to be, his best-known work. There was indeed only one disadvantage—the difficult manner in which he notated the black people's talk. It was, for example, tiresome and unnecessary that 'I shan't promise' should be written 'Ah cyan pramas'. It is, however, the book in which his brilliant touches go furthest towards being bound together into a consistent whole.

He remains a butterfly, but now, instead of continually disappearing over the garden-wall, he makes his way seriously and punctually from flower to flower. And his rhythm becomes more and more masterly. Consider this paragraph (Charlie Mouth has become separated from his family and is lost in the crowd):

> Missionaries with freckled hands and hairy, care-worn faces, followed by pale girls wielding tambourines of the Army of the Soul, foppish nigger bucks in panamas and palm-beach suits so cocky, Chinamen with osier-baskets, their nostalgic eyes aswoon, heavily straw-hatted nuns trailing their dust-coloured rags, and suddenly, oh, could it be?—but there was no mistaking that golden waddle: 'Mamma!'

Concerning the Eccentricities of Cardinal Pirelli came out in 1926, a few months after Firbank's death. It is phrased more brilliantly than ever; for example (of the Cardinal who, on his excursions, disguised himself as a matron), 'disliking to forgo altogether the militant bravoura of a skirt'. This sketch, too, is charming:

> There was to be . . . a Maiden Mass. With his family all about him, the celebrant, a youth of the People, looking childishly happy in his first broidered cape, had bent, more than once, his good-natured head to allow some small brothers and sisters to inspect his tonsure.

There are absurdities such as the young nun 'with a face like some strange white rock, who was inclined to give herself married airs, since she had been debauched, one otiose noon, by a demon'. The choir-boy who 'was fingering a score of music. He had been taking lead in a mass of Palestrina, and had the vaguely distraught air of a kitten that has seen visions'. Or, for sinister resonance, this paragraph: 'A nephew of the Dean of the Sacred College, it was rumoured that he was addicted, in his "home" above Frascati, to the last excesses of the pre-Adamite Sultans.' Individual phrases: 'Sheltered spas by glittering seas', 'a light slithery bell like a housemaid in hysterics'. But, as a whole, the book does not reach the level of its two predecessors.

This essay is frankly a eulogy. It has been my business to point out the merits of Firbank's work. To its defects—above all to its frequent incoherence and lack of construction—I am not blind. Those who are fortunate enough to have discovered contemporary books that are good from cover to cover will not concern themselves with an author whose merit lies in incomplete technical experiments and erratic strokes of wit. If, however, there exists anyone who like myself cannot discover in most modern fiction from first to last line any connection at all with literature, he will feel for Firbank's thin streak of genius an enthusiasm that admirers of our 'great' contemporary novelists will find hard to understand.

EVELYN WAUGH

Ronald Firbank

It is no longer necessary to be even mildly defiant in one's appreciation of Ronald Firbank. There is, it is true, small probability of his ever achieving very wide recognition, and even among critics of culture and intelligence there will, no doubt, always be many to whom his work will remain essentially repugnant, but already in the short time which has elapsed since his death, his fame has become appreciably stabilised so that condemnation of him implies not merely a lack of interest in what may or may not have been the amiable eccentricities of a rich young man, but also the distaste for a wide and vigorous tendency in modern fiction.

Those who delight in literary genealogy will find his ancestry somewhat obscure. He owes something to *Under the Hill* and Baron Corvo, but the more attentively he is studied, the more superficial does the debt appear. His progeny is unmistakeably apparent. In quite diverse ways Mr Osbert Sitwell, Mr Carl Van Vechten, Mr Harold Acton, Mr William Gerhardi and Mr Ernest Hemingway are developing the technical discoveries upon which Ronald Firbank so negligently stumbled.

These technical peculiarities are late in appearance in Firbank's work and are the result of an almost incommunicable sense of humour attempting to achieve means of expression. His early books are open to the charge, so indefatigably launched against them, of obscurity and silliness. When he had in *The Flower Beneath the Foot, Prancing Nigger* and *Cardinal Pirelli* fully developed his technical method the obscurity gives way to radiant lucidity and most of the silliness is discovered to be, when properly expressed, exquisitely significant. Some silliness, a certain ineradicable fatuity, seems to have been inherent in him. His introduction of his own name in *The Flower Beneath the Foot* and *Prancing Nigger* is intolerable *vieux jeu*; perhaps Firbank's sense of humour had reached a degree of sophistication when it

---

First published in *Life & Letters*, July 1929. Reprinted by permission of the author's executors.

could turn on itself and find the best fun of all in the doubly banal; if so it was a development where few will be able to follow him. His coy naughtiness about birches and pretty boys will bore most people with its repetition. He exhibits at times a certain intemperance in portraiture, indulging too gluttonously an appetite other novelists, even his most zealous admirers, struggle to repress. These defects, and perhaps some others, may be granted to his detractors, but when everything has been said which can intelligently be brought against him there remains a figure of essential artistic integrity and importance.

It is the peculiar temper of Firbank's humour which divides him from the nineties. His raw material, allowing for the inevitable changes of fashion, is almost identical with Oscar Wilde's—the lives of rich, slightly decadent people seen against a background of traditional culture, grand opera, the picture galleries, and the Court; but Wilde was at heart radically sentimental. His wit is ornamental; Firbank's is structural. Wilde is rococo; Firbank is baroque. It is very rarely that Firbank 'makes a joke'. In *The Princess Zoubaroff* there is the much-quoted introduction:

NADINE: My husband.
BLANCHE [genially]: I think we've slept together once?
ADRIAN: I don't remember.
BLANCHE: At the opera. During *Bérénice.*

Even here the real wit is not in the pun, but in Adrian's 'I don't remember'; one of those suddenly illuminated fragments of the commonplace of which Firbank's novels are full and which, Mr Gerhardi has shown, are not inimitable. Any writer with a more or less dexterous literary sense can evolve 'jokes' without the least exercise of his sense of humour. In his later work the only verbal jokes are the proper names, Mrs Mouth, Lady Something, Mr Limpness, etc. The humour is no longer a mosaic of extricable little cubes of wit. It cannot be repeated from mouth to mouth prefaced by any 'Have-you-heard-this-one?'

Floor of copper, floor of gold. . . . Beyond the custom-house door, ajar, the street at sunrise seemed aflame.
'Have you nothing, young man, to declare?'
'. . . Butterflies!'
'Exempt of duty. Pass.'

> Floor of silver, floor of pearl....
>
> Trailing a muslin net, and laughing for happiness, Charlie Mouth marched into the town.
>
> Oh, Cuna-Cuna! Little city of Lies and Peril! How many careless young nigger boys have gone thus to seal their doom!

But by its nature Firbank's humour defies quotation. Perhaps it is a shade nearer to the abiding and inscrutable wit of the Chinese. It is there to be enjoyed by those who have a taste for it, but it is too individual and intangible to become a literary influence. The importance of Firbank, which justifies the writing of a critical essay about him, lies in his literary method. He is the first quite modern writer to solve for himself, quite unobtrusively and probably more or less unconsciously, the aesthetic problem of representation in fiction; to achieve, that is to say, a new, balanced interrelation of subject and form. Nineteenth-century novelists achieved a balance only by complete submission to the idea of the succession of events in an arbitrarily limited period of time. Just as in painting until the last generation the aesthetically significant activity of the artist had always to be occasioned by anecdote and representation, so the novelist was fettered by the chain of cause and effect. Almost all the important novels of this century have been experiments in making an art form out of this raw material of narration. It is a problem capable of many solutions, of which Firbank discovered one that was peculiarly appropriate and delicate.

His later novels are almost wholly devoid of any attributions of cause to effect; there is the barest minimum of direct description; his compositions are built up, intricately and with a balanced alternation of the wildest extravagance and the most austere economy, with conversational *nuances*. They may be compared to cinema films in which the relation of caption and photograph is directly reversed; occasionally a brief, visual image flashes out to illumine and explain the flickering succession of spoken words.

> One sunny May Day morning, full of unrest, Lady Parvula de Panzoust left the Hotel for a turn on the promenade. It was a morning of pure delight. Great clouds, breaking into dream, swept slowly across the sky, rolling down from the uplands behind Hare Hatch House, above

whose crumbling pleasances one single sable streak, in the guise of a coal black Negress, prognosticated rain.

'Life would be perfect,' she mused. . . .

And the dialogue begins anew.

But nothing could be further from Firbank's achievement than the 'novel of conversation'. In his dialogue there is no exchange of opinion. His art is purely selective. From the fashionable chatter of his period, vapid and interminable, he has plucked, like tiny brilliant feathers from the breast of a bird, the particles of his design.

'I would give all my soul to him, Rara . . . my chances of heaven!'

'Your chances, Olga——', Mademoiselle de Nazianzi murmured, avoiding some bird-droppings with her skirt.

'How I envy *the men*, Rara, in his platoon!'

'Take away his uniform Olga, and what does he become?'

'Ah, *what*——'

The talk goes on, delicate, chic, exquisitely humorous, and seemingly without point or plan. Then, quite gradually, the reader is aware that a casual reference on one page links up with some particular inflexion of phrase on another until there emerges a plot; usually a plot so outrageous that he distrusts his own inferences. The case of the Ritz Hotel *v.* Lady Something in *The Flower Beneath the Foot* is typical of the Firbank method. The King at a dinner-party employs the expression:

'I could not be more astonished if you told me there were fleas at the Ritz', a part of which assertion Lady Something, who was blandly listening, imperfectly chanced to hear.

'Who would credit it. . .! It's almost *too* appalling. . . . Fleas have been found at the Ritz.'

Nothing more is said for forty pages, and then:

'Had I known, Lady Something, I was going to be ill, I would have gone to the Ritz!' the Hon 'Eddy' gasped.

'And you'd have been bitten all over,' Lady Something replied.

Twenty pages pass and then an 'eloquent and moderately victorious young barrister' is mentioned as 'engaged in the approaching suit with the Ritz.' A few pages further on it is casually observed that the Ritz is empty save for one guest.

In the same way in *Cardinal Pirelli* the scandal of the Cardinal's unorthodox baptism of the Duchess's pet dog is gradually built up. The actual baptism is described; then it is approached circumspectly from another angle, touched and left alone. There is a long scene in the Vatican, apparently without relation to the rest of the story; at the end the Cardinal's name is mentioned; another touch and then retreat. There is a social climber who wants *her* dog to be baptised. Suddenly the Cardinal is in disgrace.

In this way Firbank achieved a new art form primarily as a vehicle for bringing coherence to his own elusive humour. But in doing this he solved the problem which most vexes the novelist of the present time. Other solutions are offered of the same problem, but in them the author has been forced into a subjective attitude to his material; Firbank remained objective and emphasised the fact which his contemporaries were neglecting that the novel should be directed for entertainment. This is the debt which the present generation owes to him.

E. M. FORSTER

Ronald Firbank

To break a butterfly, or even a beetle, upon a wheel is a delicate task. Lovers of nature disapprove. Moreover the victim is apt to reappear each time the wheel revolves, still alive, and with a reproachful expression upon its squashed face to address its tormentor in some such words as the following: 'Critic! What do you? Neither my pleasure nor your knowledge has been increased. I was flying or crawling, and that is all that there was to be learnt about me. Impossible to anatomise me and find what breeds about my heart. Dissect the higher animals if you like, such as the frog, the cow, or the goose—no doubt they are full of helpful secrets. By all means write articles on George Eliot. Review from every point of view Lord Morley of Borley's autobiography. Estimate Addison. But leave me in peace. I only exist in my surroundings, and become meaningless as soon as you stretch me on this rack.'

The insect plaint is unanswerable, and if critics had not their living to get they would seldom handle any literary fantasy. It makes them look so foolish. Their state of mind is the exact antithesis of that of the author whom they propose to interpret. With quiet eyes and cool fingers they pass from point to point, they define fantasy as 'the unserious treatment of the unusual'—an impeccable definition, the only objection to it being that it defines. A gulf between the critical and creative states exists in all cases, but in the case of a fantastical creation it is so wide as to be grotesque. And in saying a few words about our butterflies and beetles we must not be unmindful of the remarks which, if they felt it worth while, they might pass upon us.

Butterflies and beetles are not always identical, and are sometimes dragon-flies, etc., too. For instance, in the paragraph above, when the phrase 'Lord Morley of Borley' slipped in, a beetle was speaking. No butterfly would probe so far. And when a Mrs Shamefoot says, in one of Ronald Firbank's novels, 'The world is

Dated 1929. From E. M. Forster: *Abinger Harvest* (1934). Reprinted by permission of Edward Arnold (Publishers) Ltd.

disgracefuly managed, one hardly knows to whom to complain', she, again, is a beetle. But when she says, 'I adore the end of summer, when a new haystack appears on every hill', she has hovered from wittiness to charm. And: 'Nearer, hither and thither, appeared a few sleepy spires of churches, too sensible to compete with the Cathedral, but possibly more personal, like the minor characters in repertoire that support the star'—well here we get both, the coloured glint, the naughty tweak. And when a gentleman who is married to a fox dreams all night of public schools for the children, and cannot think why Eton will not quite do, nor Harrow, nor Winchester, nor even Rugby, and then wakes up and thinks 'Ah! a private tutor is the solution', yet still feels dissatisfied, and finally remembers, and bursts into tears—here again we get something different, something downy and moth-like brushing the cheek, something at once countrified and sophisticated which pervades all the work of another fantast, Mr David Garnett. It is indeed impossible to decide where one insect stops and another starts; they are metamorphosed behind a rafter or in full flight, or in the calyx of a single flower, even on the very wheel of criticism, and there is only one quality that they all share in common: the absence of a soul.

With the soul we reach solid ground. As soon as it enters literature, whether in full radiance or behind a cloud, two great side-scenes accompany it, the mountains of Right and Wrong, and we get a complete change of *décor*, adapted for writers who likewise treat the unusual, but who treat it mystically or humanistically. Butterflies and beetles may survive the soul's arrival, but they serve another purpose: they bear some relationship to Salvation. Think of all they go through in *Water Babies* or Sir James Barrie! Even the Three Mulla Mulgars are not completely on their own. Whereas in the creatures considered today there is nothing to be saved or damned, their modish ecclesiasticism and rural magic bears no relation to philosophic truth, the miracles that transform them, the earthquakes that shatter, have no deeper implication than a conjuring trick. As soon as we realise that we cannot save them we shall enjoy them. But it is not easy for an Anglo-Saxon to realise so little. He requires a book to be serious unless it is comic, and when it is neither is apt to ring for the police.

In his masterly introduction to Firbank's collected works [pp. 166–74] Arthur Waley put us on the proper track. He remarked of Firbank that he 'seems as though endowed with a kind of inverted X-ray, which enabled him, not to penetrate the unseen, but, on the contrary, continually to hover, as it were, an inch or two above the surface of things'. The remark applies to this literature generally which omits not merely the soul but many material actualities, and, if taken in large quantities, is unsatisfying. The writer who hovers two inches off everything may fascinate for a time, but finally he gives one the fidgets, and the reader will be both kind and wise to imitate him, and to repair to some other book at the first hint of boredom. So, like a swarm of summer insects, feeling perfectly free and disclaiming any vested interests in the soul, let us continue to flit. . . .

Ronald Firbank died a few years ago, still young. But there is nothing up-to-date in him. He is *fin de siècle*, as it used to be called; he belongs to the nineties and the *Yellow Book*; his mind inherits the furniture and his prose the cadences of Aubrey Beardsley's *Under the Hill.* To the historian he is an interesting example of literary conservatism; to his fellow insects a radiance and a joy. Is he affected? Yes, always. Is he self-conscious? No; he wants to mop and mow, and put on birettas and stays, and he does it as naturally as healthy Englishmen light their pipes. Is he himself healthy? Perish the thought! Is he passionate, compassionate, dispassionate? Next question! Is he intelligent? Not particularly, if we compare him with another writer whom he occasionally resembles—Max. Has he genius? Yes, in his flit-about fashion he has, but genius is a critic's word, and one insect should not fasten it wantonly upon another. What charms us in him is his taste, his choice of words, the rhythm both of his narrative and of his conversations, his wit, and—in his later work—an opulence as of gathered fruit and enamelled skies. His very monsignorishness is acceptable. It is *chic*, it is *risqué*, to titter in sacristies and peep through grilles at ecclesiastical Thesmophoriazusae, and if he becomes petulant, and lets a convent or a pipkin crash, it does not signify, for likely enough we have thrown down the book ourselves a page before. Yes, he has genius, for we are certain to take up the book again, and to come across Reggie, whose voice was rather like cheap scent, or Cardinal Pirelli baptising a dog, or Miss Sinquier, daughter to a dean, who gave up all for the drama, and was killed by a mousetrap, or Mrs Cresswell, who would have been canonised but for her unfortunate mot: 'If we are all a part of God, then God must, indeed, be horrible', or Princess Elsie of England, or St. Laura de Nazianzi her rival, or the Mouth family leaving their

Negro nakedness for the lures of Cuna-Cuna, or a hundred other sentences or people (the two classes are not separable) which have been evoked by his gaiety and exoticism. It is tempting to conclude the catalogue with the words 'He was a perfect artist'; tempting but unwise, for the words have something of the heavenly extinguisher about them, and we may discover that after all he was a glow-worm, and that now we cannot see him any more.

Vainglory is a good example of his earlier manner, and *Prancing Nigger* (first called *Sorrow in Sunlight*) of his later. *Vainglory* is all tweaks and skips. It professes to describe the attempts of Mrs Shamefoot to insert herself into Ashringford Cathedral in the form of a stained-glass window. Bishop Pantry is reluctant. Meanwhile she runs a florist's shop; indeed, *Meanwhile* would do admirably as a sub-title for the book. On we read, confusing the characters with the incidents and neglecting the outcome, but tickled by the images and the turns of the talk. It is frivolous stuff, and how rare, how precious is frivolity! How few writers can prostitute all their powers! They are always implying 'I am capable of higher things'. Firbank is completely absorbed in his own nonsense; he has nothing to hide, he is not showing off, he is not (or is very seldom) polemical. When he attempts satire, or wistfulness (as in *Santal*), he falls at once, he was incapable of totting up life. But there are no attempts in *Vainglory*, it is an untainted series of absurdities, and most delightful although Mrs Shamefoot's efforts have not even a comic coherency.

It is strange that such a writer should have developed, but *Prancing Nigger* offers quite another pair of wings. The butterfly has come out, and has demanded, with such severity as it can master, a temperature and even a cage. The temperature is tropical; we are on an exquisite island which travesties Haiti. The cage is the fortunes of the Mouth family; we are bounded by them, and it is the first time we have been bounded by anything, we are approaching the semblance of a novel. Is colour, after a certain point, only to be increased by a judicious mixture of human interest? Perhaps the question presented itself to him. Certainly one comes nearer to 'minding' about Edna, Miami and Charlie than about any of his previous characters—Charlie, the glorified symbol of the writer himself, the happy black boy, passing through the customs at Cuna-Cuna with a butterfly net and nothing to declare.

The English novel, to Mr Waley's distress, is at present cluttered up with realistic lumber, and he draws a comparison between it and English painting. Fiction is mostly 'still in the Chantrey Bequest stage', and Firbank was an Impressionist, who broke away from academic naturalism by the method of selection and choice. Another reaction besides the Impressionistic is possible, namely the pre-Raphaelite, where the writer or painter throws himself into a state of mind more simple than his own, and thus raises his work from the anecdote to the lyrical. This, Mr Waley points out, is the reaction of Mr David Garnett, who is deliberately naïve; and has found in fantasy a serviceable ally rather than a fairy queen. Unlike Firbank, he wants to do something, he wants to write a story, and we are here in the presence of a much more sophisticated mind, a sophistication all the greater because it is so carefully controlled, and always kept out of doors. His art is a hybrid. It blends in a new relationship the stocks of fantasy and common sense. It is a successful experiment—unlike the art of Firbank, which contains no experiments at all. All that the two share in common is an omission: they do not introduce the soul nor its attendant scenery of Right and Wrong, they are fundamentally unserious. This disconcerts the Anglo-Saxon reader, who approves of playfulness, but likes it to have a holiday air. In the absence of regular office hours 'to sport would be as tedious as to work', says Prince Henry the prig, and the butterflies and their kindred neither contradict him nor agree—they merely go away, and allow him to ruin Falstaff and save England. Play is their business. If for an instant they swerve from it they are swept into the nets of allegory. They may or may not possess will-power, may or may not desire to hover over a certain hedge, but the will is a trifle in the realm of the lower air which they inhabit and invite us to share.

ERNEST JONES

Introduction to Three Novels

Ronald Firbank is a better and a more serious writer than it has ever been fashionable to suppose. The tiresome adulation of the claque which adores his *fin-de-siècle* wickedness and the grim incomprehension of the excessively serious have always obscured his real merits. The Firbank legend, for which Firbank himself was largely responsible, was constructed so carefully that even a quarter of a century after his death it is difficult to disentangle the artist from the delicate posturer who tried so hard—and with indifferent success—to astonish the bourgeoisie. Between 1915 and 1926, when his books were being published, the English novel seemed set for ever in the pattern of realism and a modified naturalism. Firbank's writing lacked the obvious purposefulness and the impressive documentation which Wells, Galsworthy, Bennett and Moore were bringing to the composition of seemingly indestructible fiction. If Forster, Conrad and Lawrence deviated from this pattern in ways unpopular or disturbing, still they were serious as Firbank, to judge by the surface of his writing, was not. Today, when the formulas of realism-cum-naturalism which once seemed so inexhaustibly fruitful produce only apples of Sodom, Firbank is a green bay tree. His rococo palaces turn out to have been more solidly constructed than the sedate family mansions of the Georgians and their lower middle-class water-closets. The tradition of the contemporary novel now closest to our sensibility is that established by Joyce and Virginia Woolf. To this tradition, in his own eccentric fashion, Firbank belongs.

His style, his settings, and the themes which recur in his work can be accounted for, so far as such accounting is ever possible, by his background. Sociologically he belongs to the history of sensitive young men who escape from the materialism which has brought money into the family straight into the materialism of the

---

First printed as Introduction to Duckworth's re-issue of Firbank's *Three Novels* in 1950. The author is a New York literary critic, not the famous psychoanalyst.

aesthete and the social snob. It is a flight likely to end in dilettantism, or, worse, in alcoholism and nervous disorders. Firbank encountered these catastrophes and, as an artist, survived them. Every printed story about him, whether it appears in I. K. Fletcher's memoir, or in the recollections of Sir Osbert Sitwell or Vyvyan Holland or Lord Berners—all sympathetic observers—is like every other story, testimony of his charm, his affectation, and his private distress. But he did not succumb to the luxury, the ennui and the neuroses which beset him.

His enterprising and illiterate North of England grandfather had made a fortune in contracting; his father married into the gentry, was created a knight, and lost money; the son, spoiled by a mother whom he idolised, lived variously in the pre-1914 society of the Café Royal, in seclusion, during the war, at Oxford, and abroad. Until the last ten years of his life, when, for all his flittings-about, he settled himself earnestly to becoming a writer, he was engaged in a seemingly sterile pursuit of the amusing and the beautiful. His entire career recalls that of Proust: the spoiled mother's darling, the carefully-ordered *décor* which he carried about on his travels, the inflexible pursuit of rarefied pleasures, the early dabblings in authorship (Firbank published in 1905, when he was only nineteen, a mediocre little pamphlet). And then there is the mature work, impossible but for the kind of existence he had led, of his last decade. Out of sensuality, idleness, dissipation and buffoonery he created exquisite art.

Once he had really started to work, his books appeared in rapid succession: *Vainglory* (1915), *Inclinations* (1916), *Caprice* (1917), *Valmouth* (1918), *The Princess Zoubaroff* (1920), *Santal* (1921), *The Flower Beneath the Foot* (1923), *Prancing Nigger* (1924), *Concerning the Eccentricities of Cardinal Pirelli* (1926). The *Artificial Princess*, written shortly before 1915, was published posthumously in 1934.

The settings of the novels record his flight from the world of his father and grandfather into the refinements of a new-foundland—a Haiti in which the climate does not oppress, a glamorous Spain, 'some imaginary Vienna' (his own term), populated by beautiful aristocrats upon whom, like Pater's Mona Lisa, all the ends of the world are come. Their weariness is part of their fascination. They all suffer from what, in the eighteenth century, the French designated as the specific English malady—ennui. Firbank is the first novelist to celebrate that fragmented, corrupt and anarchic milieu known today as café society. He adored the aristocracy, but the aristocracy he created is *parvenu.* It has no deeply-established roots in land or money or manners, but resembles that aristocracy of the circus described by Djuna Barnes in *Nightwood.* Its chief prerogative is eccentric behaviour; it is dominated by women, and they, in turn, are dominated by chic.

In transforming his bedazzlement into the permanence of fiction Firbank sometimes succeeded in spite of himself. He occasionally affected a fine carelessness about art. Often his prose is delightfully easy, but sometimes it sounds as if it were meant to be easy. The history of ennui among the English is the history of a fashionable pose which experience of the world is constantly transforming into the most painful reality. The ennui of *Vainglory* and *Inclinations* is, occasionally, simply fashionable; that of the later novels, particularly of *The Flower Beneath the Foot*, is realised artistically. Sex, for Firbank, was always a matter for comedy; but just as in life his infantilism betrayed him into preposterous affectation, in his novels the comedy of sex is too frequently marred by an almost obsessional bravado and schoolboy snickering. The world of his fiction, with its international élite and its splendid palaces, is a Nirvana in which homosexuals are the ultimate chic, and in which, as in *Le Temps Retrouvré*, almost everyone turns out to be at least bi-sexual. Even in his own time he was old-fashioned in his toyings with the ceremonial of Rome, his aesthetic interest in evil, 'if for no other purpose, to add colour to life', and a dandyism which would have revolted Baudelaire.

But—and this fact saved him always—he was no more self-deceived or diverted, as an artist, by his predilections than he was by the world he chose to create. There is always a tough core of common sense to his dallyings with the trivial; the wit flicks even those enchanting and world-weary figures he most loves; he merely found the substance of his art in the fantastic behaviour of the inhabitants of a fantastic milieu. If, in *Caprice*, he shares some of his heroine's excitement over the London scene to which she has fled from the cathedral close, he can also see its pretensions:

> 'And how does Mrs Smee?'
> 'So-so.'
> 'One never sees her now.'

> 'There she sits all day, reading Russian novels. Talk of gloom!'
>
> 'Really?'
>
> 'Oh, it is!'
>
> 'Well . . . I'm fond of thoughtful, theosophical reading, too, Mr Smee,' Mrs Sixsmith said. 'Madame Blavatsky and Mrs Annie Besant are both favourites with me.'

Or, if, like several of his heroines, he was fascinated with Rome, a sense of the incongruous was always calling him back to a point from which such fascination appeared slightly absurd. A conversation during a thunderstorm in *Valmouth* illustrates this gambit perfectly—a compound of religious trappings, artistic arrangement, and the masking of real concern in a giggle:

> 'Let us go,' Mrs Thoroughfare said in a slightly unsteady voice, 'shall we both, and confess?'
>
> 'Confess!'
>
> 'Father's in Nuestra now.'
>
> 'My dear, in my opinion, the lightning's so much more ghastly through the stained-glass windows!'

For all the occasional snickering, the deflating process is also apparent in his treatment of homosexuality. With the exception of Proust, Firbank is the one serious novelist of the twentieth century, overtly concerned with homosexuality, who avoids the bathos which mars even *Les Faux-Monnayeurs*. To him it is simply one more subject for comedy. Aside from the extensive account of the passion of Miss Geraldine O'Brookomore for Miss Mabel Collins in *Inclinations*, it appears chiefly in the form of omnipresent hints and jokes. In life he feared and disliked women, his mother excepted; in his fiction his entirely feminine sensibility concerned itself far more with women than with men. He is perfectly at home with their talk, their affairs, their clothes. Except for Cardinal Pirelli, half man, half woman, his heroes are perfunctorily drawn or deliberately muted. They are always beautiful, ruthless in the pursuit of pleasure, irresponsible and perverse. Because he feels more deeply about them, he never writes about men as freely as he writes about women.

He was afraid of feeling, a fear which seriously limited the range of his fiction, but which is directly responsible for his delightful ironies and flippancies. 'His work,' says a character in *Vainglory*, describing a novelist clearly meant to be Firbank, 'calls to mind a frieze with figures of varying heights trotting all the same way. If one should by chance turn about it's usually merely to stare or to sneer or to make a grimace. Only occasionally his figures care to beckon. And they seldom really touch'. They do not 'touch' as does the passion which sometimes breaks so wonderfully through the comic mask in Molière or even in Congreve. Sex is amusing, but passion is at once a stimulant and a drug, always fatal to the addict. Those who reveal it are rejected, like Thetis Tooke in *Valmouth* or Laura in *The Flower Beneath the Foot*. Thetis, who is all feeling, becomes comic as she prepares to drown herself:

> 'I shall remove my hat, I think,' she cogitated. 'It would be a sin indeed to spoil such expensive plumes. . . . It's not perhaps a headpiece that would become every one;—and I can't say I'm sorry!'

The famous twentieth chapter of *Inclinations*, in which Miss O'Brookomore laments the defection of the beloved, is comic and malicious:

> 'Mabel! Mabel! Mabel! Mabel!
> Mabel! Mabel! Mabel! Mabel!'

And there is real venom in the picture, in *Valmouth*, of the ageing Lady Parvula de Panzoust in impassioned pursuit of the reluctant dairyman.

Occasionally in the later novels feeling is not resolved in comedy. Unlike most of his contemporaries, Firbank did not have any explicit messages. Life is sad, human beings suffer, the mask always conceals anguish. These are the conditions of life even in his luxurious world. There is nothing funny about Laura's anguish when she is forsaken by Yousef, or about the unhappiness of Miami Mouth. For all the scandal of his end, there is even a triumphant, if perverse, moral grandeur in the death of Cardinal Pirelli:

> Now that the ache of life, with its fevers, passions, doubts, its routine, vulgarity, and boredom, was over, his serene,

> unclouded face was a marvelment to behold. Very great distinction and sweetness was visible there, together with much nobility, and love, all magnified and commingled.

Firbank's prose mirrors clearly the society with which he was preoccupied, his distrust of feeling, and the ironic habit of mind which replaced feeling. It has some obvious literary origins. As a young man he had read extensively in Gautier, Verlaine and Huysmans, in Pater and in Wilde. I. K. Fletcher says that his first published piece, *Odette D'Antrevernes*, was influenced by his readings in Maeterlinck; in content it is a pastiche from Francis Jammes. He was 'excessively well-read', says Sir Osbert Sitwell, in the eighteenth-century memoirs of every European country. But any account of the influences to which he so rapturously gave himself up must shift to the visual arts; there are, all through his novels, scenes which might be descriptions of Beardsley drawings or of the fragile beauties of Conder fans; there are numerous direct references to Italian painting. Here is Miss Compostella in *Vainglory*:

> A lady whose face looked worn and withered through love, wearing a black gauze gown, looped like a figure from the Primavera, made her way mistily into the room.

Again:

> ... Miss Compostella swept by them, in some jewelled hades of her own.

His careful selection and ordering of detail, his reliance on evocation and juxtaposition, are reminiscent of the methods of the Impressionists. Mrs Hurstpierpont's fête for the centenarians of Valmouth is described in such terms and recreates wonderfully that crowded, complex scene:

> There uprose a jargon of voices:
>
> 'Heroin.'
>
> 'Adorable simplicity.'
>
> 'What could anyone find to admire in such a shelving profile?'
>
> 'We reckon a duck here of two or three and twenty not so old. And a spring chicken *anything to fourteen*.'

'My husband had no amorous energy whatsoever; which just suited me, of course.'

'I suppose when there's no more room for another crow's-foot, one attains a sort of peace?'

'I once said to Doctor Fothergill, a clergyman of Oxford and a great friend of mine, "Doctor," I said, "oh, if only you could see my——" '

'*Elle était jolie! Mais jolie! . . . C'était une si belle brune . . .!*'

'Cruelly lonely.'

'Leery. . . .'

'Calumny.'

'People look like pearls, dear, beneath your wonderful trees.'

This technique has been so widely imitated by way of Joyce and Virginia Woolf and not of Firbank, who appears to have developed it independently—that it is difficult to remember how new it was in 1918.

But subject matter was even more important in shaping Firbank's prose than borrowings or influences. The world of his fiction is at once a realisation of his private dream world and a re-creation of the real, if tiny world of pre-1914 English and continental chic. Dream and reality fuse in a milieu entirely material. The trappings of circumstance, fascinating in themselves, are indices to the most complex states of the soul. Landscape, architecture, clothes—these have never quite existed; they are the product of lifelong fantasy. Conduct and conversation are real, even if they belong to the limited world of his own society. The language of his characters is private, often that of aristocrats in luxurious exile who no longer trouble much to communicate with the outer world, but who can rely on one another (and, by inference, on the reader) for complete comprehension. But it is authentic speech. (Read Firbank aloud to comprehend fully the subtlety of his dialogue.) Their conduct may be bizarre, yet too much has been made of their artificiality. They stem in great part from the rich tradition of British eccentricity, which was at its height—since it could then best be financially afforded—in the world in which Firbank lived as a young man. A glance at the sober reporting of Sir Osbert Sitwell's memoirs should dissipate any notion that their goings-on are merely extravagant invention.

The pamphlet of 1905 which contains *Odette d'Antrevernes* and *A Study in Temperament* is of interest today only because in it may be discerned, in a state of suspension, the elements out of which Firbank constructed his novels. The first piece, a fairy tale, has an evanescent lavender-pink background composed of a dim forest, a misty river, and a romantic chateau. In the foreground are a cloyingly sweet girl-child and a sentimental concern with the Virgin. *A Study in Temperament*, which sketches an attempted seduction in the most elegant London society, is all interior decoration and faded smartness. A Pateresque madonna in whose 'wearied eyelids' are gathered 'the sins and sorrows of the whole world' adorns the drawing-room of the heroine. The lover talks an imitation of a minor wit in a Wilde comedy; yet there is already a hint of something new in his speech, something which is to become the characteristic Firbank conversational tone, witty, private, entirely cognisant of the absurdities of which the speaker himself is a part. He wants to elope: '. . . let us be brave —and—and defy the evening papers.'

Ten years later, in *The Artificial Princess*, the weariness of the madonna, the wit of the lover and the pastelle landscape have been fused. Odd juxtapositions, references to the more or less *recherché* in literature and painting, and to the material chic have become the devices of this prose:

> To compose herself she thought of Carpaccio's St. Ursula in Venice, a woman without a trace of expression, with the veiled, crêpe-de-chine look of a Sphinx.

The 'crêpe-de-chine look' is out of the private sensibility, a private witticism, typical of the fashionable talk of a tiny set, and formulating the kind of perception on which Firbank came more and more to depend. It is also responsible for much of one's pleasure in reading him, for the sense of belonging, momentarily, to the charmed circle and of sharing the intimate joke. In *Valmouth* this joke has suffused the landscape:

> Through a belt of osier and alder Valmouth, with its ancient bridge and great stone church, that from the open country had the scheming look of an ex-cathedral, showed a few lit lamps.

In a world in which the artifact is of central importance, landscape improves as it imitates art. A panorama from palace windows becomes a 'deceptive expanse':

> So much, contained on so little, suggested a landscape painted delicately upon a porcelain cup or saucer, or upon the silken panel of a fan.

Hills are 'quiet, modest hills, a model of restraint'. From *The Artificial Princess* to *The Eccentricities of Cardinal Pirelli* there was no radical change in Firbank's prose, although he modified and refined it as the occasional posturings of his early novels gave way to a real ennui, to a sharper humour, and to a feeling, expressed on occasion in elegiac terms, of the sadness and mortality of all things human.

It is idle to seek conventionally-ordered narrative in writing so absolutely dependent on the momentary awareness of the beautiful, the comic, of the poignant—the Firbank counterpart of the Joycean *epiphany*. He habitually collected on cards those sentences which, in the novels, illuminate so completely an individual attitude or the mores of group, just as they occurred to him, or as, overheard, they amused him. Later he fitted them into a careful mosaic. His novels progress in a series of animated tableaux. It is failure of his that the reader must fill up the gaps between the scenes; such a demand, indeed, has, since his time, become part of the economy of fiction. Plot or movement in themselves did not interest him—his play, *The Princess Zoubaroff*, is dismal reading—although it is possible to outline the actions of his books. They burlesque themes popular in nineteenth-century fiction. *Valmouth* is in part a parody of the Hardy and post-Hardy novel of rural life. In *Caprice*, Miss Sarah Sinquier, bored with life in a cathedral town, absconds with the family silver to the London stage and the Café Royal, the Firbank variation on the flight from the provinces. In *Prancing Nigger* a Negro family on some improbable tropic isle migrates to the local capital so that mother and the girls can get into society. Here, to some extent in *Valmouth*, and in *Santal*, the brief and unsuccessful Arabian tale which bored him in the writing 'unutterably', Firbank achieved comedy by imposing English lower middle class values on a half-civilised society. The artificial princess imagines herself a Salome to a glamorous local evangelist, a *reductio ad absurdum* of all the highborn and imaginative maidens of romantic fiction. The heroines of *Valmouth*, *The Flower Beneath the Foot*, and *Prancing Nigger* take the veil, nourishing hopeless passions.

Nor was Firbank's interest in character that of most artistically successful novelists. For him the exterior always indicates an inner state which the imaginative reader must realise for himself. Interior monologues are frequent in his novels, but they are filled always with aesthetic judgements and self-deflating ironies which are contrived to evade the omnipresent anguish of the soul—an evasion endemic to a society devoted to the pursuit of fashion and the preservation of impeccable surfaces. The human countenance, even, is depicted rarely except as a mask of fashionable beauty, weary, passion-ridden, depraved. These novels are thronged with brilliant, entirely material grotesques.

Sometimes the Firbank dialectic spiritualises the material, although it usually materialises the spiritual, processes most clearly illustrated in the closing and opening scenes of *Concerning the Eccentricities of Cardinal Pirelli*: the spiritually triumphant death of the corrupt priest and the baptism of the Duquesa DunEden's police dog. Irony, which must never approach the obvious, is the universal solvent, dissolving, itself, on occasion, into half-articulated phrases. Sir Osbert Sitwell has described how, while writing, Firbank would be so overcome with laughter at the absurdity of the situation he had created that he would have to abandon work for the day. Given his double view, the enchantment and disenchantment out of which he wrote, his humour, at its best, simultaneously affirms and denies. Consider the yearnings after the finer things of life of Mrs Ahmadou Mouth, a jungle matron. 'Lordey Lord; what is it den you want?' her husband queries. 'I want a Villa with a water-closet——' Flinging wiles to the winds, it was a cry from the heart.

If the double view is responsible for many of Firbank's virtues as a novelist, it is also the reason why, for all his art, he is a minor figure in the history of English fiction. His writing is often explicitly concerned with Evil, but his sense of Evil is imperfect. It is really naughtiness that he portrays, just as those sinister figures in Beardsley drawings turn out on close examination to be merely naughty and perverse. What is Evil in the world he has created? Any behaviour, especially any sexual behaviour, which can be labelled Fun. Overtly he resolves in Catholic terms what he considers Evil; the real resolution is in terms of the moral atmosphere of the middle class into which he was born. Whenever the lovely ladies of his court circles, the Baroness Rudlieb or the Countess of Tolga, for example, embark on adventure they enjoy a sense of transgression against conventional mores. Their predestined end, associated, however, with none of the emotions usually attendant on conversion, is Rome. Certainly there are echoes here of the conduct of those great ladies of the eighteenth-century memoirs he knew so well and of those heroines of Balzac who forsake their paramours for convents. But the radical attitude is middle class watered-down Puritanism: material pleasure must be paid for with material chastisement. The last scene of *Prancing Nigger* shows this limitation clearly. The suffering and feeling Miami (whose lover has been eaten by a shark) joins a band of penitents; the unfeeling Edna, her sister, becomes the mistress of a dandy who will soon tire of her. Firbank's sympathies are with Miami; Edna, it is made clear, will come to a bad end. Evil resolved in these terms lacks stature. Not even Cardinal Pirelli is a great sinner. There are no Stavrogins in this fiction.

In an age which looked for the moral to be sharply indicated in literature, Charles Lamb excused a taste for Restoration comedy by explaining it as entertaining gossamer out of some cloud-cuckooland and totally alien to ordinary human concerns. Just as this pleading neglects the facts of life out of which that comedy arose and places it in a vacuum impossible to art, so is the judgement in error which finds in Firbank merely entertaining and delightfully wicked frippery, however inadequate his sense of Evil may have been. Essentially he is a comic writer; his chief device is a kind of romantic irony; on this level he is nearly always enormously successful. There is a consistent satiric intent in his novels, aimed at the usual objects of social satire. But there is more, more even than the joy of escaping into a perfectly realised world or of contemplating the perfect artifact. If his Evil is always turning into naughtiness, his sense of mortality is sharp and unfailing. One has only to read a page or so of Firbank at random to note his awareness of the transience of all the earthly beauty he loved so well, an awareness which makes these novels, with their curious materialism, their praises of the rich and the exotic, moving as well as comic.

EDMUND WILSON

A Revival of Ronald Firbank

New Directions has brought out an 'Omnibus' of five of Ronald Firbank's novels: *Valmouth, The Artificial Princess, The Flower Beneath the Foot, Prancing Nigger* and *Concerning the Eccentricities of Cardinal Pirelli*—with an introduction by Osbert Sitwell, a revised and expanded version of a memoir which has already twice been printed in other volumes. It is a good thing to have Firbank revived. Just before this collection appeared, I had been reading those of his novels that I had not read when they first came out, and these had led me to re-read those that I had read. A conviction had been gradually growing on me that he was one of the finest English writers of his period and one of those most likely to become a classic. In England he has been appreciated much better than over here. In America, he was introduced in the twenties by Mr Carl Van Vechten, but, while Firbank was alive, only three of his ten books were ever published in the United States, and although these had a certain vogue, they figured mainly among the accessories of what was then called 'sophistication' and were, I think, more or less confused, through no fault of Mr Van Vechten's, with Mr Van Vechten's own novels, which may have been influenced by Firbank but which were not on the same plane of artistic seriousness. Since Firbank's death in 1926, he has hardly been read over here. In England, he has always had a definite position. A collected edition of his work was brought out in a limited edition in 1929, with an essay by Arthur Waley and the memoir by Osbert Sitwell, and the next year a short biography by Ifan Kyrle Fletcher, with reminiscences by Sitwell and others. Both these were imported by Brentano's but aroused little interest in America. E. M. Forster, Cyril Connolly and Evelyn Waugh have all recognised Firbank's genius and written about him.

The story of Firbank himself is as strange and as entertaining, as full of surprising anomalies, as the queer cases presented in his

---

Dated 1949. From *Classics & Commercials* (1951). Reprinted by permission of W. H. Allen Ltd.

novels. Ronald Firbank's paternal great-grandfather—I rely on Mr Fletcher's memoir—had been a North of England coal-miner, who could not read or write. The grandfather got himself some schooling, left the mines to do railroad work and had become, by 1866, one of the biggest railroad contractors in England: a self-made man of the ruggedest mould, who would not accept foreign contracts because foreigners did not pay in English gold and who, when offered a loan free of interest, declined it with the remark: 'I values at nowt what I get for nowt.' On discovering, in the stable of his eldest son, a fine hunter among the carthorses, he looked at it sourly and said: 'Eh, lad!—that won't pull a load o' muck!' This son inherited the business, went into Parliament and was knighted. Mr Fletcher conveys the impression that Sir Thomas was rather a stuffed shirt. He married the daughter of an Irish clergyman, and their second son was Arthur Annesley Ronald Firbank.

The boy had already from childhood the tendency to catarrh from which he was always to suffer and which finally caused his death. His mother, who had set Sir Thomas to collecting French furniture and porcelain, cultivated the son's sensibilities, coddled him and was always adored by him. (There are a number of striking resemblances between Firbank's personality and Proust's.) Ronald did not last a year at a public school, but he was later sent to France, where he lived in a château and studied French, with the idea of entering the Diplomatic Service. He published, in 1905, a little book containing two items: one a fairy-tale called *Odette d'Antrevernes*, which exhaled a sickly perfume of the nineties, the other—*A Study in Temperament*—a satirical conversation piece, in which he had found already his characteristic vein. The next year he went to Cambridge but he did not finish.

By this time—rich, shy and fastidious—he had managed to transform himself into something like a nostalgic caricature of the aesthetes of the Beardsley-Wilde period, whose productions, together with those of the *fin de siècle* French poets, provided his chief literary food. He surrounded himself with cut flowers, offered his visitors hothouse peaches, haunted the Russian ballet, wore Chinese and Egyptian rings. When people came to see him, he would sometimes carry on conversations looking out of the window with his back turned towards his guests; and even with special friends, he was likely, after a witty beginning, to lapse into incoherent mumbling or to be seized by a *fou rire* which made it impossible for him to finish some anecdote or to go on reading aloud one of his stories. (Proust is said to have behaved in the same way.) When you talked to him, writes one of his college-mates, he was always 'writhing about and admiring his hands' like 'the portraits of society women by Boldini'. On one occasion, when Firbank had been brought to meet some friend of a friend, he refused—no doubt imitating Wilde, who sometimes made similar objections—on the ground that the man was too ugly.

At first glance, you might get the impression that Ronald Firbank had come a very long way from his grandfather, the rail-road contractor. Yet the rôle that Ronald played was deceptive. He had not quite left the old man behind. Though he expressed himself often like a schoolgirl in a high-pitched slithering voice, thought he fidgeted and giggled and drooped, he had sharp powers of observation and a very shrewd sense of values. He was also more practical than people thought. His friends, who had supposed him incapable of travelling from London to Oxford, were surprised when he made journeys without mishap to such faraway places as Haiti and when they learned that he had put down singlehanded a mutiny on the boat on which he had made a trip down the Nile; and they would presently become aware, as he asked them to witness deeds and other legal documents, that he was well able to take care of his business interests. The point was that he was not a weak character but in some ways a very strong one. Harold Nicolson, who evidently had Firbank in mind in the story called *Lambert Orme* in *Some People*—though he trans-posed Firbank's writings and his later career into somewhat differ-ent terms—has dramatised the contrast in Firbank of fortitude and serious purpose with apparent frivolity and softness; but it is characteristic of the difference between Firbank and Nicolson that the latter, always grasping at accepted values, inexpugnably official-minded, should have made Lambert Orme prove his mettle as an officer in the First World War, whereas Firbank had shown his toughness, not by distinguishing himself in the war, but by refusing, as far as possible, to recognise it. It required a good deal of self-confidence to repudiate the public school code, to play the aesthete at that period and to that degree. The preciosity of Firbank's books seems so conscious and calculated that one some-times suspects him, in fact, of deliberately overplaying this rôle. V. B. Holland, who knew him at Cambridge, reports that, 'seeing him once clad in a sweater and football shorts, I asked him what on earth he had been doing: "Oh, football," he replied. "Rugger or Soccer?" "Oh, I don't remember"—and a laugh. "Well, was the ball round or egg-shaped?" "Oh, I was never near enough to it to see that!" ' When the war came, he professed frank loathing of everything connected with it said he had always found the Germans 'most polite'. He was called up again and again for medical examinations and questionings by the military authorities, and was finally rejected as physically unfit for service. When, by mistake, he was then called up again, he threatened to sue the War Office for libel and elicited an apology from it. He protested against the war by shutting himself up at Oxford for a period of two years, during which, according to legend, he spoke to nobody but his cleaning woman and the guard on the London train. And for the first time he applied himself to serious writing.

The exhilaration of reading about Firbank is that which we derive from the spectacle—first, perhaps, made popular by Lord Dundreary in that old play *Our American Cousin*—of the apparently silly ass who is really superbly clever, of the sissy who ends by scoring off the world which has been making fun of him. The anecdotes about Ronald Firbank are as amusing as the things in his novels—especially his ostensibly irrelevant remarks, which so often bewildered his companions but left them uneasily wondering whether they didn't mean more than they seemed to. When one of his friends had said, 'Good night, Firbank', as he put Ronald into a taxi, 'the taxi moved off, but before I had had time to move, there was a violent rattling and banging and the taxi stopped. Firbank leaned out of the window and called to me. "I wish," he said, "you wouldn't call me Firbank; it gives me a sense of goloshes." ' When Sacheverell Sitwell complimented him on his latest novel, *Caprice*, he turned his head away and remarked in a choking voice, 'I can't bear calceolarias. Can you?' The technique of his writing is similar. One may have thought, when one first looked at his books in the twenties, that they were foamy improvisations which could be skimmed up in rapid reading. Yet when one tried to run through them, one found oneself pricked by something that queerly impressed; one was aware of artistic seriousness, even if one did not linger to find out what the writer was up to. When one returns to them today, one realises that Ronald Firbank was one of the writers of his time who took most trouble over their work and who were most single-mindedly devoted to literature. The memoirs of him testify to this. His books are not foolish trifles, scribbled down to get through the boredoms of a languid and luxurious life. They are extremely intellectual, and composed with the closest attention: dense textures of indirection that always disguise point. They have to be read with care, and they can be read again and again, because Firbank has loaded every rift with ore. The effect of his writing is light, but it differs from the flimsier work of the nineties, which, at first sight, it may resemble, in the tension behind it of the effort to find the felicitous or the witty phrase which will render the essence of something. The little dyed twirls of plume and the often fresh sprays of flowers, the half-stifled flutters of laughter and the *fusée* of jewellery fire, have been twisted and tempered in a mind that is capable of concentration. It is a glancing mind but rarely wobbles. Only in the dangling participles with which he sometimes begins his sentences and in a lack of continuity of movement of which I shall speak later does he betray a certain weakness of syntax. But phrase by phrase, sentence by sentence, paragraph by paragraph, chapter by chapter, the workmanship is not merely exact but of a quality for which the craftsman must gratuitously tax himself. It has recently been learned that Beardsley was the child of two generations of jewellers who were also goldsmiths, and, once one knows this, it is quite easy to recognise the influence of the family trade in his clear two-dimensional patterns with their tendril-like ramifications and their delicate scrollings of pin-point lines, in their wreaths and rosettes, their festoons and crests. Perhaps, in a less obvious way, the inheritance of Firbank from old Joseph counts for something here, too. Mr Fletcher asserts that the grandfather was something of an engineering genius and that his work shows a passion for perfection. Certainly the work of the grandson—decadent though its subject matter usually is—never fails to live up to the slogan, 'I values at nowt what I gets for nowt.'

This work of the grandson is also in an old and strong English tradition: it belongs to the school of comedy that had its first great practitioner in Ben Jonson, that was exploited in its purest form by Congreve and the other Restoration dramatists, and that persists through a variety of modifications in Peacock, Gilbert and Aldous Huxley. The true products of this school are at the opposite pole from the hearty and hilarious English humour (though in some writers the two are combined). It is polished and coldly reasoned and rarely admits any kind of idealism. It is occupied with worldly values and if it ever turns its attention to general ideas, it makes mock of them all indiscriminately. Though it sometimes introduces a moralist who is supposed to act as a touchstone in showing up the faults of the other characters, it usually verges on cynicism, and it is always non-romantic and non-sentimental. There is nothing, so far as I know, quite like this English comic tradition in the literature of any other country. Distinguished, unscrupulous, hard; carved, gilded and decorative; planned logically and executed deliberately; of good quality, designed for long wear; intellectual but never intelligent—no people could have developed it but the English. You may feel, when you first approach Firbank, that his talent is too effeminate to claim ancestry from this masculine line; and it is true that a number of his books are occupied almost exclusively with women, and that his writing is full of trailed dots, coy italics and little cries. Yet these latter, always calculated, are really a part of his subject: the mannerisms that go with the habits of his special group and time. You may think that this effete preciosity has little in common with the brutality and elegance of *Love for Love* and *The Way of the World*. Yet the fact that Ronald Firbank is dealing with a later and less lusty phase of the same society as Congreve should not keep us from appreciating that his formal panels are no less finely painted.

Ronald Firbank wrote one play, *The Princess Zoubaroff*, and it affords a useful opportunity to compare his methods and point of view with those of Restoration comedy. The men and women in Wycherley and Congreve are all engaged in chasing one another: they lack sentiment but have vigorous appetites. The men and women in Firbank, for the most part, have neither sentiment nor keen desires. To them marriage means as little as it does to the characters of Congreve; but the alternative is not a succession of more or less piquant adulteries: it is likely to be an adolescent falling-back on members of their own sexes. Eric and Enid, in *The Princess Zoubaroff*, have been married hardly a week and Enid is still answering congratulatory letters when they visit, at a villa near Florence, another young married couple. Both the husbands and the wives have gone to school together, and they immediately renew old relationships. Enid, who has married to escape from her family and has found marriage disappointing, is perfectly willing for Eric to go away with the husband of her friend on a trip to the Engadine. At the end of the first act, the young woman who has been married the longer conveys to her friend with ominous distaste, 'as though she were sickening for the Plague', an intimation that she is going to have a baby. In the next act, the two ladies, with others of the English colony, are recruited by a Russian princess for a sort of Lesbian convent, while the baby is left in the hands of a nurse. The husbands have now been away a long time, and the young women take in with apathy the report of a mountain-climbing accident which may mean that both have been killed. But in the third act the men drift back. They are received without excitement and are themselves very much relieved when they see the wives go off to the Princess's convent. The Scots nurse at this point gives notice, and the father is left with the baby, whose name he does not even know. His only idea about it is to send it at once to the right kind of school.

This skeleton will bring out the difference between Congreve's men and women and Firbank's. The difference in their literary methods corresponds to the difference in subject. Where the speeches in Congreve are set-pieces, where the scenes have the give-and-take of an energetic well-played game, the dialogue in Firbank is all vague innuendos, gasps and murmurs, light caresses, small digs. Yet as writing it is no less consummate—and much finer than that of Wilde when he is working in the Congreve tradition. Not that Firbank's fluttering absurdities are more skilful than Wilde's ringingly turned epigrams; but there is always in the comedies of Wilde an element of conventional theatre—of melodrama or simple farce—though in this he is of course running true to the tone of his late-Victorian time. *Lady Windermere's Fan* has passages that might almost have been written by Pinero; *The Importance of Being Earnest* is still not far from *Charley's Aunt*. Firbank's comedy belongs to a society that is as non-moral as the Restoration and quite detached from the middle-class standards that still make themselves felt in Wilde.

One finds also in Firbank, however, besides this durable old English tradition, a certain influence from modern France—notably, I should say, from *Histoire Contemporaine*, Anatole France's Bergeret series. One seems to find the Anatole France formulas both in Firbank's tricks of style and in his presentation of episodes. In the latter connection, Firbank seems also to have reproduced France's faults—for the weakness of his narratives, like the weakness of France's, is a lack of continuous development.

One chapter does not lead to another, but each makes a little vignette which, significant and finished though it is, does not always fall into place as part of a coherent scheme.

The point of view in these comedies of Firbank, though they derive from an ancient tradition, is unconventional and very personal. Evelyn Waugh, in his appreciation of Firbank, has explained his own indebtedness to him, and a comparison of these two writers brings out Firbank's peculiar strength. For Evelyn Waugh belongs to the category of social satirists who 'castigate the vices' of their time by referring them to old-fashioned virtues which they imagine to have flourished in a previous age. It is possible for a writer of this kind to describe the most fantastic occurrences and the most outrageous behaviour, and yet not to antagonise the public, to enjoy, even, a wide popularity, because he reassures the reader by implying an irreproachable standard of stability and respectability. It is the technique of Horace's Augustan odes—a technique which Ronald Firbank could not exploit. He had no real place in English life. He could not invoke old Joseph. His own career and that of his grandfather had not a moment in common. In only one of his novels—*Inclinations*—does Firbank make sound English values assert themselves to the confusion of international decadence. Here a girl from a good county family goes to Greece with a Lesbian novelist, persists in remaining unconscious of the nature of her companion's interest in her, breaks the older lady's heart by running away with an Italian count, returns to her family in England with a baby but without her husband, who is supposed to be looking after his estate but who is suspected of having deserted her, and finally, when family and friends have become completely convinced that the rascally foreigner has let her down, scores again when he duly appears and proves to be not an adventurer but an excellent fellow of limited intelligence and simple tastes like her own. It is a pity that this most satisfactory of Firbank's early books has not been included in this omnibus rather than *The Artificial Princess*, which, good though it is in its way, was Firbank's first longish story, written rather under the influence of Beardsley's *Under the Hill* and not published during Firbank's lifetime. The three novels that followed *The Artificial Princess*—*Vainglory*, *Inclinations* and *Caprice*—are all attempts, most successful in spite of their apparent fanciness, to depict English life and character. Ronald Firbank has caught certain aspects of these as perhaps no one else has done—particularly the English habit of pretending to disregard what is uppermost in people's minds and always talking about something else. In Firbank's next novel, *Valmouth*, he is dealing still with the English scene but has found his own vein of fantasy, and develops in terms of high caricature the theme of the English capacity for carrying on unperturbedly in the presence of the scandalous or the catastrophic.

Thereafter, he abandons England, and we get *The Princess Zoubaroff* (Florence), *Santal* (Algiers), *The Flower Beneath the Foot* (an imaginary European kingdom), *Prancing Nigger* (the West Indies), and *Concerning the Eccentricities of Cardinal Pirelli* (Spain), in which, though the English still figure, they become less and less conspicuous. Yet, free to go where he pleases, with no British conventions to hamper him, Ronald Firbank is not, even now, at ease in his chosen rôle of well-heeled international drifter. He obviously delights in the humours of *The Princess Zoubaroff*, but this shimmering and chiming comedy leaves a lasting and a disquieting impression. It is really an understatement of the same theme that D. H. Lawrence became violent and shrill about: the biologically sinister phenomenon of a slackening of the interest in mating on the part of the privileged classes of Europe.

Firbank's next book, *Santal*, a very short one, has attracted less attention than any other of his mature writings, but I do not agree with his critics, Mr Waley and Mr Forster, that it is altogether without merit. This is his most nearly realistic story, and the only one that is not a comedy. It is Firbank's most direct approach to the personal situation which is reflected by all his work, for it is the story of the religious vocation of an orphaned Arab named Cherif, who, discovering that he has no close ties with the relatives who have taken him in and is incapable of sharing their prosaic interests, sets out on a pilgrimage to a holy man who is supposed to live in the mountains. He finds nothing, his water gives out, and he is left in the barren wilderness reading the Koran and dying of thirst. There were few of Ronald Firbank's contemporaries who could have equalled the writing of such a passage as that which works up to the sentence: 'Beneath the pitiless sun all signs of life had vanished, and in the deep of noon the hills looked to ache with light.' But Firbank here was under the handicap of having himself been a poor little rich boy, so that it was difficult for him to manage a hero who was supposed to be a poor little poor boy. He could have known little of physical discomforts, and, though he is admirable at describing the landscape, he is unable to conjure up the sensations of a boy riding for days in the desert. Firbank said that, when he was writing *Santal*, he found that the subject bored him and that, reacting from it, his imagination flew to the other extreme and presented him with the luxurious aristocrats of *The Flower Beneath the Foot*, which he could hardly wait to begin. Yet this next book, so funny in its exquisite way, so squirming with court scandal, deals with a similar subject: Laura de Nazianzi, niece of the Mistress of the Robes, 'more piquant perhaps than pretty', whose large grey eyes 'surveyed the world with a pensive critical glance', is in love with young Prince Yousef of the Kingdom of Pisuerga, whose face, though 'handsome to tears', had, 'even when he had been a child, lacked innocence', and he apparently returns her love; but for reasons of state he drops her and marries an English princess. Laura enters a convent, and the last turn of the screw for her is that she finds the nuns too much distracted by the excitement of the royal wedding to attend to their religious duties. Laura watches the wedding procession, beating her hands on the broken glass that bristles from the convent wall.

Yet, eventually, we are told, Laura became a saint. This turning to religion from the life of the world is a theme in all Firbank's later books. If you should read *The Flower Beneath the Foot* without knowing Firbank's work well, you might think this was all a joke, that he was merely being silly and witty, as he was in *The Princess Zoubaroff*, about the fashionable aspects of religion. But that was not the case. 'I believe that in his early youth,' writes one of his friends, Lord Berners, 'he had thought of taking Holy Orders. But more than once he had said to me, "The Church of Rome wouldn't have me and so I laugh at them".' (He had, however, become a Catholic at Cambridge in 1908.) He strikes one as having nothing to fall back on save his capacity for self-dependence and the discipline imposed by his writing. Art was his only sainthood. He was solitary and must have been lonely, though when someone suggested this, he replied, 'I can buy companionship'. Though he loves all the gossip of the world he frequents, it is mainly for what he can make of it; and though his work is full of naughty jokes that combine in a startling way a pansy archness with a brutal coarseness, one feels that his interest in sex is also mainly an aesthetic one. From the discrepancies he found in himself—pathetically stunted functions entangled with admirably developed talents, childish inadequacies in personal relations alongside a mature grasp of moral values—he never seems to have had any relief except through the demoralising comedy and the grotesque pathos of his novels. These novels, in one way or another, like the limericks of Edward Lear, almost always present the eccentric at odds with established society—though established society in Firbank may be itself unconventional and the eccentric, like Laura de Nazianzi, an honest and natural person. The heroines of the early novels—the touching Mrs Shamefoot of *Vainglory*, who, married to an important public figure and not at all amused by her social set, has concentrated all her longings on having her existence commemorated by a stained-glass window in the local cathedral; Miss Sinquier of *Caprice*, the daughter of a rural dean, who steals the family silver, sells it and blows the money all in, in London—with the aid of hangers-on picked up at the Café Royal—on producing *Romeo and Juliet* with herself in the title rôle, only to be killed after the opening night as the result of catching her foot in a mousetrap and falling through a trapdoor in the stage—these are figures of an incredible drollery; but there is something behind them that is not quite funny. Even the Lesbian lady of *Inclinations*, whose frustration is represented by a chapter consisting solely of the exclamation 'Mabel!' printed eight times, elicits a certain sympathy. Later on, more and more, the eccentrics become saints. Even Miami of *Prancing Nigger*, who has removed her family from the country to the city and watched the rest of them go to pieces there and who loses her country lover at sea, is last seen as a pious pilgrim on her way to a miraculous shrine. And in the figure of Cardinal Pirelli, Firbank bent all his resources to the creation of his noblest eccentric who is at the same time his strangest saint. The Cardinal, who, having already a dubious reputation, has baptised, out of pity for a childless woman, one of the pups of her favourite dog, comes to present an eccesiastical problem and soon finds himself shadowed by a Vatican spy who is trying to get something on him. The Cardinal plans a flight from Spain, but on the eve of departure has a fatal stroke in circumstances of the most outrageous scandal. 'Now,' writes Firbank, 'that the ache of life, with its fevers, passions, doubts, its routine, vulgarity, and boredom was over his serene, unclouded face was a marvelment to behold. Very great distinction and sweetness was visible there, together with much nobility, and love, all magnified and commingled.' (Note here the ache of life that recalls the ache of the hills in the passage quoted from *Santal*.)

Lord Berners, in an account of Firbank's death, says that he was told by a man who lived on the opposite side of a courtyard from Firbank's apartment in Rome, that he had sometimes been wakened at night by the sound of his neighbour's immoderate laughter. Just as his conversation and his reading to friends would sometimes be broken off by paroxysms of mirth that were likely to end in coughing, so even when he was writing alone this uncontrollable laughter would sometimes put an end to his work. So he had been diverted from the sad little story of Cherif to the hilarious but even more harrowing comedy of *The Flower Beneath the Foot*. Ronald Firbank was the poet of the *fou rire*. That is the key to the whole of his work. There is anguish behind it all—and the more ridiculous it is, the better he is expressing this anguish. *The Eccentricities of Cardinal Pirelli* is at once his most preposterous book and the one that has most moral meaning; it combines his most perverse story with his purest and most beautiful writing. He has here expressed his ideal conception, quite heretical but not irresponsible, not lacking in serious intention, of what a Catholic priest might be, and this has enabled him, for the first time, through art, fully to accommodate his imperfections, to triumph over his disabilities. It may be that the dead Cardinal's serenity had been won by him, too, for a moment in the few weeks of life that were left him.

For Firbank himself was to die just after he had finished this novel. On his last visit to England, he told his friends that he had wanted to write a certain number of books, that he had now written them and that he would probably write no more. He was just on the verge of forty and was worrying about his wrinkles. His lungs and heart were in very bad condition, and he had been virtually condemned by the doctor. In Rome he came down with some kind of "chill". He was alone in a rented apartment, where he would not let his friends come to see him, because, he said, the wallpaper was too hideous. He had even sent away his nurse, in the belief that he was getting well. When Ronald Firbank died, Lord Berners was his only friend in Rome. He knew nothing of Firbank's family—his mother had died not long before but he had a sister living—and found the name of his solicitor by chance on a crumpled piece of paper. Not knowing that Firbank was a Catholic, he had him buried in the Protestant cemetery, curiously but not incongruously, not far from Shelley and Keats. When Osbert Sitwell went to visit the grave, all trace of it had disappeared. The sexton explained that the body had been moved to a Catholic cemetery. Thus, as Sitwell remarks, there was even about Firbank's burial 'an inconsequential as well as a tragic element'.

MERVYN HORDER

A Firbank Manuscript

A pale blue, limp cloth-bound, feint-ruled exercise-book with round corners, disinterred after thirty years in store among his late sister's papers, turns out to be the author's own autograph fair copy of '*The New Rythum* by Ronald Firbank'—the first six chapters of the novel set in New York on which it is known that he was at work at the time of his death in 1926. The manuscript extends to fifty-seven right-hand pages only, in violet ink throughout, with the author calligraphically speaking on his best behaviour —the writing is completely firm and clear, even stilted, with words often turned down at the end of the line to cram them economically into the space. He is elaborately, perhaps unexpectedly, careful with the use of double and single quotes, italics, and the general *mise-en-page*. *Rythum* is spelt that way—à la Beatrice Lillie. There are a very few corrections, and one or two alternative suggestions in pencil. None of the legendary blue postcards, from an assortment of which Firbank is reported to have strung together his early novels, is in evidence for this one.

The misspellings are persistent and ingrained, beyond anything that one could have imagined: disipated, worshiped, suceptibility, nonchallance, existance, enthuseasm, evedent, mistakeing, seriphicly, proding—on the first four pages alone. Elsewhere the second l in 'cotillion' is carefully crossed out. Superior persons may begin by marvelling that any practising author could have reached his fortieth year with so totally feminine a disregard for the formalities of orthography; but it does not interfere with the enjoyment of the work—indeed it does not matter in the least.

An incomparable, *sui generis* genius if ever there was one, Ronald Firbank has been, with varying degrees of felicity, compared by influence-hungry critics to more other authors than most: Wilde, Henry James, Huysmans, Jane Austen, Thomas Hardy, Lewis Carroll, Maeterlinck, early T. S. Eliot, and

---

First published as 'More Ronald Firbank' in *The Times Literary Supplement* of 14 July 1961. Reprinted by courtesy of the editor.

Congreve among them. To at least one reader, after a look at these curiously unsophisticated purple pages, the first name that comes to mind is Daisy Ashford—with Amanda Ros unaccountably somewhere in the background.

A great many questions which have occurred to those interested in Firbank's texts are more or less resolved by a close consideration of these fifty-seven pages—believed to be the only Firbank autograph manuscript in existence; and the fragment—which includes rather more description and rather less of his characteristic elliptical dialogue than some other Firbank novels—is certainly a substantial enough product of the author's maturity to be worth the attention of critics of his work as a whole.

ELLIS WATERHOUSE

Ronald Firbank

I fancy that most people who admire Firbank's books were first led to do so by finding them extremely funny: and most people who deplore them, do so because, on first trying to read them, they were either rapidly bemused or soon came to the conclusion that they were, as they would say, 'intolerably frivolous'. Neither type of reader is likely to give overmuch thought to Firbank's purely literary qualities: and I don't think his early apologists, who wrote the prefaces at the time of the collected edition of 1929, did him much service. Waley introduced a single 'idea'—if such it may be called—drawn from the dubious parallel of literature with painting, which was probably questionable in Aristotle's time and has become a great deal more questionable since the invention of the novel. The 'idea' was that Firbank is 'almost the only Impressionist in English fiction', and he enlarged upon this by saying that he did 'in writing what Cézanne, Matisse, Renoir did in painting'. But, alas, Waley was not aware that only the last of these was an Impressionist, and even Firbank's most fervent admirers—of which I certainly count myself one—would hardly care to press the analogy with the achievements of Cézanne. Waley then fell back on the quotation of amusing passages and the abuse of the contemporary novel. He uses, in passing (as Sir Osbert Sitwell does also in his Biographical Memoir), the word 'butterfly'—as a term of friendly praise rather than abuse: and he also goes out of his way to make a statement which is generally unchallenged by the friends and enemies of Firbank alike. 'There is no sign,' he says (p. 5), 'that (Firbank) disapproved of or in any way condemned the vapid society that he depicts.' But there are more ways of condemnation than being forthright about it.

It is amusing that Waley, in his account of the contemporary novel, should have forgotten to mention E. M. Forster. But it is saddening to observe what may have been the effect of this

From *Alta: the University of Birmingham Review*, No. 3, Summer 1967. Reprinted by courtesy of the author.

omission on that reputedly detached and balanced mind. In an article published originally I know not where (but most likely in the *New Statesman*), and much more unforgivably republished in that section of *Abinger Harvest* that deals (I quote) 'with some creative writers, mainly my contemporaries, who I have admired or loved', E. M. Forster reviewed the reprinted Firbanks which Waley had introduced. Picking up the term 'butterfly', he ranks him as half beetle as well, and wholly insect, because of 'the only one quality all insects share in common: the absence of a soul'. 'With the soul,' pursues Forster rather recklessly, 'we reach solid ground. As soon as it enters literature, whether in full radiance or behind a cloud, two great side scenes accompany it, the mountains of Right and Wrong, and we get a complete change of *décor*, adapted for writers who likewise treat the unusual, but who treat it mystically or humanistically.' It sounds depressingly like T. S. Eliot; but it is amusing that Forster should have expressed his condemnation by a metaphor from the stage, a field of artifice with which he was much less familiar than Firbank. Firbank was aware that it is perfectly permissible for the most important character to be 'off' the whole time, provided the players (and the spectator) are aware of the fact. Firbank remained a Roman Catholic, though not of the typical English sort. I fancy he was almost desperately aware that the soul was there all the time, but he accepts the convention of his society that it would be bad form (as well as unnecessary) to mention it. We should remember also that he had an appalling stutter.

The earliest of his mature books (for *Odette d'Antrevernes* is a devotional exercise of bewildering puerility) is *Vainglory* which appeared in 1915. Osbert Sitwell states that this, as well as *Inclinations* (1916) and *Caprice* (1917) were the actual fruits of *ennui* resulting from enforced inactivity provoked by the Great War. He even rather foolishly remarks that Firbank was 'in the best, and least boring, sense a war writer'—and there may be a pointer to the truth in this if we could feel certain that he had not begun *Vainglory* until after the war had begun. It is twice as long as the later books. He was not a quick writer and, in this first major effort, he had to invent his technique as he went along: but the printing and publishing of books was then so much more rapid, so astronomically more rapid than it is today, that it is perfectly possible that it was begun after the war had started.

And if this is true, the chief character in *Vainglory* which is 'off' is the Great War itself. Firbank, being very rich for an author, never thought to address any but the highly intelligent reader—it is this highly undemocratic attitude which gives additional charm to his work today—and the 'soul' in *Vainglory* is the fact that the Great War is waiting just round the corner for all the characters in the book.

It is a picture of several levels of society on the eve of the Great War, in which the highest aim, the aim most tenaciously pursued, is Mrs Shamefoot's for her own vitrification. Of the rather large number of characters with which the book deals the men (except for a bishop, a writer, a pianist and a painter) are all 'off': the action is taken by the women, who belong to two strata of society —the upper reaches, who function in both London and the country, and the upper middle reaches who function in the County Town only, where they connect at certain points with the upper reaches. Ashringford has a very strong dose of York about it—as we are more or less told in the next book, *Inclinations*, for Firbank likes to tell us something about one of his earlier books in his later ones. There Miss O'Brookomore says to Mabel, 'Hasn't the eccentricity of living near *York* ever occurred to your Mother?', and we realise at once that the city walls, the rather mangy river, Whipmawhopma Street and the distant view of the racecourse at Ashringford all point to York as the main scene of *Vainglory.* What Firbank is doing is giving us an account of the vapid character of large stretches of society on the eve of the Great War: he might almost be explaining the Great War as a reasonable outcome of the frivolously directed aims of pre-war society: the sequel doesn't upset him a bit. He is, in fact, the exact opposite to Henry James, who might seem to us, with very different artillery, to have been doing the same thing if it were not for the fact that James (according to Percy Lubbock) gave up writing *The Ivory Tower* when the Great War broke out because 'he found he could no longer work upon a fiction supposed to represent contemporary or recent life' and wrote that anguished letter on the outbreak of the war, that 'to have to take it all for what the treacherous years were all the while really making for and *meaning*, is too tragic for any words'. Yet, to a detached observer, the Great War would seem to have been the one thing which could and did justify James's view of the corruptness of the European scene in his day.

I imagine that the normal criticism of this point of view would be that Firbank's world bears no relation to society as it was, is, or ever will be: that it is a world of fantasy unrelated to the contemporary scene. Before discussing this, it may be worth while to consider Firbank's own definition of his style in its relation to his characters.

We are told this quite explicitly towards the end of *Vainglory*. Lady Anne sends, by her secretary, a book to beguile the time for Mrs Shamefoot while she is awaiting her vitrification.

> 'Tell me where is the book I'm to bear?'
>
> 'It's here: Harvester's *Vaindreams*!'
>
> 'Not exactly the kind of book, is it? to take to her'.
>
> 'Why not? He has such a strange, peculiar, style. His work calls to mind a frieze with figures of varying heights trotting all the same way. If one should by chance turn about it's usually merely to stare or to sneer or to make a grimace. Only occasionally his figures care to beckon. And they seldom really touch. He's too cold. Too classic, I suppose.'
>
> 'Classic! In the *Encyclopaedia Britannica* his style is described as *odd spelling, brilliant and vicious*.'
>
> 'All the same, dear, if you wouldn't mind carrying it across.'

Now this is an entirely serious statement. It is one of the occasional moments when a Firbank character cares to beckon: I am not at all sure he doesn't himself really *touch* the reader. Indeed, he here explains, with that hypocoristic levity which is inherent in a certain type of over-civilised Englishman, that he aims at a style in the classic tradition, a style narrowly governed by certain rules of art, which he expects to be misunderstood by the mass of British criticism (there felicitously called the *Encyclopaedia Britannica*), but which he wants to try and get across all the same.

I think we can accept this as a valid definition of the style at which he was constantly aiming, and the refinements of his technique in later works mark a certain progress. For instance, in *Vainglory*, each of the main characters is introduced by as much as a whole paragraph of explanation about their personality, mounting up to a mass of detailed information which, in the later books, is only revealed by the most studious indirectness. Take the character of Claud Harvester, the author of *Vaindreams* and thus not unrelated to Firbank himself:

> Claud Harvester was usually considered charming. He had gone about here and there, tinting his personality after the fashion of a Venetian glass. Certainly he had wandered... He had been into Arcadia, even, a place where artificial temperaments so seldom get—their nearest approach being, perhaps, a matinée of *The Winter's Tale*. Many indeed thought him interesting. He had groped so.... In the end he had begun to suspect that what he had been seeking for all along was the theatre. He had discovered the truth in writing plays....

I fancy this is a perfectly accurate account of how Firbank saw his own literary aspirations at this time—and you will notice that he says that Claud Harvester was concerned about 'discovering the truth'. We are not told as much in cold print about any of his later characters.

There is yet another clue to the seriousness of Firbank's intention in *Vainglory*, a book I linger over especially since it is the most revealing of all his books. In the wonderful set-piece at Mrs Henedge's party for the new Sappho fragment, a quite minor character, introduced only for this occasion and really an intruder from a world where artistic standards matter, suddenly declaims 'before anybody could stop her' (a most significant observation) a wonderful translation of Sappho's great ode, after which Mrs Henedge says, 'Exquisite, dear, thanks'. A little later, Mrs Shamefoot sings the idiotic mirror song from *Thais*, made more idiotic by its relentless insertion in the text in French prose as if it was all a part of the conversation, and is equally greeted with 'Exquisite, dear, thanks'. I really don't think we can agree with Waley that there is no sign that Firbank in any way condemned the vapid society he was depicting. For Firbank there was no distinction between an aesthetic and a moral judgment.

A recurrent trick in Firbank is 'inserts', as it were, into his normal style of sections in parody of some of the sillier or more popular writing of the day. They can usually be easily recognised by a change of key, but one would have to know much more about the fashionable writers of that distant time than I can claim, to be able always to identify the parody. I think there is only one such section in *Vainglory*, Chapter IV, describing Winsome Brookes and Andrew at 13 Silvery Place—and one passage in that chapter seems to me to have in mind *The Adventures of Sherlock Holmes*.

> Taking for granted the large, unwieldy furniture, the mournful carpet, the low-spirited draperies, the brown paper on the walls, the frieze, in which Windsor Castle appeared again, and again, and again, and which a patriotic landlady (a woman like a faded Giotto) would not consent to hide lest it might seem to be disloyal, let us confine our observations to the book, the candlestick, the hour-glass, or the skull.

There is much more of this in the next book, *Inclinations* (1916), where the action takes place in Greece and, significantly, in the neighbourhood of York.

The opening chapter of *Inclinations* must be nearly as baffling to a reader of it for the first time as the opening chapter of *One of our Conquerors*. Gone are the informative vignettes which introduce the characters. We are introduced at once into an odd house-party and we have to glean our knowledge of our fellow-guests from the scraps of conversation we overhear, very much as we have to in life. We have to be pretty sharp about it, and I think it is here that we first have, fully developed, that new technique in novel-writing in dialogue (or perhaps really dramatic) form to which Waley, not altogether correctly, has given the name Impressionism. For the effect is made by what is left out rather than by what is left in. Here is a nice example from this chapter:

> 'Poor Mr Fairmile seems so miserable, Mabel, since you've disappeared!'
> 'How is he to show what he feels when . . .'
> 'When?'
> 'Oh, Effie, why did you tempt him? . . .' Miss Collins asked as she dashed out.

The judicious reader can only understand this, because he has fortunately overheard, a few pages earlier, Mabel saying to Miss O'Brookomore: 'Effie overdoes her hospitality I somehow think. Placing rouge in all the bedrooms. Even in Mr Fairmile's room, poor boy!' We are also told, in this studiously indirect way, something about Mr Fairmile!

Just as I have suggested that, in *Vainglory*, it is the imminence of the Great War which is the character which is 'off' in the story and gives the moral standard by which the characters are to be judged; so, in *Inclinations*, the character which is 'off' is the noble and glorious associative element in the Greek scene against which the action takes place. There is no allusion to it at all—or only one, which is enough for the reader on his guard. In the enchanting tenth chapter, in which the ladies' maids visit the Acropolis, one of them says: 'Naturally one sees it has its old associations . . .': and, at the end of the chapter, when two of them discover that they both come from Hammersmith, come the capitalised words 'The Captive Women stared before them', and the *Troades* of Euripides are mischievously recalled. A parable does not cease to be a parable because it is idiotically funny.

Inclinations gets quite out of hand in the middle. The last seven chapters of Part I, where the action takes place in Greece (including the somewhat notorious Chapter XX, which is composed solely of the name Mabel screamed eight times) are clearly intended as parodies of some very silly literature of the period. It may be that Firbank had some particular book in mind, and I can throw out a clue from which it might be possible to trace it. In Part II (p. 143) where Mabel, after nearly two years in the Anglo-Italian society of Rome, has returned home with the sophisticated silliness which might have been anticipated from her earlier naïvety, and has become 'the Countess', she is seeing Miss Dawkins off to India:

> 'Have you a magazine or anything for the train?'
> 'I've a novel only—*Three Lilies and a Moustache*'.
> 'I like a love story,' the Countess confessed, 'so long as it isn't drivel'.

Her own love story had certainly been drivel and perhaps it is in imitation of a book whose name could then easily be guessed from Miss Dawkins's novel. (Professor T. J. B. Spencer has suggested Gilbert Cannan, *Three Sons and a Mother*, 1916.)

In the collected edition, there is printed not only the 1916 version of the remarkable dinner party on Mabel's return, at Bovonorsip, but also a considerably longer variant, found among

Firbank's papers and dated 'Rome, 1925'. It is interesting that Firbank should have wanted to revise one of the best chapters in a book nearly ten years old, but I have to admit sadly that I find the later version inferior, more explanatory, and singularly unhelpful to any estimate of what Firbank was after. I suspect he had begun to find that he must address a larger but less subtly attuned audience: indeed it seems to have been written with an American edition in mind.

Of *Caprice* (1917) there is perhaps not much comment to be made: it is in precisely the same manner as *Inclinations*, only the conversations and conjectures take place on the fringes or in the middle of the world of the stage. Of the corruptness of Mrs Sixsmith there is no doubt, and the book is a striking series of tableaux, which impinge at many points on theatrical life and don't say much about it beyond that it is artificial and often funny to the outsider. As far as they go, however, the conversations are perfectly realistic in this book, as they are also in *Vainglory* and *Inclinations*: and the world they depict is perfectly real too. In this the first three books differ from the later ones, and it is not for nothing that *Valmouth* (1919), the first to appear after the war, was subtitled 'a romantic novel'.

I can sympathise with doubts about the 'realism' of these three earlier novels. The society they depict has (except to some extent for that of the stage and possibly for a pocket, here and there, at Oxford or Cambridge) pretty well disappeared, or at least most of us move in it so little that we can hardly believe in its existence. Yet, although the concentrated sum total of all this silliness is a great exaggeration, there is hardly a section which, by itself, isn't perfectly plausible. In later books Firbank sometimes allows his fancy for absurdity to run away with him (for example, there is Miss Schnerb who wrote fashion notes 'till her nib caught fire'): but the conversations in these three books are most carefully studied. Often enough today one witnesses a situation or hears a conversation which one can only describe as Firbankian—and there is no other metaphor from the literary world to take the place of this. Firbank deserves much more credit than he has got for being an observer of contemporary speech and manners. It is only his additive methods of it which are really bizarre.

On the other hand Firbank may well have felt that he had

exhausted his vein of 'butterfly' observer of society. This use of 'butterfly' I mean to be quite different in intention from that of E. M. Forster's. Firbank's appalling stutter prevented him from having relations with anything but the set-pieces of Society (the exhibition, the first-night, the grand party), except on the private or café level. He was quite literally a highly observant and intelligent butterfly who flitted about the society he depicted in these novels. To enrich his field he seems to have tried two methods consecutively—first to take over the sort of characters or society from other contemporary novelists, the second to apply to these his own private brand of fantasy, pickling them, as it were, in his own special brine. I think this is what he has done in *Valmouth.* I can still remember how puzzled I was with *Valmouth* the first time I read it, but now it continually provides me with new sources of amusement, although a few of them are of an elaborately literary kind.

The scene is still England: Valmouth is only Falmouth very thinly disguised indeed, a watering-place where the salubrious character of the air makes everyone a near-centenarian. His fantasy has been to take, as it were, a slice of Henry James's later characters, the sort of corrupt world which lives in *The Golden Bowl* (for instance), to prolong their lives in fantasy till they are mostly more than 100 years old, and to deprive them of all the Jamesian web in which they have almost decently lived and make them communicate as far as possible only by direct conversation. The result is that they become laughably licentious and wicked, and Firbank stirs the plot even more farcically by intruding into this world a character from D. H. Lawrence. The parody of the Jamesian manner in which the note and tone of utterance of his characters is sometimes over-elaborately described, often appears in *Valmouth.* Mrs Yaj 'blandly yaps', and some lines are 'somewhat hectically hummed by Thetis Tooke. 'Is that—she dismantlingly ogled—what you're after?': and Mrs Thoroughfare 'reimportunes' her friend. The full parody appears on p. 88: 'My tongue is over-prone perhaps to metaphor. My cherished friend scolds me for it; only a fellow mystic—some saint, would ever know, she says, what I'm driving at often'. This appears to me a clear statement about Henry James's later works. Mrs Yaj, a Lawrence cat among the Jamesian pigeons, is a 'twinkling negress', and her first appearance, starting with her voice off-stage, 'a voice large, deep, buoyant, of a sonorous persuasiveness, issuing straight from the entrails of the owner' sufficiently proclaims her Lawrentian origin.

Firbank in fact has taken two novelists each of whom, in his way, has made a criticism of contemporary society, and has tried the experiment of employing one as a specific on the disease of the other, seasoning the whole with a very strong dose of Firbankian sardonic mirth. As a thin, serious, thread through the book, there is also the question, which is one which clearly much interested Firbank (and which comes into its own in *Prancing Nigger*), of the nature of the values, the more simple values, of Negro society, and the clash of this scale of values on the extremely sophisticated (and specifiically Roman Catholic) society of the other world in which Firbank moved. He constantly frequented soothsayers and crystal gazers, and was fascinated by the impact of these irrational beings on a society which proclaimed itself as rational.

The ridiculing of a certain class of Roman Catholic who was after the conversion of others at any price (not, I recall, uncommon in the years just after the Great War) is carried on into *The Princess Zoubaroff* (1920), the only one of Firbank's novels to be written in dramatic form. I suspect it was written before *Valmouth*, since it hardly exaggerates at all the eccentricities of Anglo-Florentine society during these years. What is remarkable about it—and not usually recognised—is that it is brilliantly funny on the stage, though over-artificial in reading. It is also perhaps the first book in which individual persons can be recognised by the judicious reader. I know too little about the contemporary Florentine scene to suggest a key, but Lord Orkish is presumably Lord Henry Somerset, and Reggie (whose name was probably chosen to annoy Reggie Turner, who loathed Firbank and was much in Florence at this time) is no doubt easily identifiable.

There is nothing to be said for *Santal* (1921), but *The Flower Beneath the Foot* (1923) is one of the best of the books. Firbank had begun travelling again and the book was written in 1921–2 and is inscribed 'Versailles, Montreux, Florence'. From the strictly English scene, he goes on to the European, but it is a European world in which a British Embassy and a British colony play a conspicuous and silly part. Here his characters are perhaps too thinly disguised. The Hon 'Eddy' Monteith, a son of Lord Intriguer, is clearly Evan Morgan, later to be Lord Tredegar. Harold Chilleywater (I suppose because he regarded Nicholson's gin as a chilly sort of water) is Harold Nicolson: and his wife, Victoria Gellybore-Frinton 'a daughter of the fortieth Lord Seafairer of Sevenelms Park', is all too palpably identifiable. The reason for this intense dislike remains a mystery, but it derived from Firbank's time in Madrid, and Pisuerga has much of Spain about it—perhaps with a dash of Cairo. In spite of bursts of extravagance, it is perhaps nearer to actual life and conversation than any of Firbank's novels, and its secondary theme is the perfectly serious one of the blind and bland idiocy of the English resident in the capital of a Mediterranean or Southern country. He describes all levels, from the Embassy to the lady who runs the English Library. Anyone who has lived much in a Mediterranean capital will perceive that it is by no means as frivolous or fantastic as it seems.

Two books remain: *Prancing Nigger* (1925) and *Concerning the Eccentricities of Cardinal Pirelli* (1926). The last is a very funny book, and its somewhat scandalous attitude towards the Roman Church, and other levities, gave it a certain *succès de scandale*. But it is what Gide calls a *sotie*, and I needn't bother about it in this attempt to suggest that Firbank is worth thinking about from a less indulgent point of view than is usual. *Prancing Nigger*, on the other hand, is a perfectly serious book and has qualities of the heart and the imagination which are new in Firbank. As a work it approaches perhaps nearer to something like a ballet by Diaghileff than anything else I can suggest. Written largely at Havana and largely concerned with the corrupting influence of the capital city on a rural Negro family: written in a rather tiresome pseudo-phonetic Negro dialect for the most part: one would have thought it a most unpromising prospect. The European sections are modishly written in his own style and only moderately amusing, but he seems to have found in his unsophisticated Negro world something which called forth qualities of tenderness and feeling as a writer, which one would never before have suspected. Descriptively too, parts of it are well written in what one can perhaps genuinely call an impressionist style. Apart from this book Firbank is a careless writer, except for his conversations, with which he takes immense pains; but *Prancing Nigger* shows a promise of development which he never lived to fulfil.

I suspect the present generation mainly regards Firbank as a tiresome mannered old-fashioned coterie writer, who is amusing to read if you have that sort of sense of humour, but one not of the faintest moment in the panorama of English literature in the twentieth century. Even those who have mainly praised him have encouraged this point of view, and it is doubtless rash, when everyone has indicated how brittle is the ground, to venture to tread upon the serious criticism of him at all. I agree, however reluctantly, with Forster's view that a novel is not worth taking seriously if the author is unconcerned, however unconventionally, with right and wrong: and I hope that I have indicated that Firbank cannot be put in this class. He belonged to a phase of English society which was in certain aspects strikingly corrupt—what one may call the Bottomley age. It was accustomed to fee-fi-fo-fum moral judgements—but these did not come from the upper reaches of society, who were morbidly concerned with the ungentlemanliness of expressing moral judgements at all. That could only be done by studious indirectness—and this, I fancy, Firbank has achieved.

Index of Names

High up on the outside of the East wall of the parish church, Newport, Monmouthshire (Gwent), is a crucifix and a stone plaque with this inscription

SS JULIUS AND AARON PARISH CHURCH
THIS CRUCIFIX WAS ERECTED IN MEMORY OF SIR
THOMAS FIRBANK DIED 7 OCTOBER 1910 AND
HARRIETTE HIS WIFE DIED 25 MARCH 1924
R.I.P.
REMEMBER ALSO ARTHUR ANNESLEY RONALD
FIRBANK THE DONOR OF THE SITE OF THIS CHURCH
DIED 21 MAY 1926